Provisions

Provisions

Jana Meehan

Cover and interior design by Marquee Publishing
Published by

Marquee Publishing
3901 Berger Ave. • St. Louis, MO 63109
www.marqueepub.com • 314-645-7581

Published in the United States of America

ISBN 10:0998501794
ISBN 13:978-0998501796
Library of Congress Control Number: 2017910523

1. Fiction/Suspense/Music/Family

Also By Jana Meehan

The House of David

Left Turn, Right Turn

Acknowledgments and Thanks

Many thanks to these people whose contributions to creating this story are invaluable:

Charlie Everingham
Clint Gallagher
Keith Kolander
Jo Skabo
Mark Stevens
Donna Valentine
David Williams

Chapter 1

"It's a pity when you have to budget a gum ball," Theresa Shelton remarked to her husband as she climbed into their minivan and departed the gas station where she had splurged at the gum ball machine. She held a red gum ball in her fingers and examined it before popping it into her mouth.

After a moment, Tim asked, "Was it worth the big expenditure?"

"No. Not at all. I was hoping it would be cherry flavored, but it's just ordinary bubble gum."

"Another of life's injustices."

"Hey, all we have left in life is the simple pleasures, and they should be free, or nearly free. Sunsets, blooming flowers in springtime—"

"The inevitable butterfly landing on your nose . . .?" Tim offered.

"There's no need to be sarcastic. I don't think it's a lot to ask that a red gum ball should be cherry flavored. It's a simple request. My expectations are already pretty low." Theresa tossed her thick mop of shoulder-length strawberry blonde hair in mock defiance. Her green eyes flashed with humor.

The Sheltons were laid off. Tim, eighteen months before; Theresa, fifteen. The job search had been arduous and disheartening.

"I'm so sorry, honey," Tim replied. "I want to do better by you."

"You're doing the best you can, Tim, and so am I."

The Sheltons were driving to Terre Haute on a cold November morning. It was still dark and a black sky in the east behind them was just beginning to turn cobalt.

There was a job opening at the college there, and Tim was a candidate. Tim and Theresa had driven away from their rented double-wide in Columbus early, leaving plenty of time to get there and not be late. This job interview was, in Tim Shelton's mind, like a trapeze in a circus act. He was releasing his grip on one trapeze, spinning in mid-air, and hoping to grasp the trapeze swinging toward him in the nick of time, do or die, without a net.

For months, they had been selling what they could at yard sales, with the hope that one of them would find work before the saleable items were all gone.

The unemployment benefits had run out a long while ago, and the pair had done odd jobs for quick cash, borrowed from friends, and called on relatives, but it wasn't a livelihood, let alone a life, and now the rent was months in arrears. The wellspring of family and friends had dried up, and they were on their own.

The cash on hand was enough for gas, a meal on the road, and, they hoped, first and last month's rent on a new place. But the job was far from his. If he was passed over, well, he didn't know what they would do.

A few minutes later, the pair stopped at a roadside restaurant, open all night. A teenage hostess greeted them at the door.

"Two for breakfast this morning?" she gushed.

"Yes, but before we do, we have these coupons for a free breakfast. Do you honor these?" Theresa asked, offering the coupons.

The sweetness vanished from the young woman's face, and she said, "Those are only good on weekdays."

"This is Thursday," Tim interjected.

"Well, yes, we honor those. We just want to make sure that the customers understand, though, that 'free' does not mean free."

"Well, then what does it mean? I won these by calling into a radio station. They said 'free' at the time," Tim said, growing irritated.

"Well, just because your meal is free, that doesn't mean the server works any less hard," the hostess said, ineffectively concealing her hostility. "Come this way, and I'll seat you," she continued, menus in hand.

She led the couple to a table and slapped the menus down on it just hard enough to preclude any possible misunderstanding of her intent. She turned away, back to her post without a word.

"Whew!" Tim said. "I guess if she had better language skills, she might have found a more diplomatic way of saying that."

"Or not said it at all. What, exactly, was she saying?" Theresa asked, taking her seat.

"That we should tip on the full amount the meal would have cost without the coupons."

"Oh. Can we do that?"

"It's only fair, and it's not the server's fault we're poor."

"I think I want to leave, Tim."

"What if I speak to the manager?"

"What if she *is* the manager?"

"Do you want to go without breakfast? We are too far away to go back home, and any other place will cost. This is free. Or, close to it."

"I don't want to reward people for their rudeness. That was just uncalled for."

"I suspect that girl got burned before by someone who had a coupon and didn't tip. She acted like she was almost ready for us. As if she was not ever going to let that happen again," Tim remarked.

"Fine, but you don't be rude to strangers who didn't do anything wrong. None of that was necessary. Let's go." Theresa began scooting her chair away from the table.

"Why is this upsetting you so much? Let it go."

"Why do you think it is bothering me?" Theresa glared, her face flushed.

"If you want me to guess, I will."

"Go ahead."

"You're upset because that little girl has a job and you don't. And you deserve one, and she doesn't."

"Exactly. And when you think about the thousands of people out here trying to get work, to sustain their families, it just burns me that people like her get to have jobs. If she weren't here, there would be a hundred people lined up to do her job. No question."

"Unfortunately, you are right. A hundred people would line up to do her little minimum wage job that pays her enough for mall money. She couldn't 'sustain a family' on those wages. And neither could you. She has this job because it requires very little, which is what she has to offer. Can we order now?" Tim gestured toward the server who had just arrived at the table, greeting them and smiling sweetly.

Sometime later, the couple left the restaurant and climbed back in the minivan.

"How was your meal, Treese?" Tim ventured.

"Worth every penny we paid for it."

"Not that great, huh? Mine was okay. Hot cakes were fluffy and hot."

"You get what you pay for, even with coupons," she said.

"Hey, I want to ask you something," he said, changing the subject. "How many interviews do you think you've been on? Since the layoff. You think two or three dozen? I counted 43 for myself, not counting today's."

"More than that. Lots more. I don't know what I'm doing wrong. I have what these people are looking for. I just can't pull the trigger."

"Let's hope it is better in Indiana."

"I don't know why we think it will be. It's all one country, and the economy is bad all over it. I just don't know what we're missing. Do we look dishonest, or stupid, or incompetent? Why is this happening?"

"We've talked about this, Treese. We aren't doing anything wrong. It is just the way the country is right now."

"No, it isn't. When I go on these interviews, not getting these jobs — someone *is* getting the job. Someone is being hired. It's the most depressing when they tell me I am a very strong candidate, and I get my hopes all up."

"Someone cheap is outscoring you. I told you this. You are 46, way too skilled, and employers see you as too expensive. They would rather hire a kid out of school who will work for ten bucks an hour, be molded to just that employer's needs, and who won't retire very soon."

"So, I should give up? Is that what you're saying? No one will ever want me again?"

Tim didn't respond at first, knowing he was on thin ice. Anything he said now would worsen her dour mood.

Theresa had been a legal secretary for a large firm in downtown Columbus for thirteen years before one partner after another retired. Within months her stable job was shaky and the associate lawyers and partners who remained weren't generating the billable hours. They had to let her go.

As she watched the ribbon of road zooming toward her, Theresa remembered the words of John Bishop, the partner who dismissed her: "Theresa, you are so good at your job, you'll find something in a blink. We hate to have to do this, but I am confident you won't be out long. Look at it as a new adventure."

Theresa, though, had endured enough adventure, and those words haunted her. If she is so good and so qualified, she thought, what could be wrong?

"I don't know. I don't know what to say," Tim said finally. "You have agonized over this for months, and I am not helping you see the bright side."

"Bright side," she echoed, deadpan, appalled.

"We're alive. We have our health. We are able to work when the time comes. And we have been provided for by some means, whenever the situation has been dire. Every time there has been a huge bill, somehow the money has shown up to pay it. We have a lot to be thankful for. We accumulated too many tons of stuff in the good old days. Now that times are lean, we have had those things to turn into cash. And maybe we are on our way right now to a new beginning."

"I don't see all of this. If you are expecting divine providence, well, I wish to be provided with a job so I can make my own providence. I don't want another winter like the last one where we can only pay the gas bill if it snows and the neighbors ask you to shovel their walks. You have two master's degrees, Tim. It's ridiculous."

"I hear you. It is ridiculous, sure. I never thought I would be the owner of two advanced degrees and tenured at a university, and end up paying for my groceries with state aid. But, remember, it did snow. And the gas bill was paid. And remember when the car insurance was due, and we didn't have anything like $900? Out of the blue Jim Scott offered me $1,000 for the Jet Ski and we made the payment. He didn't know we needed that kind of money. He had no idea how much we were hurting. He just wanted the Jet Ski."

While Theresa was silent, Tim reviewed that day when the vice chancellor at the college called Tim in for a chat.

"There has been a business decision, Tim," vice-chancellor Melvyn had announced solemnly. "The board has looked at the money and decided that a resizing is in order. We are streamlining three departments, including Music. I'll be happy to write you a letter of recommendation."

Melvyn, a jovial fat man with a red nose and an obnoxious laugh, was uncharacteristically cold and perfunctory. Tim recalled that Melvyn would probably have preferred to puncture his own eardrum with an ice pick rather than have this conversation, but it was of little comfort.

Tim was optimistic at the start. Letters were sent to universities across the country. With his credentials, and with the friends and colleagues he had in academic circles, he would know someone who would call him in. They say that you have to know somebody. Well, he knew lots of somebodies. But, it turned out he didn't know the right ones.

So, he began writing. An authority on music history of the 19th and 20th century, he thought an article or two on the reawakening of interest in the popular classics could be sold to some publication somewhere. Theresa pitched in, proofreading and fact-checking. Tim made calls, trying to spark interest.

One academic publication on the west coast showed an interest, but made an offer for the article that was so much less money than Tim expected, it was more defeat than victory. He abandoned the effort, feeling useless, wounded and humiliated.

About the time he threw up his hands in futility, the next blow came when Theresa came home with the bad news about her job.

Credit cards were cut up, the cable TV was canceled, professional organizations went without the Sheltons' dues, and Theresa's fondness for catalog shopping was replaced by the occasional prowl through the thrift stores. Tim let himself think that maybe they would be okay.

But the house note lapsed, and the house was sold. Tim let himself think positively even about the house, reasoning it was too much house for the two of them anyway, and they were stretched too thin by it before the layoffs.

His wife was more hurt. The house had been her dream home, even down to the proverbial white picket fence. She took its loss very personally, barely displacing her anger, blaming hiring managers and the luck of the draw rather than her husband.

Tim nevertheless felt blamed and responsible. The sense of letting her down ate at him, but he didn't tip his hand. That would only make it worse.

Each money-saving step and job search disappointment reminded Tim that his class status had changed forever. He was now one of the working poor, but he wasn't working, and the embarrassment was deep.

He recalled one of the first times he and Theresa bought food with the state aid food card. They both hoped no one they knew would recognize them in the store, but of course someone did. A former co-worker from Theresa's firm got in line right behind them. He greeted her and they chatted about the firm and the friends there that they shared. But when the time came, the computer would not read the card, and the cashier told her she would have to call the SNAP office and get it straightened out. She had to leave the groceries there for a clerk to reshelf. The cashier was sorry, but sometimes the magnetic strips on these cards go bad, and Theresa may have to get another one.

Theresa was mortified with embarrassment, and angry with the cashier for blowing her secret. Tim felt for her, and shared her humiliation.

The co-worker was gracious and reminded them both that they paid in for these benefits for years with their tax dollars, and it wasn't anyone's fault that they needed them now. But, again, it was little comfort.

As Tim was running over these moments in his mind, Theresa breathed a thoughtful sigh and spoke. "Okay; if you say so. I want to think that divine providence is looking out for us, but why doesn't it look out for us with jobs? I want to work like a normal person, pay my own bills, make my own way."

"I don't know. I really don't. What we are supposed to learn or glean or develop from this ordeal is beyond me," Tim told her. Then, "Take out the map for a minute."

While Tim flipped on the interior light, Theresa took a road map from the glove box and unfolded it in her lap, locating their place on the highway. "Okay, now what?" she said.

"State road MM takes us south through Durham. How far out of the way would it take us if we swung through there?"

"About 40 miles, it looks like. You aren't going to ask your brother for more money, are you?"

"No, ma'am. Too embarrassing. But it won't kill us to cruise through town and thank him in person for the help he's been. And we have the time. We're ahead of schedule."

"Way to mend fences, Tim."

"You don't have to like Andy, Treese. You just have to be civil."

"You mean I have to be humble while he lords over you his great business and his fashion-model wife and his house on the lake and his boat. And I have to be humble while he writes you a check that will more than clear, but will be paid back with every morsel of what's left of our dignity."

"Essentially."

There was a silence as each of them reviewed the last visit to his brother's house. Andy's wife had offered help with the mortgage. Tim had declined, with thanks. But when the visit ended, Andy had pressed a check into Tim's hand, grinning too broadly, and exuding an air of gloating superiority. Tim felt like a pathetic loser, and Andy sensed his humiliation and grinned more broadly. The grin and its meaning were lost on neither Tim nor Theresa.

"Should I take the exit or not?" Tim asked.

"If we go, Leah will offer us money."

"I will turn it down, and I will mean it."

"What if it's divine providence?"

"Divine providence can have a sour taste, can't it?"

"Sure can. I see you are taking the exit."

"I am keeping options open. If we change our minds, we'll ride through town, get back on the interstate, and they'll never know the difference."

State Highway MM was a barren two-lane highway. The couple passed a truck stop at the interchange, three fast food restaurants, and a few farmhouses, before the signs of human life fell away. The road took them through a wooded area of the countryside at the most beautiful time of year. The leaves were on fire – golden, red, purple — and breathtaking. The sunlight was right on the horizon, trickling through the trees. Theresa looked across Tim and through his side window at the lightening sky. They drove in silence, each appreciating the vista.

Lost in thought and the beauty of the surroundings Tim muttered, "As I remember, the turn off to their house is real hard to see. And I don't remember it being this far. I wonder if I've missed it."

"I'm thinking we've missed it," Theresa confessed. "None of this looks familiar."

The state highway's two lanes had narrowed and were crowded by the woods on either side. The trees hung over the road, shiny and golden, making the road a tunnel, vibrant with color on all sides. Fallen leaves littered the road, making it a patchwork quilt of gold and red.

Tim slowed the vehicle and pulled off onto a clear space near the road to turn around. As he began to pull the car back onto the road in the opposite direction, Theresa spoke:

"Wait! I see something."

"What?"

"Not sure. There is something in the brush. It's large and it's moving. Look there, it's not fifteen feet off the road."

"I have to reposition this car or we'll be creamed by the next car that comes around that bend."

"I'm betting not many cars pass by through here. This is really isolated."

After a few minutes, the van was parked off the side of the road in the clear space, and the pair got out. It was then that Tim saw the movement in the brush, but it seemed camouflaged by fallen leaves and underbrush. He crept closer, but an uneasy Theresa stayed back, wishing she'd kept quiet.

Tim crept closer, wary that there were copperheads in these woods, and with Andy's lake but a few miles away, there may be water moccasins as well. But the movement in the brush was far too large to be a snake.

Confusing the issue was the sunlight breaking into dawn, and throwing long shadows through the trees and underbrush. The November sky was clear and the streams of sunlight were bright and piercing.

After a moment, Tim said, "Well, darlin', I have to disagree with you. There was at least one car that passed through this area recently. Apparently, it hit this deer and kept going. It looks like his leg is broken. I think he's been here a while. He looks awful."

"Oh, my lord!" Theresa exclaimed and picked her way through the underbrush to her husband's side. "Don't get too close. It's an injured animal. It will fight to protect itself. And don't go near those antlers. He can hurt you with those."

"I think he's too weak to raise his head, Treese. But you may be right. That jug of water you brought along? Bring it here."

Theresa went to the car and returned carrying a milk jug full of water and a plastic dish. "You think he's thirsty?" she ventured.

"I'm guessing. Don't know how he couldn't be."

She poured water in the plastic dish and handed it to her husband. He eased the dish closer to the deer, fearful it would try to run and hurt itself more, or come at him in defense. Tim dropped to his knees and reached the dish forward as far as he could. The deer stared at him, apparently helpless, afraid. A little animal cry escaped his throat as Tim paused a few feet away from the deer's head. Leaning forward on one hand, he slowly lifted the plastic dish over the deer's mouth and trickled a little water.

The deer moved. Flailing in the brush, the deer tried to right himself. Tim scrambled back, spilling the water on his coat and putting distance between himself and the animal. But the animal failed, and after a few moments of kicking and struggling, he calmed himself.

Theresa poured more water in the dish and Tim tried again. The deer seemed to understand what was happening now, and his thirst partially overcame his fear. He raised his head and drank from the plastic dish as Tim hunkered back, watching.

After a few minutes, as the deer drank, Theresa went to the car again and came back with a covered plastic dish. She uncovered it and handed the dish to Tim. It contained sliced apples.

"Aren't these our lunch?" Tim asked.

"What's your point?" she countered.

He considered her for a moment before saying, "Okay, I'll try."

As he neared the hurt deer, the animal again struggled, trying to escape, and as Theresa had predicted, Tim had to duck out of the way of antlers. But in the end, with patience and slow determination, the deer let Tim near it.

The deer ate an apple slice from his hand.

A quiet, astonished "Wow" escaped Theresa's lips as she stood several feet away.

"What do you want to do? We can't just leave him here."

Wordlessly, Theresa went back to the car, and as he offered the animal another apple slice, he heard her voice. She was on the cell phone, calling for help.

Tim could hear little of the dialogue until she raised her voice to a shrill, angry "No, thank you!" and tossed the phone into the front seat.

"What happened?" he asked her as she returned to the site. He tried to keep his voice low and even to not frighten the deer, but her reaction had him very curious.

That was the state department of conservation. They promised me they would send someone with a gun to kill the deer."

"What?! Did you tell them where we are?"

"No, I hung up at that point, but it leaves me out of ideas. Is he still eating?"

"No, not really. He is really scared, and I'm not sure a broken leg is all that's wrong with him. But he is thirsty."

"The conservation guy hastened to tell me that what we are doing is very dangerous, that these animals are unpredictable, and so on. He rold me about a woman feeding a wild deer. The deer swung its head at the wrong moment, caught its antler in the woman's mouth, and tore her cheek apart."

"Good to know. I'll take great care," Tim remarked, shuddering, "But we are committed now. I am not going to leave him here to die of thirst or hunger. And I am not killing him. There has to be something else we can try."

Tim leaned back on his heels, giving space to the deer. He just watched it, as Theresa did. The deer's eyes were haunted and terrified, and it was in pain, Tim was sure. He searched his mind for ideas, but nothing came to him.

He found himself wondering if anyone had seen that helpless, haunted look in his own eyes.

Musing, considering, Tim watched the animal as the sun rose.

Abruptly, the deer began moving. It was flailing with his good legs as though trying to run sideways, and the pair wondered what was wrong. Then they heard. A vehicle was coming up the road toward the north, toward the interstate. It was loud, in need of a muffler, and as it came around the bend, it slowed to a halt near the minivan. It was a rusty silver SUV, dust-covered and aged, and driven by a woman about Theresa's age. She got out of her car and approached Theresa who went to the edge of the road to meet her. She had a kind face, greying hair, and wore a military surplus jacket and jeans. Theresa thought she must be a local, and was glad to see her.

"You two got car trouble?" she said.

"No, we have deer trouble," Theresa replied and explained the situation and the quandary they were in.

"Yeah, they'll sure kill the deer if they find it," the woman agreed. "I wouldn't be telling them where it is. This happens a lot. These deer live all their lives in these woods and never get a pinch of traffic sense. And Lord! Can they ruin a car when you hit one!"

"But we can't just leave it, and we can't stay here," Theresa repeated, her voice rising. "What can we do?"

"There's an outfit with headquarters in Durham called Wildlife Rescue. They have vets to volunteer and they take care of injured animals that people find."

"Do they destroy the animals?" Theresa asked.

"Well, not if it can be helped, but if they do, they give them a merciful shot. I'm Megan McKinney, by the way."

"Theresa Shelton. That's my husband, Tim, over there with our friend. How do I reach these people?" she said, striding toward the van and the cell phone.

"I guess you ask for Wildlife Rescue for Durham County."

It took an hour and a quarter for help to arrive from Wildlife Rescue, and by the time it did, Tim Shelton was exhausted, cold, and his head was splitting. But he kept an eye on his deer. He felt a certain comradeship with the animal. It had been blind-sided, as well. And he meant to see this thing through.

Megan McKinney had gone on her way, and Theresa warmed herself in the van. The air had an autumnal nip to it, but the sun was high in the sky and the golden leaves glowed in it. The natural beauty didn't stop her from weeping quietly. She wept for the deer, the situation they were in, her sense of futility, and for her compassionate husband who lacked the good sense to be angry at his life.

The help came in the form of a red pick-up truck with two big guys and a smaller one with a medical bag. First name introductions were made: Jake, Bill, and Dr. Ed, who scolded Tim about trying to feed the deer. Tim got the impression that it was the thing the vet was supposed to say, but that he was glad for the deer to have had food and water.

Tim told the three men that the conservation department was intent on killing the deer.

"Yep, they sure would," Jake retorted. "And they'll fine you a piece of money if they catch you helping it, taking it, or killing it out of season or without a license."

"But we're helping it now," Tim said.

"Yes, we are."

"And if they find out, there'll be a fine?" he asked.

"They'll know," Dr. Ed remarked. "They know we do this all the time."

"How will they know?" Tim said.

"They watch our facility, and they'll see the deer."

"And then they'll fine you?"

"Yes."

"And what will you do?"

"Pay the fine."

Tim examined the three men for a moment, digesting this news, until the vet spoke.

"I'm going to tranq the deer and apply a splint. Then the four of us are gonna lift the deer into the pickup truck. I won't be able to tell until I get him back what other injuries he has. Does that sound like a plan to you all?"

"By 'tranq the deer' you mean knock him out for the trip, right? You aren't going to kill him, right?" Theresa demanded.

"Yes, ma'am. We won't kill an animal if it can be saved. That's our purpose. I won't make promises, but if the deer can be saved, we'll do our best. And we'll keep the animal in an enclosure until it can walk well enough to make its own way. Hell, it will probably be laid up with us all the way through deer season."

That statement sat well with Tim and Theresa.

"How are you funded?" Tim wanted to know.

"Private donations, mostly, and the vets donate time and materials. There is never enough to save every hurt animal, but we do the best we can."

"Sometimes the best you can do is the best you can do," Tim muttered under his breath. Then, aloud, "Let's go. This animal is hurting."

While Tim knelt a few feet from the deer and spoke to him in low tones, trying to keep his attention, Dr. Ed circled around behind the deer near the hindquarters, out of reach of the antlers, and administered a shot. The animal's breathing slowed, his eyes closed, and in a few minutes, he was asleep .

When they were sure the animal was unconscious, Tim and Theresa petted the deer.

"I expected it to have a softer coat," she told her husband.

"It's not a kitty cat, not domesticated. It's a wild animal. There is no advantage in the wild to having a soft coat."

The veterinarian then put a temporary splint on the leg and Bill brought a canvas gurney from the truck. The four men strained to lift the deer onto the canvas and carry it to the truck. The effort left them all breathless.

Theresa thanked the team warmly for their help. Hands were shaken all around. As the three men climbed back into the truck's cab, Bill turned to Theresa thoughtfully. "Thanks aren't necessary." He gazed at her for a moment, as if trying to see inside her soul. At last, he said, "You realize these animals often reach a level of population that some of them have to be killed. They exhaust the food supply, begin starving, and die in misery. Sometimes it's best to let nature take its course."

"This wasn't just for the deer this time," she replied. "My husband needed to do this. It's a part of surviving to the next stage."

A moment later, the pickup truck headed south toward town as the Sheltons waved them off.

Wordlessly, they climbed into their own vehicle and drove north toward the interstate, through the tunnel of golden trees. They each thought of the deer, wishing him well.

After a few miles, Theresa remarked, "It's okay with me that we don't have time to see Andy and Leah."

"Yeah."

"What are you thinking about?"

"The deer."

"Of course, but you are very quiet."

"I'll tell you one thing, Theresa. When that animal ate that fruit right out of my hand, that was about the most amazing thing that has ever happened to me. It was worth the time and the effort and the cold, and the headache, and the skipping lunch. It was worth this whole trip, just to have that happen. That was amazing."

"I didn't tell you, but I was furious when that conservation idiot wanted to kill him."

"The 'conservation idiot' was doing his job, too. They have reasons for their stupid rules. Bill said that sometimes it's best to let them die for the good of the others."

"I don't care."

"Yeah."

They emerged from the golden tunnel to the junction with the interstate and headed west for Terre Haute.

Chapter 2

The Sheltons' first view of Terre Haute left them with an unsettled sense of dichotomy. The town boasted an odd mixture of modern architecture, and old style buildings out of the turn of some century. Theresa wasn't sure what century.

"Wow," Theresa said as they passed the Indiana Theater, "if we had time, I'd want to just take a long walk in this part of town. Look at that theater. It's so, I don't know, it looks so . . . "

"Garish?" Tim volunteered. "If it were a hooker, it'd be a 90-year-old hooker with a pound and a half of mascara trying took look like she's still young." He chuckled at his own observation.

The front of the historic theater faced a corner of Ohio Avenue. Its facade sported three upper level round-topped windows inside a larger domed exterior. Theresa mused that, in its heyday, this theater probably hosted entertainers as far back as vaudeville.

"I wonder if we could go in," she mused.

"Go in where?"

"Slow down. I wonder if we could go around the block and park and see if we could look inside the theater. What time is it?"

"Eleven-thirty. We've got an hour to kill."

"And the university is five minutes from here according to the guy at Quik Trip, right?"

"Right. But what do you want to go in for?"

"For my brilliant man. Honey, we can't have lunch; we fed it to the deer. I regret that because we were in the car for four hours and you should eat. I don't care if I eat or not, but you should have a blood sugar boost so that you are at your smartest for this interview. In lieu of lunch, I don't know, I just think the interior of that theater would get your creative juices running. I'm sure there has been music here through the decades that you would find stimulating. Can we find out?"

He considered his wife for a few seconds before he began looking for a parking place.

As the couple approached the box office in front of the theater, Theresa spied three middle-aged men near a light standard. They were dressed alike in red tuxedos with white lapels and black cummerbunds, white tuxedo shirts, and silver bow ties. Their shoes shined. They appeared to be waiting, and she wondered about them. She paused, looking at them, as Tim tried the door.

"There's no one inside, ma'am," one of them volunteered. He was a caramel-skinned man of perhaps fifty with a friendly, smile and broad, open face.

"Are you out here waiting for the owner or manager or somebody?" Theresa ventured.

"Yes, ma'am. My friends and I have a vocal group. We've been hounding this booking manager for a shot to audition, and when he gave in, he told us to show up here, but I'm starting to think we were stood up again."

"How many times has he stood you up?" "This'll be the second, but he had a good excuse the first time. But if he's playin' games, I got better things to do."

"What do you sing?" The voice came from Tim.

"Some of everything. We sing a little country, we sing a little soul, songs of love and romance, and a little rock and roll. That's our slogan."

"What do you sing the best?" Tim wanted to know. "I'm a student of music, and I'd be interested to know. My wife and I are just in town for the day, so we wouldn't get a chance to hear you, but I'm still curious."

"What do we sing the best? Hmm. Hard to say. We sing everything the best, but I guess my main focus is on the Sinatra style stuff of the 30s through the 70s or 80s. Quincy over there, well he does r&b. He kills The Temptations and Drifters — that kind of thing. Forbes, we call Mr. Versatility. He can do anything."

"I see you are the public relations front man. I'm Tim Shelton. This is my wife, Theresa."

All three men stepped toward the couple and offered their hands in greeting.

"I'm Cole Renshaw, by the way," the front man said. "Here are my partners, Quincy Garland, baritone-bass, and Forbes Wilson, tenor-baritone."

"Let me ask you this," Tim ventured, "What kind of venues do you play most of the time?" An idea was forming for Tim, and he stuck his toe in this uncertain water.

"We started out slow three years ago by doing a lot of nursing homes, senior centers and so on. Those folks love our music, and the pay wasn't bad for not much work. Since then, we've worked some nightclubs, and several of the golf clubs in the region. I've got a brochure in the car. Wait a minute."

Cole was parked five cars down the curb. As he stepped to his vehicle, Theresa remarked to the other men, "Your partner is quite a salesman, huh? If I were this aggressive selling myself, maybe I wouldn't have so much trouble finding work."

Tim's body language made clear his disapproval. She didn't notice, but the two men did. The one named Forbes looked at her. His gaze softened and bore a note of sympathy. "We've all been there. Every one of us." His voice was gentle and soft. The fears rampaging through Theresa's mind quieted themselves when he spoke, but she chided herself for revealing her jobless state to strangers.

"How long have you been looking?" he asked.

"Almost a year and a half."

"Yeah, I know. I was laid off once for two years. It was tough. What you have to do in the end is make your own job."

"How do you do that?" she asked skeptically.

"Now I'm a cab driver."

"A cabbie by day and a crooner by night?" Tim's remark wasn't exactly condescending, but Forbes took it that way.

"Yeah, you just don't know — yet," Forbes replied.

At that point, Cole returned with a handmade brochure that had been run off a desktop printer. It was nice, though. A color photo of the three men and a readable font decorated the piece. Tim affirmed his perception of Cole's marketing attempts.

"So, I started to ask about your music. Looks like from the list here, you've played a lot of places. Who is your accompanist?" Tim ventured.

"We use digital music. We find that it provides a more realistic memory for the audience, and it costs less for the venue holder."

"You mean you sing to karaoke. Is there a market for that?"

The three singers glanced at each other with a knowing here-we-go-again stance that told him they had faced this opposition before.

"Well, partners, whaddya think?" Cole said with resignation. "It doesn't look like we're gonna audition for Lambert today. Let's show, um, Tim and Theresa what we would have showed him.

The three planted their feet shoulder to shoulder, and the one named Quincy opened his mouth. "The . . ." he sang in a perfect, strong B flat, as the other two joined him for the next note, an octave jump "Eeeevee-ning breeze caress the trees, tenderly. . ."

The harmonics were riveting, Tim thought. As the three held their tonic-third-fifth interval harmony through the Walter Gross standard, Tim was both enjoying and analyzing the performance. "Tenderly" was among his favorite songs from the 40s, and the thought could not escape him that unexpected, uncalled for treats like this were just why Tim loved music.

Theresa, meanwhile, smiled to herself. She had wanted to take Tim into the historic theater to get his mind on music and get him psyched for the interview. That wasn't happening, but this was much better.

When the three had finished one verse of the standard, Tim and Theresa applauded.

"I'm impressed, gentlemen," Tim said. "I imagine, with a good accompanist, your talents could take you places. I wish you all very well. By the way, I've never heard that arrangement of 'Tenderly.' Did you do the arranging yourselves?"

"No, man," put in Quincy. "We are fans of The Flamingos. That's their interpretation. We've been covering them for years."

"Covering them? What does that mean?" she asked Tim.

"Doing their songs."

"Oh."

"See," Quincy continued. "We've been singing off and on together for a long time, but my partner, Cole, met the Flamingos a few years ago and they talked us in to reforming the group."

"So, what I'm thinking," Tim mused, "is that your karaoke music limits your arrangements and holds down your creativity, am I right? What if you could write your own vocal arrangements by using an accompanist? That could be an advantage."

"I know what you're thinking, honey," Theresa interjected, "but I don't agree with you about an accompanist. I'd sure rather hear digital music that sounds like a 30-piece orchestra accompanying a great vocal performance than a three-instrument combo that may or may not show up for a performance. We've seen plenty of that."

Theresa referred to the early years of the marriage when Tim attempted to form such a combo and would be forced to scramble at the last minute, making adjustments for musicians who didn't show up."

Cole interrupted the couple's discussion. "Oh, you don't know the half of it. Sure, we interviewed some musicians. It was the Flamingos' idea to use digital music, and we took their suggestion after we found out that most of the musicians out here want to charge us $200 to rehearse!"

"That's ridiculous!" Theresa agreed. "I never heard of such a thing."

"That's not completely right. If you have a gig lined up already, they'll rehearse for the gig for free and wait to get paid for the gig," Quincy explained.

Cole finished his thought. "But the problem is that our complex vocal arrangements require a lot of rehearsal sometimes, and musicians have to make a living, too. The digital music is the best option."

"Gentlemen," Tim interjected, "my wife and I must go. We have another appointment." Tim was both disheartened by his failure to take the discussion to a place that might get him some work, and annoyed at Theresa for not supporting him.

"Well, it was nice to meet you," Theresa allowed to the three singers. "I enjoyed you, though briefly."

"Yeah, right," Cole said. "Say, we've got a gig tonight in a hotel lounge. You are sure both invited to come in, have a drink, holler out a request or two and we'll see if we can fill it."

"Thanks, but no thanks," Tim replied, trying to conceal his dejection. "Like I said before, we're just in town for the day. We'll be on the road by the time you get to your gig. But you guys have potential. I regret I can't actually be your accompanist." He nodded at the three before turning and walking toward the van, Theresa at his side.

Chapter 3

Once at the van, Theresa snatched the clean and pressed dress shirt from the back and handed it to Tim as soon as he had stripped off his polo shirt. He put the shirt on hurriedly; the November air was nippy. He then chose one of three neckties — the one with the print of Van Gogh's Starry Night on it — and then got in the back of the car.

"We aren't rushed," Theresa said noting the time.

"I know, but you drive and I'm gonna change pants while you do."

By the time Theresa pulled into the parking lot next to the Performance Arts building, Tim was sharply dressed and ready. His spit-polished dress shoes and American flag lapel pin were the finishing touches. He crossed his fingers and silently wished for a good outcome before getting out of the vehicle and grabbing his brief case.

Theresa came around to his side and kissed him for luck. She started to tell him needlessly that this interview is the precipice. But he knew that well enough.

She got into the passenger front seat and dug a book out of her tote bag. The book, by comic writer Tony Roland, had a blue and purple cover, and could have lifted her dour outlook, but didn't. Precipice indeed, she mused as she flipped to her bookmark. If this goes badly . . . a fear welled up in her. She tamped it down as best she could.

Tim, once inside the building, rode up an escalator to the second floor. He found Room 213 promptly, and checked his watch. It was 12:45. He was 15 minutes early, just as he intended. The door was of dark wood, classy and expensive looking.

The whole building smelled of money. A large indoor fountain had greeted him when he had entered downstairs. The floors appeared to be genuine marble, and even the plaque next to the door, identifying the Music Department, was expensive.

"I'm going to step through this door into my future," Tim whispered to himself. "Please," he begged some unknown deity, "don't let me go home a failure. I don't think Treese could stand it."

He pushed the door open, wearing his most confident smile. A receptionist raised her head from her computer screen and seemed to mimic his pleasant demeanor.

"I'm Tim Shelton," he said as he approached her. "I'm a little early for a 1 o'clock appointment with Dr. Glenn."

The young woman appeared to blanch white. Something was wrong, and the look on her face put a hollow feeling in his stomach.

"If you'll have a seat, Mr. um Shelton, I'll find someone who can . . . just wait here."

Tim sat down in a lushly, upholstered easy chair. His mind spun with possibilities. They had already hired someone without telling him. That must be it. They didn't even call to cancel. The panic rose inside him. *No, no. Stop thinking that. You can't let on that you are scared out of your . . . stop it! Stop panicking! Relax. Don't freak out until you know you should freak out.*

The woman didn't return for three unanswered calls to her desk phone. Tim counted. The sense of unknown terror gripped him as he maintained the plasticized pleasant expression. When she did peek around the corner, she was sheepish and apologetic.

"Um, Mr. Shelton, Dr. Fuller is going to sit down with you. He'll explain the confusion. You want to come this way? Dr. Fuller is the associate department head. I'm so sorry you can't meet Dr. Glenn."

She took him to an office whose door sign said, "Dr. Francis Glenn, Department of Music." Tim glanced around the room. It was moneyed as well as the lobby. Mahogany furniture with leather upholstery surrounded an entertainment center set into the wall. The stereo was softly playing an Anton Webern piece that Tim recognized. Dr. Fuller rose from behind the desk to meet him.

"Tim Shelton?" Fuller said, offering his hand. "I'm Lloyd Fuller. There's been a little problem with your interview today. You see, Dr. Glenn was called away. He flew out this morning to Denver. His son was in a car accident out west and is badly injured. We are so sorry. There wasn't time to call you before you left home. We should have rescheduled, but there wasn't time.

"I'd at least like to meet you, and if you are willing to reschedule with Frank, um, Dr. Glenn, we'll set a date and time."

Tim's sense of panic rose. He could feel that his plasticized smile was cracking around the edges. "Did you know, Dr. Fuller, that I drove in from Columbus?"

"Oh, my God, no. Oh, my. I'm so sorry. Okay, I'll have to fix this. Please wait here for a moment. I'll be right back."

He was gone in the outer office for several minutes while Tim clung to hope that somehow, he could wrestle this situation to some kind of thready, tentative victory.

When he returned, Fuller said, "Well, here we go. Tim — may I call you Tim?"

"Sure."

"Here's what I've got. Frank definitely wants to talk to you and he expects to be back tomorrow. He won't trust me to do it. I guess the job is too important to leave to the help." He did finger quotes in the air around "the help," and grinned facetiously. "So, I am authorized to invite you to be our guest. The university would like to put you up overnight, buy you dinner and breakfast, and lunch tomorrow so that you can meet Dr. Glenn about 4:00 tomorrow afternoon. We realize this is a lot to ask, and a huge inconvenience, but it's the best we can do out of a terrible situation. What say?"

Tim's mind was racing. He didn't take the time to think it through, but responded immediately. "That would be acceptable, Dr. Fuller, and I appreciate your hospitality. I am so sorry Dr. Glenn has had this tragedy, and I wish his son the best outcome." His platitudes sounded as wooden as they were. He went on, "My wife and I would love to explore Terre Haute until tomorrow."

"Ah, your wife is here. Where is she? In the lobby?"

"No, she's waiting in the car with her book."

"Let's go get her," Fuller said with renewed friendliness. It seemed to Tim that Fuller was embarrassed by the miscommunication, and, having resolved it, was anxious to let his hair down. "Have you had lunch? I haven't. Let me treat you; we may be colleagues pretty soon." His seemed genuine and Tim began to relax just a little. The remark about someday being colleagues was balm to Tim's soul.

Theresa looked up from her book in time to see her husband stroll to the car with another man. She assumed failure. Her natural response after so many failed job interviews — especially when so little time had passed since the interview was scheduled — suggested to her that this man approaching with Tim had also been rejected for the job and the two were walking to their cars together.

The other man was taller than Tim, dark-haired, but sporting a salt and pepper full beard. His tummy dipped over his belt, and his shirt buttons strained to hold him in. He looked entirely academic. As the two neared the car, she could see that Tim's gait was light, and he seemed happy. "What the . . .?" she thought. She rolled down the window.

"Treese, this is Lloyd Fuller. He's taking us out for lunch, and I'll explain what's happened." Theresa's eyes widened with surprise and curiosity.

Tim turned to Lloyd. "Hop in the front, Lloyd. This is my wife, Theresa. I'll get in back. If you're buying, we're flying."

Chapter 4

Sal Romano was a creature of habit. He turned the sign on his pawn shop door to "Closed" and attached a Post-It Note with a scrawled "Back Shortly" on it. He walked across the street to a sandwich shop and ordered a roast beef on rye with a side of chips and a Coke. He took the sandwich back to his shop just as he had done every day for three years. He had bought the store on time right out of the Army, and was making a go of it.

Re-entering the store, he switched the sign to "Open" and sat behind his register. The morning had been so busy that he'd taken lunch later than usual, when the store went empty. He congratulated himself. He had sold a camera, a pair of crystal candle holders, a pair of emerald earrings, and a brass soap dish only this morning.

It was a shame about the emerald earrings, though, he thought. He could have gifted them to Sandra, girl. That might have made an impression. What a beauty she was, he considered. Bling like that could have looked great on her and also, hopefully, sealed her to him.

Sal worried that his girlfriend was the object of desire for every man alive and that he, a slight, wiry, short man with thinning dark hair and a crooked nose, wouldn't measure up.

It was in a bar fight nine years ago that the nose had become crooked. It had been smashed flat and a little to the right when he had been defending the honor of Simone, his girlfriend at the time. That guy had no business in her face, humming on —

It was that moment when Sal, while lifting the sandwich out of its paper sack, noticed the light blinking on his answering machine. He had a call. He took a bite of sandwich and a sip of drink before he hit the button.

"Salvadore, this is Sandra. I'm real tired of you. Last night when I went to the show with Dardene and Lenora, you followed me, didn't you? I was so embarrassed in front of my friends, and I have had enough of you stalking me and following me and showing up everywhere to check on me."

The voice on the recording ratcheted up in volume and ardor as the young woman spoke.

"You stalk me at my job, and my boss is sick of you. My father sees you parked outside our house at all hours, just sitting there watching the house.

"So, here it is. We're broke up. Period. Don't call me again."

He knew it, Sal thought. He just *knew* it. It was that guy at her job. He knew she was seeing that guy. He should have stepped in. He should have shown up in her office and given that guy a word up. *Dammit! What was I thinking?*

Sal threw the sandwich in the trash, then kicked a cabinet door until it cracked.

Chapter 5

It was late in the afternoon when Cole came home. His wife, Shara, greeted him with a hug and kiss. "How was your day? Did you get a lot done?"

"Not a huge amount. How was your day?"

"I wrote copy. I designed a brochure. I ordered deli food for a doctor's conference set for January. I did marketing stuff. Same old, same old.

"Oh, I just remembered. Your mother called."

"I just left her," he remarked with his brow knit. "What's wrong?"

"Oh, you forgot to bring her a hot dinner."

"Oh. I sure did. I dropped off the groceries and came home. Too much on my mind, I guess."

"So, you took her a ton of groceries, including, no doubt, a large number of microwaveable dinners, but she isn't happy unless you bring her restaurant food also?"

"I guess not."

"Cole." Shara paused. She gathered her thoughts to frame her words just right. "This has got to stop. Doesn't your mother get it that you work? Just because you own your business doesn't mean you can take off any amount of time at all to go run errands for her. Owning a business means you have *less* time, not more time, to do non-related things." Shara's voice was timbre mirrored her deep frustration.

"I know, but she's old and she doesn't understand. Just try to be patient."

"Patient. Really. How many doctor's appointments have you taken her to in the last month?"

"I don't know."

"Seven. Seven appointments. And since she can't get her butt out of bed before 1 p.m., and she wants a restaurant lunch after her doctor appointment, and since the 1 p.m. appointments always interfere with the venues that don't open until 11:00, you lose the entire day's work every time she goes to a doctor."

Cole looked at his wife with a hurt, helpless expression.

"What do you want me to do, Shara? I can't just not take her."

"Tell her to take a cab."

"A cab? There's no way she would do that. She wants me to take her."

"I realize what she wants. But as the song says, 'You can't always get what you want.' I think you need to explain to her that you lose a day's work every time she calls the doctor. And what are these appointments for anyway? Does she actually need to go, or is she just making appointments so you take her out to lunch?"

"I don't know."

"Oh, I think you do know, honey. I think you know that I talked to that doctor after every appointment and nothing is wrong with her. Yeah, she's old, and she has a bad heart. But, her blood work is fine, her prescriptions are fine, her physical exams are fine — she's fine. But she's had to go in seven times in three weeks. It's wearing real thin, Cole. You better talk to her because if you don't, I will, and I won't be so nice."

"Shara, we have to get ready for this job. I'm going to change clothes and load the car."

"I already loaded most of it. It's just the speakers I need help with."

The couple prepared for the hotel gig and drove to it, the elephant in the room notwithstanding.

Chapter 6

Shara talked to the concierge and was told to unload her equipment at the door to the rear of the building. Back at the car, she quipped to Cole, "Hey, do you feel like Nat King Cole in the 50s? He couldn't go through the front door of the hotel he was playing either. You're in grand company.

Her husband chuckled.

The couple pulled around and went in the stage door in back. It took 45 minutes to set up the speakers, head, mics and assorted electronics to put on a show. Cole glanced at his watch often, wondering where Quincy and Forbes were.

"Honey, they're not here and they aren't going to be here until all the heavy lifting is done. That's their way. If you stood up to them and made them do their share or else give up part of their pay, they wouldn't walk on you the way they do."

"Shara, I have told you, I can't do this without Forbes. I can't. I have to have him help me."

"But he doesn't help you, which is what we're discussing."

"Shara, you have been on me a lot lately. A lot. Why do you do that?"

"Because I believe in you more than you do. You're the best baritone, the best salesman, the best everything at all you do. I believe that, and I don't like to watch you be a doormat for these men. Or your mother."

"Okay, we can't argue now. People are trickling in. We're supposed to start singing in —" He glanced at his watch again. "— ten minutes. If they do show up when it's time to start, they won't have time to get dressed."

His worried face stoked his wife's impatience. "So, you'll start singing alone, too. Fine by me. What do you feel like doing? Nat King Cole?"

"Why? Because we came in the back entrance?" He chuckled. "Actually, I feel like doing Jerry Butler."

"Does anyone remember who that is?"

"Shara, for heaven's sake!" Cole's patience was also wearing thin.

"Honey, I don't mean to ride you. I hate being a nagging hag. I do. It's just that you are such a soft touch that people take advantage of you. It's tiresome."

"I realize what you're saying. But when you speak to me like this, I'm the one who gets beat up, not the people you say are walking on me."

"As I've said many times, I am more than willing to speak to your mother and to your singers. I don't much care if they hate me."

"And as I have said many times, I would really rather you did not." His tone of finality was inarguable. Shara let it go.

Chapter 7

Lunch with Lloyd Fuller was filling. Theresa ordered a heavy, carb-loaded meal, uncertain when she would eat again. Tim was also plenty hungry and he enjoyed his roast beef sandwich, mashed potatoes and gravy immensely. He and Fuller talked about music.

"What is your teaching focus, Lloyd?"

"I teach a course in history through the Renaissance, Baroque, Classical and Romantic periods. It's an overview course, obviously.

"Sure," Tim agreed. "Josquin through Haydn. I taught a course just like that at my last position."

"I saw that on your resume. My question is this: why would you say Haydn instead of Mozart as your personification of the Classical period.

"'Because Haydn deserves more credit than he gets,'"

"Agreed. But you know that Haydn took the hit when John Lennon failed to ever rip him off."

Tim's eyebrows went up. "I didn't know that John Lennon ever ripped anyone off. What do you mean?"

"'Ripped off' is too strong a word, I guess. Let's say he lifted, or he borrowed, or he, I think the kids say, 'sampled' from Mozart. Ever listen to 'You've Got to Hide Your Love Away'?"

Tim looked down and sang the song in his mind for a moment. Then, "Oh, wow. I never realized that before! That's right out of Mozart's Jupiter Symphony. Ha!" Tim realized fully that Lloyd was testing his musical knowledge. This lunch was a very casual job interview, but it was a job interview nevertheless. He hoped he had named the right Mozart piece.

He looked at Fuller. The satisfied, half smile the professor was wearing, and the slow nod told Tim that he had. He looked over at Theresa and winked at her.

"And even the Jupiter Symphony's fourth movement, if I'm not mistaken, kind of tips its hat to Josquin's Pangue Lingua, does it not, with the C-D-F-E progression?"

Lloyd's exuded sincerity, if nothing else, and Theresa relaxed for a moment.

"Hey, I've got to get back to my office. Come on in with me. Gabriela ought to be done getting you a voucher for accommodations tonight, and a gift card to the restaurant there for dinner."

"Really appreciate, Lloyd. This takes off some pressure," Tim told him.

"I can see you're under some pressure. I'll do what I can to help."

Theresa wondered what the cryptic remark meant, but it was Tim's interview, not hers. Not her place to butt in and ask. But the remark stuck with her. She wondered which of the two of them had been tipping their hand. Her fear went up one notch.

Later, Tim and Theresa relaxed in their hotel room. Tim had the news on, and Theresa took a hot shower. She used the hotel's soap and shampoo, conscious of the savings to her dwindling resources.

When she stepped out and dried off, she called out to her husband, "How are you feeling about the lunch and the interview?"

"Well, as I told you, it wasn't supposed to be an interview — although it was — and, I really don't know how I feel. The guy was really cool. I liked him and if I get the job, I'll probably make friends with him. But that will be then and this is now. My worry is meeting the department head. With his son in an accident, his mind won't be on me." "Look here. The restaurant's menu looks like they've got great food. The chef comes from the Hong Kong Hilton, this says, and this Asian menu looks fantastic."

"It only looks fantastic because it's free. You know full well I can live without Asian food."

"Ah, but you will eat it tonight with appreciation, and so will I. When do you think you'll be hungry?"

"Not very soon. This has been a long day. Let's take a nap and be fresh for a late dinner."

Theresa lay down next to her husband. She wore only the hotel towel that was wrapped around her. Her fingers walked up his thigh as he sat on the edge of the bed. The evening news was coming on. "You could turn that off for a while," she hinted.

"In a minute. I just want to see the national news." He took her fingers in his hand and held them.

"You don't have much appetite either lately," she remarked. Tim patted her hand, still looking at the television.

That's all there is to that discussion, she told herself. She closed her eyes.

When her eyes opened, it was 8:30 and she definitely felt hungry. She slipped on clothes, applied lipstick, and woke her dozing husband.

The couple entered the lobby and looked around. There to the left of the elevator was the restaurant entrance. A large neon sign topped the entrance with the name of the place: "Tin Pan Sally's."

"I love it! I just love the name. Hilarious." Then Tim noticed the large sign on a tripod announcing live entertainment would be playing tonight. On the sign, a photo showed the three men Tim and Theresa had met earlier in the day.

"What a small world!" Tim enthused. "Whadya know about that?"

"So, 'The Cole Renshaw Trio,' huh? They'll probably be as surprised as we are since we told them we were leaving town."

"Let's see."

The two stepped into the establishment and looked around. The decor was just a little jarring to Theresa. The walls were a rather unpleasant ecru, and the appointments were of a burnt sienna hue. Mismatched and ugly, she thought. Orange and white bunting was draped across the ceiling, held in place with hooks. Theresa saw this as a lame and ineffectual way of hearkening visitors back to the Sands in Vegas where Sinatra and musicians of his ilk performed back in the day.

Small cabaret tables covered with ecru plastic tablecloths were littered throughout the floor, surrounding a stage on the far side of the room. Black steel chairs with orange upholstery were set around each table.

The hostess, having greeted the pair, began to lead them to a table, but Tim stopped her and requested a table near the music. "I'm a musician," he advised.

"Sure," she intoned. She led them to seats near the foot of the stage.

The three men on stage were singing a standard that the couple recognized easily. "'At Long Last Love.' *Cole Porter, circa 1935*, Tim recited to himself.

Theresa knew it best as the turtle song.

"Is it the good turtle soup/or merely the mock?" Cole, singing lead, crooned.

Tim intended to enjoy this evening. As he held out Theresa's chair to help her get seated, Cole saw him from the stage. He laughed between lyrics and pointed to Tim, welcoming him.

Tim recognized instantly that Cole was schmoozing the club owner, signaling that Tim and Theresa were here to see the singers — that the three men were the draw. Smart marketing.

The irony and improbability of the coincidence even coaxed a smile out of Theresa, Tim noted. Good to see her relax, calm down. The thought flitted through his mind that he couldn't give her a relaxed, calm life anymore. He blamed himself.

More than that, he was trying his level best to conceal from her exactly how panicked he was about the immediate future. He had intercepted a piece of mail back at the double-wide: an eviction notice. This weighed on him, and his darkest fear was that the interviewer the next day would sense his desperation. The cheerful, optimistic face he was wearing tonight for Treese was plastic — thin and unsubstantial as cellophane.

"Yes, ma'am," Treese was saying to the server. "Would you mind checking this gift card to see how much money is on it? We need to know how to order. Thanks." The server took the card and walked away, silently rolling her eyes.

As the song ended, Cole said, "Now, we've got another stump-the-stars trivia question. Remember, you all out there are the stars, and we're gonna stump you. This is a tough one, so I'm gonna bring Quincy up here to tell you what you'll win. Quincy?"

Quincy took a step forward. "First prize, if you get this right is — a two-gallon jug of home-made pork gravy and four — get that — four soppers!" His voice, filled with humor, was taken seriously by no one. His facetious grin was reflected by many in the crowd.

A female voice came over the speakers, and Tim and Theresa looked around for its source. "Did you say four soppers?" The couple then noticed a woman at the side of the stage behind a table filled with electronics.

"That's what I said," Quincy continued. "Second prize is a full color autographed photo of Cole in a bathing suit. Third prize is a hand-crafted pot holder woven out of chewing gum wrappers by my nephew at Bible camp!"

Cole then spoke into the mic, "All right, folks, these great prizes can be yours. We'll sing a song, and you'll have to guess who had the hit on this song. Listen carefully!"

As the music came up, Tim began to listen. He knew the "contest" was a joke, but he wanted to play the game anyway.

Theresa saw Tim perk up. His eyes were intent on the stage and he looked engaged. This was good.

The three singers launched into a lovely ballad Theresa had never heard before. She looked over at Tim. His brow was knit. He didn't know who recorded it, and that took her by surprise. Her husband was a self-styled expert on the Tim Pan Alley music of the early 20th century. But this didn't sound like that era to her. Not surprising he was a star who was stumped. The song was apparently named, "Then You Can Tell Me Good-bye," she gathered from the text.

When the song ended, she wondered if Tim would shout out a guess as to the identity of the artist. But he didn't. This was exactly the kind of intellectual exercise that Tim loved to compete in. She was a little disappointed.

Somebody in the audience, an older man in an Elvis tee shirt and a badly fitted hairpiece hollered out a guess.

"No, sir, not The Classics IV, but that's a good guess. It was a vocal group, and its name did begin with a C. Who else?"

Cole pointed into the crowd, looking for raised hands. "You, right there in the red shirt — That is correct. The Casinos recorded that song in 1967. Right after the show, see Quincy about your four soppers." The crowd offered a modest laugh. "We're gonna take a little pause for the cause right now. Be back soon. Don't go far away. We'll be back with some great hits from the American Songbook!"

The three men and the woman at the soundboard descended the short set of steps and worked their way through the audience. Quincy paused at a table and signed an autograph, as the woman beat a path to the outside and the restroom. But Cole and Forbes went directly to Tim and Theresa.

"Hey, guys, I'm so glad you came out. I was up there singing and couldn't remember telling you where we'd be playing. Sure glad you remembered."

"We actually didn't remember, or ever know. The outfit that is interviewing me for a job at the college tomorrow messed up and the guy missed the interview. So, they put us up overnight in this hotel. Funny coincidence."

"What's the job?" Forbes asked. He was looking at Theresa mostly with a curious expression on his face.

"I'm going for a music professorship at the college."

"Good luck," Forbes continued. "I heard they have a great music program."

"I'm a music lover, and surely a lover of the American Songbook. It's fortuitous that the hotel we got happened to have a place like Tin Pan Sally's. I love the name."

"Remind me of your names again?" Forbes queried.

"Tim. And Theresa."

"Oh, right. I won't forget again, I promise." He flashed a warm smile. "How long have you been out of work?

"A while. Things have gone pretty badly. We both got laid off and it's been a struggle."

"How long?" Forbes insisted.

"Fifteen months for her; eighteen for me."

"Sometimes we have to give up looking and make our own job," he repeated.

"What does that mean?" Tim asked with just a whisper of defensiveness.

"Hey, I've been where you are. I was laid off from a factory job almost two years ago, and I went through all of this with the endless job applications and the call backs for jobs I couldn't even do, or that were so low paying that it costs more to do them than not, or were in another state, or required a college degree, or that I couldn't physically manage or something. At the end of the day I gave up trying. Now I drive a cab and sing at night. Quincy works in a grocery store, and Cole's wife works while he runs our group. We're all struggling. Every one of us, but it looks to me like you both have had a real hard time."

"Why do you say that?" Theresa interjected.

"Look, I don't know you and I don't want to be untoward. It's none of my business."

"No, really, I want to know why you think that," she pressed.

Forbes looked in his lap for a moment and formed his words. "Well, ma'am, you seem, I mean, you just look a little, I don't know, haunted."

Theresa was mortified. She stared at the two men with her lips parted in surprise and fear. She turned to her husband for his remark. He just pursed his lips slightly. "You think so, too, don't you?" he said to Cole.

"I don't blame you for that, ma'am," Forbes went on. "The fear wears on you, and it can't help but come out on your face sometimes. Your secret's safe with us," he promised.

Cole changed the subject. Turning to Tim, he said, "What instruments do you play?"

"With varying degrees of competency, I play cello, violin, sax, bone, organ and piano."

"Really? What is your varying level of competency on keys

"When I was in college, in what seems like a lifetime ago, I started a jazz combo — a cello, drums and keys — with myself on keys. We did some original pieces. Why?"

"Sweet. Well, I have to tell you that some people agree with you about the digital orchestration we use. I am getting pressure from a lot of the club owners I see who want live instruments. I'm with your wife; I think the digital music sounds better and is less expensive to use, but the pressure's on anyway.

"I want us to bill as primarily singers. I don't want to be a 'band.' But getting booked is becoming tougher and I may need to hire a musician. Since you're out of work, I was just thinking."

"Honestly," Tim replied, "when I met you in front of that theater, I was thinking along the same lines."

Forbes interrupted. "Cole, we gotta go." Then, to the couple, "Will you stay for the set? We can talk more."

"Yeah, stay," Cole agreed. "Who knows, maybe you'll win a tank of pork gravy and four soppers." Cole appeared serene, but looked meaningfully at Forbes. Something passed between the two. Forbes nodded at his partner. Both Tim and Theresa noticed it, but didn't ask.

The two stood and approached the stage. The woman was already at her soundboard, and Quincy was returning from his pit stop.

"Hey! We're back, ladies and gentlemen. Remember, if you have a favorite song from any era, make your request to Shara on digital orchestration. If we know the song, we'll do it for you.

"Here's your next Stump the Stars challenge. We'll sing you this next song, and you have to tell us who had the biggest hit and who wrote the song and in what year the song hit the charts.

"Yeah, this one is a tough, but the prize is no joke. I have here a gift card for $300 from Walmart that I will give to the first person who can tell me the artist, composer, lyricist and year it came out. Good luck to all!

"And by the way, any contestant using a smart phone will be disqualified. That's cheating, you all. If I see a smart phone, everyone at that table is left out of the game."

When Cole mentioned a $300 gift card, Theresa's eyes got wide. She looked over at Tim, but he was staring at Cole, anticipation filling his eyes.

Cole continued, "Now, singing lead on this Stump the Stars is this man." He turned toward the singer named Quincy. "Let me tell you about Quincy. I can drag Quincy out of bed at 4 in the morning wearing pajama bottoms and plush velour slippers that look like zebras, shove him on stage in front of a full auditorium, cue a song he's never heard before, and he can still kick it to the moon, and all this — while he's in a coma. Here he is, Quincy Garland."

The opening music began and Quincy stepped forward with his mic.

Theresa was making a clenched fist in her lap. As she did, though, the phone went off in her purse. A text message had arrived, and she started to follow her instinct and read it. "No, no," she scolded herself. "Whew! Almost blew it!"

Quincy sang the song. Theresa studied her husband carefully for a sign. It came when he glanced at her briefly and winked before turning his attention back to the stage. She relaxed just enough to admit this singer was powerful on the song. "Teach Me Tonight," was the title, but that's all she knew about it.

At the conclusion, Cole stepped forward, and said to the crowd, "Okay, ladies and gentleman, let's see how stumped you are. We need composer, lyricist, artist who had the first big hit and year the hit was released. Whaddya got for me?"

Theresa noticed that Cole looked right at Tim, as if expecting a response. Tim had one.

He raised his hand. "Yes, sir, here in the front," Cole pointed at Tim.

Tim, acting nonchalant, said, "Gene DePaul wrote that."

"Correct. Gene DePaul. And who was the lyricist?"

Tim's palms got sweaty. He was 85 percent sure, but he could blow it on that fifteen percent. "Here goes," he told himself.

"I'm gonna say Sammy Cahn."

"Sammy Cahn is correct, brother. You're almost there. Who had the first big hit on the song?"

Cole's delivery reminded Theresa of a game show host.

"The DeCastro Sisters, I think."

"Correct again!" Cole announced triumphantly. "And in what year?"

Again, Tim was unsure. Of course, it was a hit song in the 50s, and lots of artists did it through the decade. "Hmm," he thought. Sinatra sang it, but later.

"Okay, I'm not sure, but I'll say 1955," Tim announced loudly to Cole and the crowd.

Cole paused for a half of a second before he announced, "Correct again! You're a winner! Please see Shara on digital orchestration for your $300 gift card to Walmart!"

On stage, Forbes' and Quincy's eyes met, Theresa noted, but she didn't care if the contest was rigged. That gift card would be a hug benefit. She squeezed Tim's hand.

Tim arose from his chair and went to the side of the stage where the woman's soundboard was set up. "Yes, I'm here for the — "

Shara presented the envelope, and Tim was as nonchalant as he could manage as he lifted it from her hand. His hands trembled a little, but he hoped she didn't notice. He wondered if he would be any more excited if he had won the Powerball. Extraordinary, he told himself, how desperation and poverty change a person's values.

"While I'm here," he whispered, "can I make a request?"

"Sure. What would you like?" Shara asked.

"Give me some Van Heusen and Burke."

"Can you be more specific? We do a lot of Van Heusen and Burke."

"You do?"

"Of course. They're iconic."

Tim looked at the woman with admiration and a realization of their shared passion. "Okay, then, but you pick. I never heard a bad song written by those guys."

"No worries. And good luck with that gift card. Enjoy."

Tim returned to his seat, handing the envelope to Theresa, who tucked it in her purse. The Van Heusen and Burke standard that began playing next was written for Bing Crosby in 1944 for a movie, Tim told her. The up-tempo "Swinging On A Star" mirrored the mood Tim was growing into. He had a good feeling, suddenly, about everything.

At the end of the evening, the three singers returned to the Sheltons' table and thanked them for coming. Cole handed over a business card with his contact information and told Tim that, if he wanted to be an accompanist, the three singers would line up an audition, depending on the outcome of the interview.

"Okay," Tim replied. "But if it goes badly, as I hope it won't, we'll head back to Columbus."

"Let's keep a good thought," Forbes said.

"Yes, let's," Theresa agreed. "It was nice to meet you all," she intoned. Theresa had enjoyed the music, but mostly she enjoyed the effect it was having on Tim. These three men appeared to have shoveled a load off of Tim's shoulders, and she was thankful. "We're going to head on up to bed now."

Theresa had forgotten all about the text message.

Chapter 8

Suzanne Renshaw, 83, loved to talk on the phone. There was little else she could do for entertainment. At her age, getting out and about was a chore, and her front stairs leading to the street were a challenge. Best to go out when her son could take her. She would hold his arm on the way down the steps, and that made her feel warm and safe. She could hold the hand railing, of course, but she'd rather hold him.

"When Cole gets here, I'll have him go to the store and get some Liquid Plumber for the face bowl in the bathroom. Then he can also get me something for dinner, and I'll hope he'll change the door lock. He bought the new lock, but had to leave last time he was here before he put it on."

This Sunday, she was chatting up her friend, Alice Bonner, from church, who had a grown son of her own.

"Girl," chimed in Alice, "if your boy doesn't work, what does he do that takes up all his time? I don't know why he can't take you places you want to go! My boy works for Chevron, so I know why he can't drive me places during the day!"

Suzanne mentally acknowledged the ninetieth time her friend had mentioned her son's good job with the oil company. Alice was always focused on getting the topic back on herself.

"I don't know what that child does," Suzanne continued. "Oh, he has his singing thing, but that's in the evening, so I just don't know why he never comes over unless I call him and make him come."

"He has that wife, hasn't he?"

"Sure, girl, and she's a sweet little white girl. But she works. She's the one who's a breadwinner. So, it's not because of her he won't come over. I guess he just doesn't love the mamma who birthed him."

"Oh, sure he does, Suzanne. Who wouldn't love you, sweet girl," Alice cooed.

Suzanne was thinking Alice was as phony as a rubber chicken. But she didn't let on. "Oh, you're too kind, Alice. Ooh, ooh, I have to hang up. I hear Cole coming in the front. Bye."

Hanging up without waiting for a reply, Suzanne stood, grabbed her cane, and shuffled to the entryway where Cole stood.

"This is the same old lock, Mamma. I thought you were going to have that handyman put on the new lock I got you."

"Oh, my, no!" she emoted. "He wants $20 just to put it on. I told him to forget it. I'd just wait for you to put it on."

"Mamma, I told you this. I have never put a lock on a door in my life. I would have no idea what I'm doing. It would be far safer and more secure if you had — what's his name, Derek? — put it on for you."

"It can't be that hard. Won't you just do it for me?"

"Mamma, again. I don't know how to do it. For me it would take two hours. For Derek, it would take fifteen minutes. I'll call him. What's his number?"

"You can't stay with me for two hours? What's so important you won't sit with me?"

"I'm happy to sit with you for a few minutes, but I do have some venues I want to go to while the breakfast buffets are still open and their managers are on duty."

"Good. Let's go out to brunch together. You can talk to your managers and I'll have a hot meal."

Cole conjured a mental image of taking his ailing mother into the elegant patio restaurant at the four-star hotel in town and making a positive impression as he retrieved plateful after plateful from the buffet for the house dress-wearing, swollen-ankled, gray-haired, shuffling octogenarian. Nope, wouldn't happen. But, he couldn't tell her that.

"Sure, Mamma. Get ready and I'll take you to eat." Once again, business would be put off for another day or another week.

Chapter 9

"Frank, it's Lloyd," Professor Fuller said as soon as the department head answered his phone. "How's Frankie doing?"

"Hello, Lloyd." His tone was somber, a tone contrary to the boisterous, ebullient demeanor Lloyd's boss usually presented. "We're on some pins and needles waiting the test results. It looks like he may have a ruptured spleen, a laceration in one kidney, and his jaw is broken in three places. His air bag didn't go off, and he'll be in for lots of reconstructive surgery — if he makes it at all."

"Frank, I'm so sorry. How did the accident happen?"

"He ran off the road and plunged into a ravine. We don't know why. Someone was with him who wasn't injured badly. Her airbag deployed. Something happened to take his mind off the road. We won't know what until, well, he can tell us."

"What did you find out? Did you talk to Shelton?"

"I did. I took him to lunch. His wife is in town with him, so I met both."

"What do you think, so far?" the department head asked.

Lloyd Fuller thought for a minute before answering. He had to frame his words well. He had to be very subtle and manipulative, and his boss was a long way from stupid.

"Well, he's got some chops. I didn't do an audition, but we talked and his musicianship is fine. He certainly knows his field very well . . ." Lloyd left the end of the question up in the air.

"But? I hear a 'but' coming."

"No 'buts.' He's fine. He'd be a fine addition to the department. I just think you have some very strong, younger candidates you haven't looked at very seriously and before you narrow the field down too far, you should call in a few more people."

"Such as?"

"Well, did you see the credential of this woman, Barbara Baxter, out of Missouri? She is about to earn her doctorate in music history, and her field is 20th century classical music. For her doctoral thesis, she examines the correlation between personal idiosyncrasy and musical genius with a close examination of Glenn Gould. She looks very interesting. Plus, several others. I've taken some time today to look over some resumes.

"Wow, I'm impressed. You know all about one candidate's thesis. You've done a lot more than just read resumes," Glenn said. His ears were perked up. Something about this was off. But he couldn't name it.

"Just trying to pitch in while you're out. You'll be back Friday afternoon for the 4 o'clock meeting?"

"I've got an early flight. See you then."

When the two hung up the phone, Lloyd gathered a short stack of resumes he had set aside and took them in Frank's office to set on his desk. He put Barbara Baxter's resume on top with pride. He wouldn't let on until it was too late to change it, but he wanted the best advantage for his baby girl. She had told him only this morning that she intended to apply. Any effort he intended to make for Tim Shelton was now moot.

Chapter 10

"Your mother called during the show," Shara told Cole as the couple picked up sound equipment and secured it on a hand truck. "Did you not tell her we have a show?"

"Sure, I told her. What did the message say?"

"She wants you to come by after the show."

"Okay."

"You're not going, are you? It's midnight," Shara appealed.

"Oh, she doesn't care if it's late. She's up all night anyway. We won't stay long."

"We won't stay at all, Cole. Why does she not understand that the world does not orbit her?"

Cole paused and looked at his wife, considering her reaction. "I'll just tell her you're tired and want to go home."

"Then she'll want to know why you don't come by yourself."

Again, Cole considered Shara's growing unease. He often felt trapped between these two women, and that he was the rope in their long-standing tug of war.

"Okay. We'll just go home. You have to work tomorrow, don't you?"

"Of course, I do. Plus, I keep thinking that if she wouldn't stay up to the wee hours every night, she might could drag her keister out of bed before noon."

Cole looked at his singing partners. Quincy was sitting at a table with his cell phone to his ear. Forbes was winding microphone cords on a spindle. After every show, Quincy always had an emergency phone call to make while Forbes, feigning helpfulness, did the light work, leaving the speakers and heavier equipment for Cole and Shara to lift. Cole had accepted defeat on this matter long ago.

"I know what you're thinking," Shara told him.

"You do?"

"You're thinking that Quincy and Forbes are lazy. I'm thinking that, too. Are you sure you don't want to be a solo act?"

"I told you many times, I can't do this without Forbes."

"I disagree. I heartily disagree."

"Help me get this speaker down, will you?"

While Cole lifted the speaker off its pole, Shara removed the pin and let the pole telescope in on itself. Then she helped him ease the speaker to the floor. "These things get heavier with every show," she remarked. She picked up the pole, collapsed its tripod, and slid it into its case.

Shara took the case down the short flight of steps and set it by the hand truck. She'd carry that herself out to the van. She turned to go upstairs and nearly bumped into an approaching woman. Shara guessed she was in her early 70s. She wore a sweatshirt with a silkscreened message extolling the virtues of blackjack, and a pink golfers hat studded with rhinestones. Her lips were decorated with bright pink lipstick that matched her hat.

"Oh, I'm sorry. I almost crashed you," Shara apologized.

"Oh, hello, dear. I just wanted to tell you how much I enjoyed the show. We got here right at 7 and have been here ever since. My husband just loves their singing. How on earth did you get a job doing this?" The 's patronizing inquiry struck Shara a disingenuous at least, and unnecessary at most.

"Oh, the gig kind of came with the man, I guess. The leader of the group is my husband, Cole," Shara explained.

The woman's face darkened. "You're married?"

"Yes, to that man there," she gestured to the stage where Cole was detaching a speaker wire from the floor monitor.

The woman seemed taken aback. Her mouth opened slightly as if to speak, then closed, then opened again. Shara had seen this plenty of times before and could virtually script what was to come next. Lacking patience owing to the lateness of the hour, she plunged in to get it over with. "You know, ma'am, this is the 21st century and some of us whiteys do marry black folks. And, I guess I haven't been spat on in ten years. Why don't you try to catch up to the times, huh?" With that, Shara moved to the edge of the stage to take the floor monitor from Cole and put it on the hand truck. When she turned around again, the woman was gone.

"What was that?" Cole said, leaning down to her.

"Nothing. She likes your singing."

"Well, I'll go invite her to the Claymont show tomorrow."

"Um, honey, don't bother. Really."

"What do you mean?"

"I'll tell you later. Is Quincy off the phone yet?"

"Now, you know he isn't going to hang up that phone until the work is done."

"Fine. Scoot that speaker over here and I'll lift it down."

Chapter 11

Theresa luxuriated in the king-sized hotel bed until 8:30 in the morning. She was still full from the meal at Tin Pan Sally's, but she vowed to be up, showered and ready before the continental breakfast offered by the hotel was cleared away. She noted with satisfaction that there was enough money left on the gift card that she and Tim could eat lunch, too. Good. She could send Tim into this interview with a full stomach so he could be at his best. She tried to ignore the butterflies already fluttering in her stomach about the interview this afternoon.

She wished she had a change of clothes. She had washed out her underwear and socks in the bathroom sink last night and put them on the forced air heater to dry. They were stiff, and would be uncomfortable to put back on, but were clean. Her blouse and slacks were another matter.

Tim was up and sitting in the corner of the room in a chair. He was studying the copy of the job description he had printed off the Internet. The hotel's printer had come in handy. The couple had let their printer go for $10 at some long-ago garage sale.

The importance of acing this interview wasn't lost on him either, Theresa acknowledged, and a warm glow filled her as she watched her husband concentrate.

"Hey. I'm gonna jump in the shower," she told him.

"Sure," he answered, his mind on his task. "I got mine earlier."

She took her purse into the bathroom with her clothes. She noticed the phone in her purse, and then she remembered the text message.

She sat on the toilet and dug the phone out. The message was from Dorothy Pratt, their nearest neighbor in the trailer park. It read:

Sheriff here puttn u out. Ur stuff all over lawn. Kids pickin thru. Locks changed on door. I saved a lot of ur clothes 4 u. Call me.

The familiar fear and panic wrapped around Theresa's heart like a python, and squeezed. She was homeless, and the realization of what that word meant was suffocating. She flashed on images of homeless men and women in downtown Columbus, filthy, stinking, desperate and frightening. At certain intersections in the city, they would assault her car, hands on her windshield, and ask for money. She was now one of them. She sat there in the bathroom, frozen, afraid to move, staring at the message for a long time.

"You okay, honey? I don't hear shower noises. We better get going if we want the free breakfast."

In that moment, Theresa made the decision to keep this news from Tim. She deeply feared that his desperation would show on his face during the interview just as it had registered on her face when she spoke with those singers. Keeping the news from showing on her own face was going to be a trick, but she'd do the best she could. That way, the pressure would be piled on her, but not him, until the interview was over.

Chapter 12

Sal stopped in a hamburger joint on the way to the store. A fast-foodie kind of place that had recently opened for breakfast, he noticed immediately the young woman who stood at the counter. She was new, he guessed. He hadn't see her before.

"What can I serve you," was her canned greeting. Read right off a script given to her on her first day, she nevertheless seemed friendly. There was just a slight whisper of flirtation to her tone. Just a slight one.

The woman was young; maybe 20. Her hair was pulled back in a bun on the back of her head, and a beret naming the restaurant covered most of her scalp.

She was not much more than a kid — the kind of young woman a guy like Sal could coach and guide. Maybe, he reasoned, she would be more conciliatory than that hateful Sandra had been.

His grin was flirtatious, not threatening.

"Do you have hush puppies?" he asked, his eyes gleaming.

"Um, not for breakfast, sir. Usually you can get hush puppies in fish places, not places like this, and then, just for lunch."

"I see. Do you have hash brown casserole?"

"No sir. We have hash browns, but not in a casserole."

"Do you have collard greens and grits?"

"No, sir," she laughed, "and you are bustin' my chops just a little."

"Aw, you caught me. My name's Sal, and I just think you're cute as a button. What's your name, Marie?" He pointed at her name tag.

"Yes, sir," she countered. "Can I take your order?"

"Yes, please. I order you to let me take you to dinner tonight. What do you say?"

The young woman's pleasant smile vanished immediately. "Sir—"

"Sal," he corrected.

"Okay, Sal, I would have to know you a lot better than I do before I would consider such a thing. May I take your order?"

Sal ate breakfast each of the following five days and talked to Marie each day. Each day he asked her for a date, and each day except the last, she side-stepped his efforts. On the last day, Marie agreed to coffee with him. Only coffee, that's all, she insisted.

Chapter 13

"Hey, man," Cole greeted Forbes when the doorbell rang. C'mon in. Quincy called. He can't get here. He's at work until 3, and will go straight to the Claymore, so I figured you and I would work up some arrangements and let him put in his own part later."

"Sure, man. What're we doing?"

"'The Lady is a Tramp.' Here's what I'm thinking. You and I will sing the melody like we're having an argument and one of us singing, 'the lady is a champ' while the other sings tramp. Is she a tramp or is she a champ? Kinda fun. Get it?"

"Okay, man" Forbes said agreeably. "Let's see what you got."

The music came up on the digital system and the two men, having sung together for decades, picked their own entrances based on instinct and gesturing to each other. This song was going to be easy to make stage-ready, they agreed.

When that was complete, Cole told his friend, "Okay, now you sing it all the way through just like I'm singing it with you, but I'll show you this descant I came up with for Quincy to do."

"You know he won't like doing a descant."

"Then I'll do it. Or you can do it. I don't care. Just tell me if you like it."

Shara was in the kitchen listening to the two practice. It was always a treat to hear her men sing together, but she was still aware of a few things that bothered her. Cole was too easy on the others. Sure, their friendship predated their singing group — and her marriage — and Cole was reluctant to tighten the screws on them, but a little professional distance would make him more of a leader. And less of a door mat

She popped a bag of popcorn in the microwave, poured it in a bowl, and took it into the living room. They liked salty snacks when they sang. Seemed to help their voices.

Forbes thanked her for the snack by nodding as he sang the song.

She smooched Cole on the forehead.

Shara's dissatisfaction stemmed, in part, from her husband's failure to see himself correctly. He had just as good vocal chops as the other two. Better, in some ways. While Quincy had that great, gravely r&b thing going on, and Forbes had the amazing three-octave range, Cole had what her own marketing brochures described as "a voice like melting chocolate." He was smooth, velvety and sexy. She couldn't stand it when he readily turned over to Quincy or Forbes yet another lead on a song.

She liked the Rogers and Hart standard, and was glad the group was developing it. It was easy to hear, she could tell, and would be ready as soon as Quincy got his part down.

Now, while Forbes was singing it, Cole weaved in an alternate melody, singing, "The chick is a champ," over and over, that went up when the melody went down and vice versa. It was cute. It would work.

She sat down at the desk near the singers and began to hand scribble a possible program for the show for Sunday night. There was a beer garden across town that wanted the group to entertain for the after-hours crowd. The group would play from 8 until 11, and so another late night would rob her of sleep when she had to get up and go to work the next morning.

She admitted to herself that she loved this meaningless part-time job for her husband's singing group, in spite of the endless low paying gigs, personality conflicts, ego-management strategies and frustrations getting work. She was so proud of her man and his friends that every performance was a treat, even when everything didn't go right. Until they became world-renown and loved by millions, she would pay the bills with her little job, and revel in their success, such as it was.

Chapter 14

Lloyd Fuller called Missouri to talk to his daughter before his boss got back from Denver. He wanted her to have a heads up. "Hey, little girl," he greeted her when she answered.

"Hi, Dad, how are you doing?"

"I put in a word for you on that job at the college here."

"You did? Did you do it without revealing my secret identity?" The cheer in her voice and her reference to the superhero comic books they had shared when she was a youngster made him laugh.

Barbara Fuller Baxter was at her church in Rolla, down the street from the University of Missouri campus, working on a medley of sacred music for Sunday. She sat at the organ, cell phone in hand, happy to hear from her father and best friend. She had been practicing a setting she had composed herself for Advent, "Wake, Awake, For Night Is Flying." The sixteenth century classic had always been her favorite.

Barbara was a beautiful woman of 32, blonde and curvy. She had been married only five years before facing widowhood following an industrial accident. Her husband, Bill, had been an engineer developing technology to automate a dangerous function in the assembly of automobile parts. He had gone to the plant to test a prototype when the factory was shut down for the weekend, had severed his hand on the machine, had gone into shock, and had bled out before anyone found him Monday morning. His wife, in Terre Haute to visit her father, didn't know he hadn't made it home until someone from the plant reached her.

The accident, coming two years after her mother's death from cancer, had brought the father and daughter to a much fuller closeness. They talked every day. Barbara had high hopes of getting this job at her dad's college. There was nothing for her in Rolla now. Not without Bill.

"I just pointed out your superior qualifications," her father was continuing. "I talked about your doctoral thesis, and your experience in composition."

"Dad, do you think he found it plausible? I mean, how many doctoral theses do you read as a general rule? Won't he figure out that you and I are kin? Or at least that we have more than a job applicant/professor relationship?"

"I didn't really think of that," Lloyd confessed.

"So, did Professor Glenn get a lot of applicants for the job?"

"Two hundred and seventy-seven."

"Holy smokes!" she emoted.

"It's not that bad, baby," her father retorted. "Only a handful — a dozen or so — are suitable, and of them only three or four are worth interviewing."

"Three or four besides me or including me?"

"Including you." He went on to explain the gaffe with one applicant who was scheduled for an interview when the department head was out of state. "Boy, was my face red when that guy showed up," he told her.

"Dad, look, not to change the subject, but I'm thinking of coming home."

"You are?"

"Yes, I am. Whether I get this job at your college or not, well, I'm homesick and there's really nothing keeping me here. My thesis is in; the committee will bestow the doctorate or it won't, and then I'm free as a bird. I've gotten rid of all of Bill's belongings, cleaned up the condo, and I'm ready to move no matter what. Could you use a roommate?"

"Sure, honey. This is your home, always. But I don't want you to sit at home and mope once you get here. You need to find a good job that will challenge you. This one at the college is perfect for you, but the school has strict rules about hiring relatives in the same department. I have to keep my influence on the down-low, as they say."

"My lips are sealed. I'm probably going to hire a moving van for two weeks from tomorrow."

"Hey, what about your present job? Did you give your notice?"

"Not yet. But it won't much matter to the church. There are probably a million Lutheran church organists out there looking for music directorships. These jobs are hard to come by. The church won't have any problem filling my position."

Chapter 15

"I'm meeting with that club owner at noon, Forbes, so I hope you can get this done in time for me to be there."

"Sure, man, but give me credit, will ya? This isn't my first door lock."

"Yeah, well, it would have been mine, so I owe you for this." Cole approached his mother's front door, key in hand. As he let himself in, with Forbes carrying a small tool box, he checked the clock on his cell phone. It was 9:30. Plenty of time for Forbes to change the lock before Cole's appointment.

"Ooh, it's the doctor!" Suzanne cooed as she came into the foyer and spotted Forbes. "How have you been, young man?"

"Real good, Mrs. Renshaw. You know I've never been a doctor."

"You're a doctor to me, Forbes, after you saved my husband's life." Her vitriolic glance at Cole was intended for only his eyes. "You found his nitroglycerin just in time to save him that time. I'll never forget it. He was clutching his chest and you were here with my son, and you dug out the pills from his pocket and got one under his tongue. I'll never forget it."

Forbes noted that the incident with the nitro pills was in 1977, and yet Mrs. Renshaw insisted on bringing it up each and every rare occurrence of him visiting her house. It was tedious to the point of predictability. "Mrs. Renshaw, Cole and I are here to change out your door lock. I understand you have a new replacement lock?"

"Oh, yes, just a sec." She shuffled into another room and in a few moments produced the new lock. Cole, meanwhile, cleared her dirty breakfast dishes from the dining room table and put them in the sink for her. When Cole returned to the dining room, his mother was poised in her favorite chair watching Forbes work. As predicted, the lock replacement took Forbes eighteen minutes, and he was happy to complete the task and move on. "You ready, man?" he said to his friend.

"Yeah, sure. Hey, we're goin', Mom," Cole hollered over his shoulder. "I've got a business meeting."

"Okay," she called back. "Are you sure you don't have time for a cup of coffee, both of you? I made a fresh pot."

"No, thank you, Mrs. Renshaw. Cole needs to drop me off before he heads to his meeting, and my place is in the opposite direction."

"Oh, okay," she murmured with a calculated mournfulness.

"Wait a minute, Forbes, I left my keys somewhere." Cole was sticking his hands in and out of pockets to his pants and jacket. No keys were found.

"Well, where'd you leave 'em?"

"Don't know. Wait a minute." Cole traced his steps. He'd been to the dining room, but the keys weren't on the table. He'd taken dishes to the kitchen sink, but no keys appeared on any kitchen counter. Back in the dining room, the keys weren't on the buffet, the end table next to the lamp, the ottoman leading into the living room, or the sofa. Suzanne watched from her seat at the table, happy for the company to stay longer.

Cole checked the spots he'd already checked. Having eliminated all the obvious places, he started on non-obvious places. He checked between the sofa cushions. He put his hand between slits in the radiator. He went back into the kitchen and checked the refrigerator, toaster, microwave, and silverware drawer. Forbes, with an impatience he dared not reveal, went into the bedroom where he knew Cole hadn't been, and checked the bed, nightstand, chest of drawers, and dresser. He went in the bathroom and looked on the toilet tank because that's where he often laid his own keys. Forbes went into the study and looked around on the desk.

While he continued, Cole gave the dining room one more going over. Wracking his brain, he could not remember going into any other room. This was getting bizarre. Time was growing short as he checked his cell phone. It was almost 10 o'clock. He needed those keys.

Forbes gave up. He sat down at the dining room table and Suzanne repeated her offer of coffee. With nothing else to do, he accepted and offered to bring her a cup. "Oh, yes, please. With a little half and half from the refrigerator." While Forbes found coffee cups in the usual cabinet of this home he had visited so many times, Cole continued his search. On his fifth trip into the kitchen, Forbes said, "Coffee?"

"No, man. I need these keys and to get out of here."

"I know, man. Did you go back in your mind and look every place you went since we got here?"

"Of course, man. Don't act like I'm an idiot."

"I'm not, but I don't know where you've checked. I'm gonna sit down with her and wait till you figure things out. What's that bulge in your pants pocket?"

"It's a little box of ibuprofen pills and I'm gonna eat some of 'em in a minute."

"I heard that." Forbes sat with Suzanne as Cole scoured the downstairs again and again, and again. The keys were nowhere. He had them when he came in, he reasoned. Otherwise he couldn't have opened the door.

Stopping himself in mid-stride, he turned around and marched to the front door. He flung it open and checked the lock just in case he'd left the keys hanging there. But no. Not at all. *They're in this house,* he told himself. *They have to be.*

As he walked through rooms glancing around, he repeatedly stuck his hands in each pocket obsessively. The old adage about Einstein flitted through his mind: the definition of insanity is doing the same thing many times and expecting a different result. This was maddening. At a quarter to 11:00, Cole stopped the search, and gave in to fate. He was going to miss his meeting. He was aware Forbes wanted to start his shift in the cab at about the same time, so the pressure was on Cole to drop Forbes off at home for more than one reason.

Allen Parker, owner at The Dark and Stormy Nightclub was going to be a hard sell anyway, and strolling in late would look bad. A sigh of resignation escaped his lips. He lifted his phone from his pocket and called The Dark and Stormy.

"Hey, is this Allen?" Cole said. He hoped his joyful, confident demeanor would come through in his voice. "This is Cole Renshaw, and I'm trying to get on over there to you, but it doesn't look like I'm going to make it today. Yeah, it's been a wild day. Can I come by the same time tomorrow? No? You won't be around? Wow, that's tough. Can I call you next week? Okay, then. Have a good one."

Cole disconnected. "I lost the gig, Forbes. I was on thin ice with the guy because of the karaoke anyway, and he used this excuse to not see me."

"Well, then, you have time for coffee, don't you?" Suzanne squealed from the dining room. "I'll get it." When she hoisted herself to her feet and shuffled into the kitchen, Forbes and Cole spied the car keys sitting on the chair where Mom had been sitting.

"How on earth did she not know she was sitting on those?" Forbes asked his friend. "You carry five dozen keys."

" "I know," Cole said quietly. "We're not going to mention this to Shara. Square?"

"Why not?"

"Because Shara will say Mom *did* know she was sitting on them." "You think she did?"

Cole shrugged his shoulders.

Chapter 16

The Sheltons checked out of their hotel room right at 10 o'clock as the hotel required, but lingered over their continental breakfast. Theresa enjoyed three cups of coffee even though the breakfast fixings had been removed by staff. With hours to kill, they sat in the restaurant and considered alternatives. They could sight-see. Or they could drive around and get the lay of the land. Or they could use their cell phone to examine local housing just in case there was reason to stay in the area. There wasn't a lot possible without spending money, though.

The usual dose of guilt rested on Tim. He couldn't even take Theresa to a movie or a shopping trip to the mall or buy her a rose from a gas station to show her he loves her. Everything was wrong, and his attempts to fix it were inconsequential.

Fumbling in his pocket, he pulled out the business card Cole had given him. Well, here's something to do.

He asked Theresa for the phone and called the number.

A man answered.

"Is this Cole?" Tim asked.

"Yes. Who's calling?" The voice was overly friendly — like a salesman, Tim thought.

Tim identified himself as the man who won the Walmart card the previous night.

"How'd the interview go?" Cole asked. His upbeat timbre seemed to expect good news.

"I don't know yet. It's rescheduled this afternoon. We've got some time to kill, and I wonder if you have a little time. Maybe we could talk about music and the accompaniment you're looking for."

"Um, sure. That'd be fine. I've got a show tonight across town, but not until later. Why don't you come by? We can talk, but I don't have anything for you to play."

"Actually, I've got a little electronic keyboard in the back of the van. Fortuitous. I just didn't think to unload it the last time I took it for an audition."

Cole was quiet, unsure for a moment. Tim considered that the other man may not know what "fortuitous" meant.

Theresa, meanwhile, was most thankful Tim had not unloaded the instrument. The only item they still owned of any value, the three-thousand-dollar piece of equipment, thereby, was not tossed on the lawn back at the double-wide, and no-doubt removed by a neighbor who would sell it on eBay very promptly. She tried not to let her relief show.

"Do you want to come over now?" Cole was asking Tim.

"Um, sure. I'm not familiar with the city, so I'll need directions."

As Cole explained the route to his home, Tim started the engine. Theresa was unsure why she and Tim were doing this; her main thought was for Tim's piano. This marked a rare, unexpected good turn of fortune, she reasoned. This and the Walmart card — maybe they were due for a little good luck.

Fifteen minutes later, Tim parked in front of a modest frame home on Terre Haute's south side, not far from the interstate.

The front door opened as Tim and Theresa approached it. The portly, middle-aged man with the wide brown eyes and impeccably trimmed mustache greeted them. He invited them into a large living room where sound equipment was stacked in cases as if ready to load up for a show. More equipment was poised on a table, and a song was playing with the volume low. Cole turned up the sound, picked up the microphone, and sang a Van Heusen and Burke ballad, "But Beautiful," with aplomb.

"Shara told me you like Van Heusen and Burke," Cole explained at the song's conclusion. "Come on, I'll help you get your keyboard out of your car. Quincy's on his way over, which is good. I have no memory for lyrics at all, which is why I like a teleprompter. But Quincy's never forgotten a lyric in his life."

"Quincy is the one who does the r&b, right?" Theresa asked.

"And, how," Cole affirmed. "Have a seat. Your husband and I will be right back."

As the two men went back outside, Theresa looked at the sofa. It was covered with pet hair of some kind. Oh, well, so what, she told herself. Her clothes were already dirty. What would it hurt? So, she sat on the sofa and the fur, and it wasn't long before a beautiful Siamese cat sauntered into the room and took its place in her lap.

Delighted, Theresa stroked the animal on the head and back. She remembered her cat, Pixie, an orange tabby she had taken to a shelter a year before. She loved the cat dearly, but times had been so lean that she gave him up rather than spending improvidently on food and litter. She had cried all the way home that day as Tim had tamped down his own tears. The memory was fresh, and it provoked Theresa to lift the cat into her arms and bury her face in its neck.

The cat didn't seem to mind. It had been well-loved, it seemed.

Lost in the memory, Theresa was startled a little when Tim and Cole came in carrying the piano and its stand. Cole set up the stand. Tim set the keyboard down and plugged it in. Turning it on, he tested it with a few chords.

"Here," Cole said, handing him a wire. "This goes into the head."

The men cooperated in interfacing Tim's equipment with Cole's. Cole fetched a chair from another room for Tim to use.

Turning to Theresa, he said, "I see you've met Papa Kitty. He's my wife's cat. He has made cat hair the bane of my life. Don't worry, though. I buy lint rollers by the gross. I'll get you cleaned off before you leave."

"Papa Kitty is a sweetheart," she acknowledged. "Hey, I have a question."

"Name it."

"How did you get that Walmart card to give away. What gives with that?"

"Oh, well, Shara and I go to church with a guy who manages the Walmart on State Road 46. Once a month, he gives me a card for give-away, but I promise to mention his store from the stage to give him the free advertisement."

"Oh. Okay," she murmured.

Tim and Cole played with some songs, and Cole made suggestions about the type of music usually preferred by venues that resisted the digital orchestration.

"I guess you can expect that if you try to play a piano bar, they may actually want you to use the piano," Tim suggested.

"You're right about that. There are a couple in town that I've approached, but, I'm thinking . . . " he trailed off and stared at Tim.

"Yes?" Tim said.

"My wife is constantly telling me that I should be a solo act and not work so hard for Quincy and Forbes. She has a point. They've both got some issues. But if I did go solo, at least part of the time, I could pick up lower-paying gigs. Would you consider doing a piano bar with me sometime?"

"Well, as you know, I expect to drive back to Columbus tonight and I have no idea if I'll be back, or when," Tim reminded him.

"I think you should take him up on it," Theresa put in. "I think we should assume the best and say you got the job at the college, and I think we should just stay here."

Tim looked at his wife with astonishment. "Really, Treese? We have to go home to get our belongings and everything. What are you thinking about? What brought this on so suddenly?"

She didn't have to answer his question. The doorbell rang, and Quincy strode into the house. He waved greeting to the couple. He took a seat on the sofa near Theresa without appearing to notice the cat hair.

Theresa noticed that Quincy smelled of marijuana.

"So, what're we doin', man?" Quincy addressed Cole.

"Just going over some material. We may need to pick up an accompanist, and Tim here may be interested."

"Why do we need an accompanist — another piece of the paycheck?" Quincy's timbre was suddenly confrontational. He didn't want the money divided into smaller piece, clearly, and Tim understood.

"Hey, I'm just trying this on for size," he explained. "I don't know that it will happen at all. I may end up back in Columbus in a trailer park and never see you guys again. We're just kicking around ideas here."

"But I'm pretty sure we're moving here," Theresa interrupted. "If we can find a place to live in the budget. Otherwise, we'll live in our van."

The two singers looked at each other meaningfully. Cole remembered that the couple was on the edge of something. His heart went out, and he wanted to help.

Quincy, noticing Cole's change in body language, stepped in and said to Tim, "Hey, man, did you spend that Walmart card all in one place yet?"

"No," Tim replied, "Why?"

"My sister, Marietta, has some rental property across town. It's nothing fancy. Kind of low-rent — literally. But if times are that tough, I might be able to get her to take that Walmart card as first month's rent. Would that help out?"

Theresa's heart rate quickened. She had been considering all the things to use the Walmart card for since she learned she was homeless. Food, clothes, a guest pass to a YMCA to use the shower — an endless list, surely. But first month's rent may be a godsend.

"Wow, um, Quincy. That really could. We may know this afternoon what's going to happen. Thanks so much for that generosity. Wow."

What is going through her head? Tim thought. *Theresa was jumping the gun on all of this.*

"Yeah, sure," he agreed, demurring to her. "We'll be in touch on that."

As the three men settled in and rehearsed songs with the piano, Theresa retreated into her own thoughts. She was on the threshold of a new life, of course, but what form it would take was still shrouded in darkness. Theresa, whose father was a doctor, was well-educated, and had always been comfortable until the last two years. She had filled her life with few black people, or people of any different background from hers. She could not name one black friend from high school, college, or even her work experience that she had ever grown close to.

She didn't think of herself as being bigoted. Her politics were liberal, and one of her friends had once told her that she was a "quintessential bleeding heart." But this was very different. She was apt to actually become beholden to people who were fundamentally different in background. This may, she was thinking, become a meaningful precipice in the evolution of her life. It could redefine her.

Since the layoffs, Theresa had resisted the idea that her actual class had changed. She was still a proud member of the middle class, but just temporarily displaced. But that self-perception had worn thin after a while and she was forced to the brink of reassessing herself as poor. She was letting strangers help her in a palpable way, strangers whose views of the world must be different in innumerable ways.

The thought occurred to her that she could learn a lot if she kept her eyes and ears open. And her mind.

Yet, her basic nature was to resist. She had been so comfortable in her old life, and her intellect whispered that was gone, but her emotions cried out that it wasn't possible.

Lost in thought, the minutes clicked by. The three men tried several songs with the piano, and Tim surprised Theresa by jumping in on a harmony note that would have been Forbes's if he had been there.

"You've got a good ear for harmony," Cole remarked to Tim at one point in the rehearsal.

"Thank you," he said simply. He wondered quietly how one could be an accomplished musician and not hear harmony, but he said nothing further. Perhaps it was early in the friendship, and that Cole didn't yet understand how accomplished Tim was. The fleeting thought ran in contrast to Theresa's. Tim had lost all confidence in his accomplishment, she thought.

Theresa then noticed Quincy giving Cole a look as if to warn him away from whatever he may be thinking. She was not worried on Quincy's behalf, and she admitted to herself that, while her husband was a good singer — always on the right pitch — he was no performer. His voice wasn't pretty or pleasing to listen to like these men's voices were. Tim mounted no threat to any of them.

Absent-mindedly, Theresa looked at her cell phone. It was quarter to three! *Where had the time gone?*

"Tim! I lost track of time. We've got to get back to the hotel and eat lunch and then get to the interview."

"Oh, crap!" Tim responded, standing and removing the wire to the mixer. He quickly picked up the keyboard and headed toward the front door.

Quincy cut him off and held the door open for him and Cole picked up the rear with the piano stand.

Theresa followed the men out. "Hey, thanks, Quincy, again for your offer of an apartment. I've got Cole's number and we will be in touch about your offer." She shook Quincy's hand.

In the car, Tim told his wife that he really wasn't that hungry and maybe they should have stayed longer.

"I insist you eat, Tim. I want you at your best. I want your brain to do this interview when it's good and fed. Be quick on the uptake. Be on. It's important."

Tim knew she was right, but he admitted to himself that he had really enjoyed playing for those two men. They seemed like nice enough guys. Quincy was stoned, but Tim didn't care. "I know it's important," he agreed. "But doing that today with those guys was just what I needed going into this interview."

"You betcha, it was. It put your mind right where I want it to be: close to your skills and passion, lubricated for the questions and answers, and brimming with confidence. Just like I like my man to be." She flashed him a grin, and he returned it as he pulled out into the street. His doubts about his own equity, he kept to himself.

Chapter 17

Lunch at Tin Pan Sally's was quick. They split a chicken salad sandwich and a bowl of soup. Afterward, Tim changed into his suit in the men's room and the two hurried to the interview. Fortunately, they knew exactly where to go with no uncertainty. This time, Theresa didn't come around to the car and kiss her husband for luck. The clock was ticking.

As he entered the office on the second floor, only seven minutes early, he was relaxed (as much as possible) and enjoying his full stomach. The receptionist he had seen the day before rose to greet him, and then disappeared without saying a word.

In mere moments, she returned, followed by a gray-haired man with an impeccably trimmed Vandyke beard and wire-rimmed spectacles.

The man stepped forward and extended his hand. "Frank Glenn," he said. "May I call you Tim?"

"Of course, Professor. I've been looking forward to meeting you. How is your son?"

"That's the sixty-four-dollar question, I'm afraid. I'm so sorry I missed our meeting yesterday. I know you understand."

"Sure." And so it began for Tim: the escalating level of fear. Should he have not asked about the son? Would that put the situation on Glenn's mind more than the interview? But he didn't want to appear indifferent. But he didn't want to distract the interviewer. He second-guessed himself in a running commentary in his head of what he must and must not do. He vaguely wished he could turn off the commentary and just complete the interview.

As he entered the now-familiar office, he was pleased to see Lloyd Fuller sitting in one of the upholstered chairs in front of Glenn's desk. "I hope you don't mind that I invited Professor Fuller to sit in with us," Glenn was saying.

"Oh, not at all. I enjoyed meeting Lloyd yesterday." He looked at Lloyd and said, "Hi."

Lloyd's smile, Tim noticed, was less open and friendly than it had been the day before. Well, maybe, the running commentary told him, Lloyd didn't want to reveal how much support he was offering Tim. Maybe he wanted to keep it subtle, conceal the reality that the two of them were already nearly friends.

Professor Glenn launched into the amenities. How had Tim's stay been? How does he like Terre Haute so far? Did he have enough money on the gift card to have a good meal or two? Would he like anything? Coffee? Water? A Diet Coke? Had he had time to look over the materials the college had emailed him?

All of these questions were so routine, so standard, that Tim, having endured them dozens of times on dozens of interviews, sought to conceal his resentment of the waste of time they represented. He wished the three men could dive right in.

As if reading his mind, Glenn gestured toward the seat next to Lloyd's, and began. "We're looking for someone for a full professorship, and the job description indicates, and your resume seems to highlight a number of items that are of interest to us. What is your interest in 20th century classical composers?

"I have nearly none, Professor," Tim responded, perhaps too quickly. "My understanding is that your classical music department is fully staffed with what I have learned is a noteworthy stable of experts in the field.

"You don't need me for that. You need me for a program in contemporary popular music through the same century. I am proficient in the construction of what many call the popular classics from Irving Berlin to Johnny Mercer. I am also qualified and experienced in teaching music theory."

"Music theory. I see," Glenn noted, scribbling something on a pad. "What can you tell me about yourself to highlight your achievements in theory?"

The question was oddly worded, Tim thought. He judged that the question had not originated with the professor, but had been put in his mind by someone else. He wondered if the someone else was Lloyd Fuller.

"When I was in college, I won a national competition in composition writing."

"From, let's see," Glenn looked at the resume on the desk, "The University of Missouri — is that right?"

"Correct," Tim replied.

"Play it," Professor Glenn ordered. He gestured at a piano in the far corner that Tim hadn't noticed on his first visit. He rose and sat on the piano bench. It was a lovely grand piano, a Petrof, he noted, one of the finest in the world.

He played the piece. He added a few flourishes and concluded with a sweeping hand gesture that he hoped portrayed confidence. He stood and returned to his seat as the other two men offered polite applause.

"You wrote that in college?" Professor Glenn repeated. "When in college?"

"I was nineteen at the time. I played the piece in Chicago at the awards ceremony before an auditorium full of spectators, mostly the families of the other contestants, and none of them were very happy about it." Tim grinned with just a whisper of pride.

"Understood." Glenn mentally assessed the piece, but Lloyd didn't seem to react, Tim noted.

"So, what's your greatest love?" Lloyd interrupted.

"Well, my wife, but I don't think that's what you mean," Tim replied, trying to coax back his new friend's warmth. The temperature in the room had just dropped. Tim wondered what he had said or done.

"It's not," Lloyd said without tone. "I mean which area of study impassions you the most? Theory? Twentieth century composition? What tickles your fancy?"

Again, Tim noted, the question was oddly phrased. He detected just a very slight something — a slight scent of vitriol he hadn't caught on their first meeting. It made him afraid. He'd come into this today with the assurance that if nothing else went his way, he had the support, and possible friendship, of this professor. Pretty clearly, though, he didn't. What in hell could have happened in twenty-four hours?

The two men questioned Tim for the greater part of an hour, and made other requests of Tim on the piano, but Lloyd's change in demeanor had largely taken the wind out of Tim's sail. He answered completely every question posed. Many questions were such often-asked bromides that he had answered them well and often on previous interviews. The good side was that he had the answers down pat. The flip side of that coin was that he chanced offering answers that were too "cooked" — too practiced by a man who hadn't gotten hired in many, many attempts — the man he was. The sense of a black rock was forming in his gut. He wanted it to be over. The need to redeem the situation was acute, of course. He refused to allow himself to consider failure, but his instinct and history was front and center of his perception.

How would he face Treese? And what would they do now?

On the way to the door, Professor Glenn patted Tim on the shoulder and walked out with him. In the reception area, Tim asked the standard questions. A decision would be made within a week. If hired, Tim would start immediately making lesson plans, learning the ropes of the department, and setting up his office. Classes would start on January 2.

Glenn was so positive and upbeat that Tim couldn't help but leave the office with some hope. He wondered again why Lloyd Fuller had been so cold. Lloyd wasn't the decision maker, so maybe it wouldn't matter. But after so many failed interviews, Tim couldn't shake his sense of foreboding.

"How do you think it went?" Theresa asked him immediately.

"I honestly don't know," came his answer. "It seemed to be fine. I answered questions pretty well. They asked me to play a couple of pieces, and they seemed warm enough, or, at least the department head did.

"But that guy we had lunch with yesterday, the one who was so positive and reassuring — I don't know. He was different this time. He was colder and not on my side at all. I wonder what I said that turned him off."

"Maybe nothing."

"If, by that, you mean that his perception of me is totally out of my control, we've both been there before. How many jobs have you interviewed for, that you would be perfect for, but didn't get because of something that had nothing to do with you?"

"I lost count a long time ago."

"Do you want to eat a light dinner back at the hotel, and then hit the highway?"

"Um, Tim, we need to talk about hitting the highway." Theresa was tentative, and her tone got his attention.

"We do? What do we need to say about it?"

"Well, I got a text last night from Dorothy Pratt while we were at that club."

"Who is Dorothy Pratt?"

"The lady who lives across the way from us. You know; with the geraniums."

"Okay . . . ?"

"Tim, we were put out last night. The sheriff was there with some deputies, and they put our belongings out on the lawn and changed the locks. We're homeless."

Tim then looked in his lap, afraid to meet her eyes. "I knew this was coming."

"I thought that, by law, they have to give you official notice," Theresa complained.

"They did give us notice. I hid the notices from you."

"Why? Why didn't you tell me?"

"For the same reason you didn't tell me today. You wanted to keep the stress off me. You did everything you could to help me relax and be mentally prepared for today."

"Yes, I did," she affirmed. She took a breath. "Dorothy rescued some of our things. I talked to her while you were interviewing. She threw some clothes into trash bags. She picked up a box of your books and sheet music, your hand-held digital recorder, and four cans of tuna. Neighborhood kids got the rest. Not that there was much to steal, what with all we've sold in yard sales. There's really hardly any point in driving back home. She said she'd keep the stuff until we can get it, but . . . "

"But apparently, we've relocated. Welcome to Terre Haute, Treese. Are you ready to be a Hoosier?" His expression was bleak.

"Hey," she said, a thought just occurring, "Do we have renter's insurance?"

"No. I let the premiums lapse months ago. It was a good thought, though."

"Typical," she replied cynically. "It's a feature of being poor, I'm learning. It's like a double whammy. We can't afford our rent or the insurance to help us when we're put out for not having the rent. It's so damned expensive to be poor."

"That it certainly is."

The couple availed themselves of the dollar menu at a fast food joint. They drank water, sat, and talked until a noisy group of teenagers descended, fresh out of classes. Tim and Theresa left and walked to their car, their new home.

Chapter 18

"So, what's your take on Shelton?" Frank Glenn said to Lloyd Fuller when Tim had left. "I like him myself. I think he'd be a great fit in the department."

"Uh, he's okay, I guess," Lloyd Fuller replied with deliberate, calculated nonchalance. "I think we have better candidates. I wish you'd look at some of them up close before you rush to judgment."

"Who do you think is a better candidate than Shelton? He's perfectly matched to the job description with his area of expertise, his knowledge of theory, and his mastery of percussion, strings and brass instruments."

"I just don't want you to rush to judgment," Lloyd repeated, "until you do some more interviews."

"You've said that twice, and I really don't know how I'm rushing. We've looked at resumes and held interviews for three weeks. So, now I'm asking you: Which candidate do you want me to interview?"

Lloyd strode to Frank's desk and picked up the stack of resumes he had placed there early in the day. "Look here at this woman on the top of the stack. Barbara Baxter. She's a doctoral candidate in music history from University of Missouri, which is where Shelton graduated. I believe she deserves a look. She competes with Shelton in almost every area. She only has some weakness in the area of contemporary popular music. And she's only 32 — considerably younger than Shelton."

"How do you know she's only 32?" Frank asked suspiciously.

Lloyd lost color in his face. This could be a grave error. He must not reveal his connection to his daughter. "Well, I'm extrapolating. She graduated with her bachelor's degree when she was probably 22. It was ten years ago, so I'm guessing she is 32."

"You are assuming that she's 32. And we can't make a judgment based on age. The lawyers will be up one side of us and down the other if we hire on that basis."

"Oh, I know we have to be politically correct, but I honestly think Baxter is a candidate you need to look at."

"Fine," Frank said with resignation. "Tell Gabriela to call her and book her for an interview early next week."

Chapter 19

A little after nine that night, Cole Renshaw looked up from his audience and saw Tim and Theresa enter the Claymore Room.

The small room was narrow and long, but its telling feature was darkness. Each small cabaret table featured a lone candle, and tiny white lights, such as one would hang on a Christmas tree, decorated the artificial foliage around the room. The bartender prepared beverages by the light of an under-counter dim fluorescent, and Shara ran her equipment with a clamp on light she'd picked up at Home Depot. The windowless room was otherwise dark, and Cole only recognized Tim and Theresa in silhouette as they stood just inside the door.

Cole expected the two as Tim had called him earlier, said their plans had changed, and they needed to talk to Quincy about his sister's rental property.

Cole had then called Quincy, and Quincy had called Marietta, his sister.

Marietta was sitting by herself at a table that sat five when the Sheltons came in.

Cole, seeing the couple, waved. He then pointed to Marietta's table, and with a gesture, signaled Shara.

At the end of the song, Shara picked up her microphone and announced, "And now, ladies and gentlemen, Mr. Cole Renshaw." Cole then stepped forward as his solo began. Quincy and Forbes left the staging area and approached the table. They got to it moments before Tim and Theresa did.

Marietta signaled Quincy and he leaned down to hear her over the music. "Quincy, you didn't tell me these are white folks."

"Something wrong with white folks' money?"

"Nothing. I just don't know if they'd want to live in that neighborhood. They'd be kind of out of place, I think."

At that moment, the couple came to the table and Quincy made introductions. Forbes kissed Marietta on her cheek and sat next to her. Quincy also sat, and the group listened as Cole completed three solos. At the conclusion, Cole intoned, "Thank you so much, ladies and gentleman. Now I'd like to present again, Forbes Wilson — Mr. Versatility!"

The audience clapped, as Forbes stood up and strode toward the staging area. As Cole took his place at the table, he leaned toward Theresa and said, "My wife wants to talk to you."

Theresa looked at him, startled and uneasy, but Cole just gestured toward the soundboard where Shara was waving and gesturing with a curled finger for Theresa to see her.

As Theresa approached, Shara said to her quietly, "You and your husband will stay at my house tonight, okay? And tomorrow, you'll hook up with Marietta about an apartment." It wasn't an invitation so much as an assumption. Either these people knew far more about the Sheltons' situation than Theresa was comfortable with, or they could just smell the desperation. Either way, Theresa was humbled and grateful. She thought for a moment of Tim's oft-repeated metaphor about letting go of one trapeze, spinning in air, and catching the other trapeze. She simply thanked Shara and turned back to the table.

Chapter 20

"Baby girl, can you be here Monday morning at 9?" Lloyd spoke to Barbara as soon as he was back in his own office. His office looked out on a grove of maple trees on the campus property. It was golden-orange with the turned trees. The pathway between them was littered with golden stars. A memory flooded him of his departed wife strolling with him in a park on a beautiful autumn day just like this one. He started to choke up, but tamped down the impulse. "Eyes on the task!" he told himself. He totally missed Barbara's reply.

"You there, Dad?"

"Yeah, sorry, say again."

"I'll have to leave here after church Sunday, stay the night with you, and go in with you Monday morning."

"No, no. You won't go in with me. We are concealing our connection, remember. You drive by yourself."

"Yeah, okay. I don't like the subterfuge, though."

"You want the job, don't you?"

"I understand."

Chapter 21

Tim and Theresa helped the vocalists pick up equipment and load it in the van at midnight. Theresa was exhausted and wanted badly to lay her head down somewhere. It was mostly stress, she knew. She hadn't done much other than drive and worry.

The two followed Cole and Shara back to their house and helped unload the equipment. There sure was a lot of it, Tim mused to himself. It would be easier, if he were the accompanist, to just carry a digital piano, a small mixer, and speakers, especially for a tiny room like the Claymore.

Shara observed Theresa thoughtfully. Once the work was done, Theresa plopped on the sofa and gathered the cat in her lap. Her body language spoke of fatigue and defeat.

"Theresa?" Shara said, approaching, "Let me show you where the bathroom is and the guest room so you can get some rest. I put a couple of pairs of sweat pants and tee shirts in there on the bed for you all to sleep in. In the morning, if you want, I'll wash your clothes."

"Oh, wow," Theresa replied with some relief. That would be great. All I have to wear, I'm wearing, and I've had it on since yesterday."

Tim and Theresa crawled into the small guest room bed. The room sported a small dresser and mirror and what appeared to be a small closet. Yellow-flowered wallpaper was peeling around its seams and appeared to have been assaulted at some point by cat claws. The room smelled slightly dusty and clearly was not used often. Next to the bed, a small braided throw rug in a cacophony of dull earth tones sat. A tiny end table held a lamp that glowed to illuminate the room. It was inornate and poor. Theresa thought briefly of the home she had owned in Columbus. It had two lavish guest rooms with private bathrooms and thick, soft carpeting. She'd had it decorated with lovely silk flowered wreaths she had bought at crafts fairs and later sold to strangers in yard sales for a fraction of what she'd paid.

How the mighty have fallen, she mused, as she closed her eyes.

Chapter 22

"I don't want them here until this afternoon." Marietta was barking to her brother on the phone. "I've got too much to do in this apartment. Your son, Isaiah, told me he cleaned this apartment, and I paid him. It's filthy, and I can't stand to let it to anyone, let alone snooty white folks."

There were so many things wrong with his sister's remarks that Quincy didn't know where to begin. This couple was on the edge right now, and they might have a lot to learn about being on the edge, but they weren't snooty, not that Quincy could tell. And when Marietta had paid Isaiah to clean the apartment, she had given him fifteen dollars to do about six hours' worth of work. Quincy hardly blamed Isaiah for the lick-and-a-promise he had given the place, and was personally offended because Marietta had been so cheap.

He let all of that go. It was a matter at hand. "'Etta, girl, the Renshaws are sleeping in. We've got another show tonight, so Cole and Shara'll be resting for a while."

"What has that got to do with — ?"

"The couple is staying at Cole and Shara's house. I doubt they'll rise very early."

"Oh, okay. I just wish I didn't have all this to do by myself, and — "

"I gots to go, big sister. I'm pulling up in front. Talk to you after a while. Let me know how it goes, and thanks for taking that Walmart card for rent." Quincy disconnected his cell phone. Marietta could really flap a jaw, he told himself. And she could whine till daybreak about one thing or another. And if these white folks were ever ten minutes late on their rent, she'd be calling him, not them, to complain about it.

Well, it's family, he reminded himself. Ain't nothing but family, with all its joys and terrors, and he'd be in a big trick if he didn't have Etta.

Quincy parked his green, rusty station wagon in front of an apartment building on Terre Haute's north side. It wasn't far from Marietta's apartments, but it wasn't that close either. As he walked toward apartment 2C, he fingered the cash in his pants pocket. Tonight, he'd be singing for four hours, and he'd want to be mellow. A whisper of guilt grazed his ear because he planned to be far mellower before the show to be of much use setting up. Another thought grazed by that, with the day off, he could go over to Etta's apartments and help her clean. The thoughts were fleeting, though. He'll get himself just a little herb.

Chapter 23

Theresa awoke to the smell of brewing coffee. She was surprised how well she had slept in a stranger's bed — a stranger to whom she was now thoroughly beholden. She stepped out of the room, used the toilet, and wandered into the kitchen where her hosts were entertaining Tim at the kitchen table. She sat at the table with Tim and Cole. Shara, at the counter, lifted the coffee pot in invitation and Theresa nodded.

Theresa dolled her coffee up with cream and two spoons of sugar. As she looked around the empty kitchen table, Shara seemed to read her mind. "I'm afraid I wasn't expecting guests and didn't lay in breakfast supplies," she told Theresa. "Then I've got to beat a path to work."

"You work Saturdays?"

"It's become a habit. I miss work through the week because of music jobs, so I make it up Saturday mornings. That way I only irritate the boss slightly."

"Hey, why don't I make breakfast? I see right there in your pantry that you have pancake syrup," Theresa offered.

"I don't have Bisquick," Shara said apologetically.

"No problem. Do you have flour, eggs and milk?"

"Sure."

"I'll make them from scratch. Show me around the kitchen?"

In a few minutes, four stacks of pancakes and warm syrup graced the breakfast table. Theresa dug in as if she hadn't eaten in a while, and Tim munched down hungrily as well, recognizing his wife's recipe. Cole and Shara ate too, and watched the others as they ate, speculating on the unknowns about this couple.

"You're from Columbus?" Shara ventured. "What did you do there?"

"Well, I used to be a college professor, and Treese used to be a legal secretary. But the economy turned and we both got laid off. Poverty is quite an education," Tim answered.

"Poverty is far more educational than college," Cole agreed. "If I had a choice between a four-year degree and four years in financial crisis, I'd take the crisis because, in the long run, the crisis teaches more, gets you more and wears on you more. But it costs less. I've been blessed to have had both."

"What's the best thing you've learned?" Tim asked.

"Well, how to manage without," Cole told him. "The short cuts, the needful greasing of wheels when you're poor are fundamental, and utterly beyond the comprehension of the folks with money.

"I came up in a black neighborhood, but we stuck out 'cause we had money. Then my dad passed when I was sixteen, and Mom and I got poor pretty quick. The camaraderie I gained from that — the close, bonding friendships — were also laced with a measure of competition and frustration.

"One time, a factory was opening in midtown, and it was going to hire 300. Quincy, Forbes and I all went down there, and of course, when we arrived, there were 300 guys already there—times three or four. On one hand, I want all of my friends to get hired, and I want to share that love equally. But a part of me wanted me to get hired first and to hell with the closest of my friends. When people get desperate enough, they change. When they are desperate for a long time, they change a lot."

Cole tapped his spoon on the edge of his coffee cup thoughtfully.

"My dad was a lawyer, and he did pretty well, but when he was gone, my mom changed. We both felt like we had no hope. Then his firm called us in and let Mom know that Dad had set aside for my education, and I could go to college. I know my mom thought of using that money herself, but she didn't. I *know* she was scared his life insurance wouldn't be enough. He had a lot saved, though, and I don't know how he got to where he was in that firm.

"I know he did some tricks, 'cause he rose up in his law firm faster than most black men ever could, back in the day."

"What kind of tricks? You never told me this." Shara said.

"Don't know what kind. All I know is that there was terrible pressure on him to perform. That's always true, you know. The old adage that a black man has to be twice as good to be regarded as half as good — that's never changed. It led him to an early grave, and my mother went on without and got *her* education about not just being poor, but being poor and old."

Theresa wiggled in her seat as if preparing to speak. "I keep hoping that we won't stay poor long enough to get too much more education. If Tim gets the job at the college, we'll be back on our feet in no time. We don't have to hold down a mortgage, a car payment, or any other major expenses, so the money he brings in should go a long way."

"Like the song says, 'Freedom's just another word for nothing left to lose,' huh?" Cole offered.

"Kris Kristofferson, had it going on," Tim agreed. "Once you let go of things, of having things, life gets simpler and the things you do have get most precious." He looked at Theresa.

"Until you lose them, too, right?" Theresa said dourly.

"You leaving me?" he asked. "I was talking about you and me."

Cole and Shara, uncomfortable, stood and cleared the table. "More coffee?" Shara asked, waving the pot in the air.

Theresa pushed her cup forward on the table and nodded with thanks as Cole sat back down next to Tim. "So, how is your knowledge of 60s and 70s rock? Is it as good as your take on popular classics? Oh, and by the way, you blew the answer to the question about 'Teach Me Tonight.' You got the year of publication wrong."

"So, the game was fixed," Tim grinned. "I suspected as much."

"Oh, it wasn't very fixed. You were only off by two years, and no one else had any idea about the song, so you won fair and square. Now answer my question."

"Yeah, I've got some chops with 50s and 60s rock — 70s and 80s, too, for that matter. Why?"

"I've got a club downtown that is hiring, and if I bought digital music that they want from that era, it would cost more than the job would pay. I was thinking, if you're up for it, you and I could do it together. It doesn't pay well enough for Quincy and Forbes, but it would be a buck and a half each if we split it.

"We've got an hour before I have to get you two to Quincy's sister's place. Let's get your piano."

The two men fetched the piano. Cole found a notebook of lyrics he had compiled and the two set to work on a repertoire. Meanwhile, Shara set the dishes in the sink and soaked them. Then she gestured to Theresa to follow her into the bedroom. The unmade bed was unkempt and piled with clothes. Shara didn't seem to care.

"Theresa, I've put on 20 pounds, and I need to get it off. But I probably won't. Taking it off is so much harder than putting it on. So, I figure, maybe you can use a few shirts and pants that I can't wear anymore to hold you over until you start getting paid. I've got to leave for work, but I want you to use the room, try on these clothes, and help yourself to whatever you can use. I am being very serious. Don't be shy and don't hold back. When you pick out what you want, Cole will give you a trash bag to pile it in."

Theresa stared for a full ten seconds. Then, "Shara, thank you. I'm stunned. But you hardly know me, and you have been terribly kind, far kinder than our level of relationship requires. Why on earth would you make me such an offer?"

"Because I believe in Jesus Christ, and He calls us to love one another."

Theresa's reaction was slow in coming. When it did, it was not what Shara had hoped.'

"Okay, thank you," she told Shara with a faint note of dismissiveness.

"I'm outta here." With that, Shara left.

As Shara closed the door behind her, Theresa's emotions were conflicted and difficult to organize. She was thankful for the clothes. Her mind flitted back and forth between the garments here and the ones she imagined strewn on her front yard in Columbus. And as she went through the pile on the bed, they appeared to be in very good shape. A couple of the blouses still had the tags. But she couldn't stop feeling a little suspicious of all that kindness. What is all that, anyway? Shara is doing this because of Jesus Christ? What has religion got to do with anything? She abruptly decided she didn't like Shara very much, kindness notwithstanding. And she didn't trust her.

Chapter 24

Tim and Theresa followed behind Cole's car as he led them to Marietta's apartment building. The trip took 20 minutes, and the matter was not lost on Theresa that, as the journey progressed, the neighborhoods looked worse and worse. Clearly the poor side of the tracks, she told herself. Then the thought came to her that in the economy she was now in, the poor side of the tracks is her new normal. She flashed again on her beautiful home in a Columbus suburb she had sold and left for a ratty double-wide that she couldn't afford either. She shook the memory off.

"You've got the Walmart card with you?" Tim asked unexpectedly.

"Sure. It's in my purse."

"All right. It looks like Cole is pulling over. I guess we're here."

The building was a two-story affair of blonde brick. Four apartment doors were visible on the first floor, and four on the second floor. A crumbled sidewalk led to the bottom of stairs that went up to the second-floor walkway. Each apartment door sat next to a front window that looked across the street to the loading dock of what appeared to be a factory of some kind.

Cole led the couple up the stairs to apartment 2B, and he knocked. A moment later, Marietta opened the door. She was dressed in baggy jeans and a tee shirt. Her hair was knotted up in a bandana and she was perspiring.

"Oh, hi," she said in greeting.

"Are we early?" Cole asked. It was clear from Marietta's demeanor that she wished the visitors had given her more time.

"Oh, no. You're fine. I had gotten behind on getting ready for you because I thought the apartment was clean, but my nephew, well, come on in."

The couple entered. Exploring the apartment was brief, as the place was tiny, and the amenities few. There was a bedroom, living area, a tiny kitchen and tiny bathroom. Everything was painted green or beige. The beige carpet in the living room had seen many, many better days. A lingering scent of cigarettes wafted from the carpet and drapes.

Theresa looked around in the kitchen. She told herself not to mind that there was very little storage space because she had nothing to store. The faucet was dripping and she tried to shut it off, but failed. Rust lined the burners on the stove, which was brown and crusty with dried food and grease. She opened the oven. Yep. As she expected. It was crusty with grease also.

Marietta watched the other woman examine the kitchen. Too embarrassed to tell her that she hadn't cleaned it yet, she hedged, "I was supposed to have some help today, but Quincy didn't show up. What he and I worked out, though, was that I usually ask for first and last month's rent."

She saw the couple look at each other. Fear registered in the woman's eyes. "But Quincy and I talked and I agreed to take your Walmart gift card for the first month and skip asking for the last month. So, I'm going to let you clean your own kitchen. If you want the place.

"That's most kind, Marietta," Tim said a little too sweetly. He knew Theresa was miserable, but he didn't know what alternative there could be. "Let us talk this over just a minute, okay?"

Cole spoke up. "Marietta, I want to invite you to a Christmas show we're doing at a senior home not far from here . . ." Cole motioned with his eyes for the couple to take advantage of the distraction. Tim, noticing, guided Theresa by the elbow into the bedroom.

"I know you're upset, but I don't know what else we can do," he began once he had Theresa out of earshot of the others.

"There isn't anything else we can do. We can't crash at Cole and Shara's again. Let me be plain: I *won't* crash at Cole and Shara's again. We're out of options. It's a terrible little place, but it's what there is. Tell her we'll take it. Here's the Walmart card." She reached into her purse and snatched out the treasure, handing it to her husband. She blinked back tears, turning her face away.

"Treese, listen to me," Tim said. "This isn't permanent. And we're lucky to get it. We're lucky to have met these people."

"Sure," she admitted. "Give me the car keys. I'm going to bring in my lovely wardrobe of new clothes." Her sarcastic timbre irritated Tim. He handed her the keys.

Theresa mustered a pleasant face for Marietta as she went past her and down to the car. Tim returned to the living room and told the landlady that they were good to go. He handed her the Walmart card.

Marietta took the card, saying, "Cole tells me you have little furniture other than a piano. I hope you'll use the piano quietly because you have neighbors. If you need furniture, I have a little you can use: a mattress and a table and chairs. Would you like that?"

"Yes, ma'am."

"I've sanitized the mattress. It's a full size, so . . . "

"We are most thankful."

"Cole and Quincy have vouched for you, so I'm skipping the background check. See you next month." With that, Marietta pulled the bandana out of her hair, shook her head, took a deep breath, and exited the door with Cole on her heels. The two passed Theresa on the stairs. She was carrying the garbage bag full of clothes Shara had given her. Cole stopped, took the bag, and carried it up the rest of the stairs for her.

Cole told Tim, "I'll meet with that club owner tomorrow morning and see if I can line up that show for you and me. If I do, we'll need at least 30 songs. Think we can do that?"

A warm sense of gratitude filled Tim. "Sure," he said to his new friend. "Thanks for everything you've done for us. I'm touched, really, by your generosity and thoughtfulness. Do you want to rehearse tomorrow? I'll come over."

"I'll call you. Anything else you need?"

"Oh, there's tons we need," Tim laughed. "Can you direct me to a thrift store or second-hand shop or someplace we can get some bed sheets and a few dishes, and soap?"

Theresa, now standing near her husband chimed in. "Toothbrushes, toothpaste, and perhaps some food."

Cole explained that two streets over a small strip mall contained a thrift store and an everything's-a-dollar place. There was also a small grocery, but, he cautioned, the prices weren't that good. He mentioned a supermarket on the main drag toward the highway.

Cole noticed that, while Tim seemed fairly relaxed and even relieved by the change in circumstances, Theresa seemed as tense and unhappy as ever. Cole excused himself and made his departure with a succinct, "See ya later!" He trotted down the stair somewhat relieved to be out of there.

Tim put the garbage bag of clothes in the bedroom, returned to the living room and gave Theresa a warm hug. She shook him off.

"What's the matter, Treese? I thought you'd be happy. We aren't homeless, and we have the means to maybe make a little money and start our life again. We should be thankful."

"Thankful? I'm living in a sty, I have no bed, and $300 per month, which used to be what we paid for our mobile phones and cable TV, now seems like an unapproachable amount of money to raise in a month. Further, you seem to really like these music people we've met. I do not, and I don't want to spend any more time with them than I have to. But there's nothing to do but go with you to shows and rehearsals, so I'm stuck." She sat down on the floor, but got up again immediately. "Plus, the carpet is sopping wet!"

"I guess Marietta just shampooed it," Tim offered. "Why on earth don't you like Cole and his friends? Is it because they're black?"

"No, of course not. I like them okay. It's Shara, the one I can live completely without."

"I'm confused. She gave you a huge bag of clothes, put us up for a night, fed us, did our laundry, and showed an interest in our lives. What on earth is there to dislike?"

"It's why she did all of that," Theresa complained.

"Okay. Why did she?"

"Because of Jesus Christ. That's what she said."

Chapter 25

Barbara Baxter arrived in Terre Haute at 7:30 on Sunday evening. The drive to her father's house was pleasant as her mind filled with many childhood memories that the landmarks inspired. As she pulled into the driveway of the house where she had grown up, there was more than a sense of coming home. There was a sense of coming full circle, of returning to the point of origin, of having a life with a marvelous husband, having that life ripped away, and being returned to a past that provided only a small comfort for her grief.

She walked to the side door adjacent to the driveway and let herself in with her key. "Daddy?" she called out.

"Up here, baby," her father's familiar voice coaxed. "I'm in my office."

His office, which had once been her bedroom, bore no resemblance to the rainbow and unicorn motif of her childhood. It was now paneled with wood: darker, masculine, and foreign. She wondered vaguely where she would sleep now that she was home. Her mind flitted very briefly across the memories of her collection of unicorn figurines. What ever happened to all of those?

Her father rose from his chair and hugged Barbara hard in greeting. She returned the hug with a passion fed by grief and relief. It seemed like every single thing she did lately was fed by grief. She made a mental note to shake it off. She had to start a new life. *Let it go. Let it go.*

"You hungry? I've got leftover fried rice and egg rolls, or we can go out and grab a bite," Lloyd offered.

"I could eat. I'll drive. I'm blocking you in the driveway."

The two were seated in a booth at a nearby Applebee's. "Here's how I want to do this, Barbie," he began. "I gave the department head who will interview you a number of questions I think he should ask. If he uses them, and I'm sure he will because I made a convincing argument that he should, I'm going to tell you what answers to offer to these questions. It should help you ace the interview. Yeah, it's dishonest, but if it gives you a leg up — "

"It is certainly dishonest, Dad. I don't think I want to get the job by cheating."

"Then how can I help you?"

"Just refresh me on what the guy is looking for, or, better, what he's looking for now. I know expectations change during any hiring process as the interviewer meets candidates."

"Fair enough. The guy who leads the pack of candidates convinced Dr. Glenn that his take on the popular classics of the early and mid-20th century would be useful. He's a good candidate, I admit, and his areas of expertise lend themselves well to where Glenn wants to take the department. You need to be better."

"But I'm not better, Dad. I know next to nothing about Berlin, Porter, or Rodgers and Hart. I can hum a few tunes; that's all. "Do you think there's any chance he'll ask about Ralph Vaughan Williams?"

"It's not impossible, but Williams wrote hymn tunes and symphonies, so his contributions hardly overlap the standards Glenn is interested in. Barb, please understand that, while I know you love sacred music, this is a secular school. Ralph Vaughan Williams' hallmark tune for 'For All the Saints' will be of little use in this department.

"I'll help you at home. We'll fake it until you make it. Youtube is our friend. I can show you some patterns that appear in many of Cole Porter's songs that you could familiarize yourself with and exploit to prove you know more than you do. I centered several of the suggested questions on Cole Porter, so we've got until the interview to make you an expert on the subject."

Barbara agreed–, but she still felt an amount of guilt about her inside track on the interview. But she reminded herself that her father was her only reason for coming home, and this job was the only way to stay. In for a penny . . .

Chapter 26

"It's all on me, Cole. All of it, and I need help," Shara complained to her husband.

"The music is working, sweetheart. We're getting more popular, the bookings are increasing, and in just a little more time, the pressure will come off of you."

"That's what you say, but there is always one obstacle after another. Plus, you could take a day job, even if it's part time, doing something to help out. You admit that when you go to venues, you almost have to go at night because the managers aren't there in the daytime. So, you could work days. I can't pay for everything, and I shouldn't have to — "

"You don't. I pay for the music we use, the equipment, the costuming — "

"Right. You eat up all the money you make buying stuff to make more money — which you use to buy more stuff. And you only take a fourth of the total payday even though you take all of the expenses on yourself."

"We've been through this, Shara. If I took a portion of Quincy and Forbes's pay to buy equipment, then they would have a say in what equipment to buy. I don't really want them with that much control."

"I wholly agree with that, but the fact remains that there isn't enough money coming in the house. You still haven't explained why getting a part-time day job is out of the question."

"I need my days free."

"Why?"

"I just do."

"In case your mother needs you to take her to some appointment, right?"

"That, too."

"I want her to understand that I need you to contribute to the household. Every day you take her somewhere, it takes the whole day, and you don't get anything booked and you don't get anything else done. She takes the whole, entire day."

"I heard you the first seventy times."

"Oh, Cole, I don't want to be a nag. I don't want to be one of those women who nag their men. I'm just trying to simply ask you for help. What about Don Litvack? Did you talk to him anymore about letting you work in his store?"

"Organizing thousands of boxes of used, discarded vinyl LPs? No, I haven't talked to him."

"Should I talk to him?"

Cole simply looked at his wife with a sardonic "what-do-you-think?" expression. "I've got to go," he concluded, and headed for the car. As he stepped outdoors, he shook his head with self-recrimination. That was a narrow escape, he told himself. It wouldn't be long — the handwriting was on the wall — before he had to tell Shara the "stuff" he was buying was more expensive than she knew, and his share of the paydays wasn't going very far. He had been getting money from Mom.

Chapter 27

It came as some surprise to Theresa that the grocery store accepted her SNAP card so that she could buy food. The card, which she had thought was provided by the state of Ohio, could easily not work in Indiana. So when the debit off her food account registered, she breathed a sigh.

She didn't buy much. No frozen food, surely. When she checked the freezer in the apartment, she noticed that the ice cubes in the tray were not entirely frozen. Oh, joy, she told herself. This awful, tacky apartment already had something wrong with it the first day. It wasn't impossible that Marietta had filled the trays a short time before Theresa noticed them, but Theresa wished to pout. She pushed that possibility aside.

The debit card from the Columbus bank worked, but she made a mental note to get a new bank account first of the week. Not that her old bank in Columbus would miss her ever-diminishing balance. At the dollar store, she bought plates, and flatware. At the thrift store, she scored a frying pan, saucepan, and a set of well-worn bed sheets in a dour and ugly goldenrod color. But they were the right size. Pillows would be a problem, but they could sleep without for a while.

She hoped Marietta would make good on her promise of a mattress.

Tim and Theresa had spent so many months guarding every nickel that even a small purchase on their debit card filled them with dread. With no projection of when another deposit could be made, there was great unease accompanying every expenditure.

Tim crossed his fingers for the job at the college, and for the job with Cole. Let something come through soon, he told the sky.

When they returned to their new digs after the shopping trip, they found a mattress in the bedroom and a rusty Formica-topped table from the 50s with two chairs in the living room. Neither chair matched the table or the other chair, but they were happy to see the furniture.

The couple ate rice and beans for lunch Sunday with more rice and beans for dinner. A jar of salsa dressed it up, but Theresa regretted having bought the cheap kind with the high fructose corn syrup, rather than a healthier choice with less sugar, salt and fat. The healthy kind was surprisingly dear. This was another way, she remarked to Tim, that it's expensive to be poor. There is cost to our bodies when we can't eat healthier.

After each meal, it felt good to brush her teeth with her new toothbrush and a tube of Pepsodent that had set her back a dollar.

The couple turned in early simply because there was nothing to do. No television, books or other amusements.

Another note to self, Theresa told herself: get a library card.

Before dozing off, Tim kissed his wife deeply. He said, "I love you."

"Love you, too."

"Hey, when are you going to tell me why it bothers you that Shara Renshaw was kind to us because of her religion?"

"When I figure it out myself," she intoned. She rolled over to face away from him and closed her eyes.

Chapter 28

The phone rang early Monday morning. Cole caught it on the second ring and answered in his friendliest voice, just in case it was a customer. Turns out, it was.

Simon Seloff was on the phone. He identified himself as the marketing manager for some company Cole didn't recognize. He wanted to hire Cole and his singers for a home and garden show at the convention center.

"Let's see if we can play that, Simon. Hold on while I look at our schedule. What's the date of the event?"

It's Thanksgiving weekend. Friday, Saturday and Sunday. I can offer you $4,500 for the three performances, but you need to be there from open to close. It turns out to be quite a lot less money than it seems when you consider the 12-hour day."

"Sure does," Cole said. I don't know that I can ask my guys to sing for 12 straight hours . . ."

"Oh, no," Simon interrupted. "No, you sing every two hours for about an hour between presentations. See, these vendors who are selling their furniture or their fireplaces or their hot tubs or whatever will want to be on stage promoting their businesses. You'll be in a huge room lined with vendors at tables. Every once in a while, one vendor takes the stage and does a little speech about whatever special is being offered. Between these presentations, we want music. Understand?"

Cole certainly did. It would be the worst possible scenario for him personally. He liked to compare himself to a major-league baseball pitcher whose arm, once warmed up, could be ruined for the day by a rain delay. Too many long breaks, and he'd struggle to finish the show.

Nevertheless, Cole Renshaw had never turned down a job and wasn't about to start now. He told himself he'd have to lean on Quincy. Quincy could sing Bocelli while drowning.

"That sounds fine, Simon. So glad you called."

"What will you need from us in the way of set up?" Simon asked.

"Electricity."

"I think I can manage that." Simon's humor could be heard in his voice.

"If you'll be in your office this morning, I'll run over there with a contract."

When Cole was off the phone, he called Shara and told her about the booking.

"That will be exhausting," she told him. "But the money won't be bad. That's great, honey. How did the guy hear about us?"

"He said he saw us that time last summer when we did that country club."

"Oh, yeah, I remember."

"Shara, he offered me the money. I didn't even have to bid the job."

"It's a good thing, because you would have bid it for a lot less."

"You're right, I would have. Okay, I'm going to go and call Quincy and Forbes."

When Cole arrived at the convention center with the contract, Simon greeted him with a handshake. "Let me show you around the facility. See if there's anything else you'll need."

The center was huge. Cole knew it was large, but he hadn't been inside for years, and his perceptions and recollections were way off.

Typically, he and Shara brought all of the sound equipment with them to jobs, but they had nothing that could handle this space.

"Simon, I'll need to interface my sound system with yours . . ."

"Of course, you will. I'll show you the board."

The sound room for the center was intimidating. Endless channels, multiple heads, and a plethora of equipment that Cole didn't understand turned this job into a problem. He'd have to hire a sound engineer, that's all. And with that, the money for this job just got quite a lot smaller. A good, union sound guy would want two-large per day for a job like this. It wouldn't be worth doing.

But he didn't let on to Simon.

"Simon, thanks for the look around. I'm going to leave the contract with you, and I'll pick it up tomorrow. I got someplace to be and I lost track of the time."

He knew he sounded lame, and Simon knew it, too, but Cole beat a hasty retreat out of the center.

He called Shara and told her he may have to turn down the job.

"It's the best paying job we've ever had," she told him unnecessarily. "Why don't you call around and find out for sure what a sound engineer would cost?"

"Not a bad idea."

He hung up the phone and paced the floor for a few minutes, dreading what he would find out. While he was pacing, the phone rang. It was Tim.

"Hey man! How're you all doing? How does it feel to be a Terre Haute dweller for the first time?" His positive, happy timbre sounded phony to his own ear.

"Well, we survived the weekend, that's all I can tell you. Look, Treese is at the library, so I wondered if you want me to come by and go over some material."

"Oh, hey, that's great," Cole replied. "I'm kind of on a mission today, though. We just got booked to do a home and garden show at the huge convention center downtown, and I'm going to have to hire a sound engineer. The soundboard for this place is vast. I know Shara won't know how to use it, and I don't even know where or how to hire a guy."

"Why can't you just use the sound engineer that works at the convention center?" Tim suggested.

"Well, because I will have to interface my equipment with the equipment there, and I don't know how that could work."

"Why?"

"Why what?"

"Why do you have to interface your equipment? Just use his board."

"How will I get the music to play? I have to run my cdg player — what you like to call my karaoke machine — through his board, but it has to be done remotely, I think, so I can communicate with Shara on the stage."

"You'll have to put her in the booth with the sound engineer and use cell phones to communicate."

"There's an idea," Cole said thoughtfully. "But I'd rather put her on stage and let her communicate with the sound guy by phone. Good thinking."

"Glad I could help. So, working on material is off for today?"

"Not necessarily," Cole allowed. "Let me make some calls and see what I can see.

"Hey, when will you hear from the college?"

"I'm going to call over there and check in as soon as I get off with you."

After disconnecting, Cole felt chagrined that he hadn't thought of asking for the convention center's sound engineer to work for him. *Nuts*, he thought, *they probably have a staff engineer already set up to work the weekend. I am such an idiot. Glad I talked to Tim*, he mused, *before I hired someone, or, worse, couldn't hire someone and turned down the job.*

He called Simon and explained.

"Well, sure, I'll have a sound guy here and of course he can run your sound. I don't know how he'll interface with your equipment, but I'm very confident that he will," Simon explained. "His name is Bob Norton. Let me find his phone number."

"Bob is scheduled to work the whole weekend, but none of the rest of the audio staff are available because of the holiday. He has no family, so he doesn't mind. So, it's all on Bob, but he's a good guy. Worked here for decades."

Cole disconnected and took a large, cleansing breath.

Chapter 29

Barbara got up very early Monday morning and made a nice breakfast for her dad. The ham and eggs went down well, and Lloyd was delighted to have his little girl home. He gazed at her across the kitchen table, smiling.

"What are you grinning about?" she teased.

"Nothing. Nothing at all. We need to head out of here in 45 minutes for me to be on time. I'm going to drop you at the student center and you kill an hour until time to walk to the music building."

"Then I better get hopping. I'll clean up the kitchen later. Going to jump in the shower," she promised.

She wore her powder blue suit, and a bright yellow scarf with the tiny blue blossoms. The suit brought out her blue eyes, she thought. She decreed herself elegant, yet professional-looking when she joined her father in the car.

As per their plan, Barb walked to the music department, arriving at a quarter after eight and greeted Gabriela, the receptionist. She took a seat as instructed and said a prayer for the success of this venture. The prayer was disingenuous, she knew. No matter what happened, she wasn't going back to Rolla. She was in Terre Haute to stay, to build a new life, and to grieve with her father for their lost loves.

Abruptly, she mentally returned to the moment and flew through some of the facts about Cole Porter that her father had coached her on last night. Her focus was off, she knew. A small voice inside her head warned her that Cole Porter wasn't going to matter in this interview. She could only do the best she could do.

And, so she did. When she met with Dr. Glenn, she was chirpy, upbeat, full of conviction, and determined to communicate her belief that a strong music program makes better students and better graduates.

She talked about Josquin DesPrez, the 14th century father of classical music. She spoke of the contributions of liturgical composition to all genres of music. She made a case for the inclusion of Bach, Beethoven, and Brahms in the study of modern rock and roll. Glenn questioned Ms. Baxter about 20th century composers, and she felt obligated to talk about Ralph Vaughan Williams even though her father had cautioned against doing so. Williams was the modern composer she knew best. She had studied his nine symphonies, and she prayed silently as she spoke of them, that she was leaving a good impression.

Lloyd Fuller had excused himself from the interview on the grounds that he had agreed to take another professor's class this day. Secretly, he told himself that he feared tipping his hand in Barb's direction. Or, that he feared she would fail before his eyes.

In the end, she left Dr. Glenn with a sweet taste in his mouth. A very sweet one, in fact. As she thanked him for the interview and shook his hand, he was just about convinced that his second-in-command, Lloyd Fuller, had the best instincts. Glenn was mesmerized.

But he stopped to think. Did this woman impress him so much because of her rhetoric, her credentials and her talent, or was it simply because she was beautiful? The old bromide about the snow on the roof and the fire in the furnace came to his mind.

He had told Fuller that they couldn't discriminate according to age. Could they discriminate according to beauty?

Frank Glenn came away good and confused.

While he was in his musings, Gabriela's phone rang in the reception area. She answered promptly.

"Music department, Gabriela. How may I help you?"

"Hello, Gabriela," came an overly friendly voice. "This is Tim Shelton. I'm a candidate for your teaching position and I'd like to check in with Professor Glenn if he's available."

"He's available, Mr. Shelton, but I can tell you that a decision has not been made. I will expect him to have a decision by the end of the week. Why don't you call back then?"

The impatience, revealed by the timbre of her voice, the effort to get rid of him, the friendly, business-like, cavalier dismissal were all too familiar. He'd had this conversation fifty times in the last two years. He wasn't going to be put off that easily this time. Way too much was at stake. He flashed in his mind on the grimy apartment, the acute unhappiness of his wife, and the hopelessness of their future. He insisted.

"Sure, I'll do that, Gabriela, but I'd still like to just holler in Dr. Glenn's left ear for a minute, if I can. If you don't mind." He was homey and endearing, he hoped.

"Yes sir, please hold." Her demeanor was not at all hostile, Tim noted, but the uncertainty, the creeping unease wouldn't leave him alone. This too, this post-interview follow-up call was such an oft-repeated protocol that it bordered on the tedious.

Dr. Glenn answered his phone, and Tim identified himself cheerfully.

"Oh, yes, Tim. I was just thinking about you. How are you doing?"

"Very well, Dr. Glenn — "

"Call me Frank."

"Okay, Frank. I'm just calling to check in and see how the decision-making process is going on the teaching position, and if I can offer any other credentials to you."

"No, no, I think we have all we need from you. You are an impressive candidate. Someone will get back to you by the end of the week. Thanks for calling."

"And I wanted to check on how your son is doing."

"Too soon to tell," Frank dismissed. "Thanks for asking. I'll talk to you by week's end."

Frank hung up. Tim was left with the same helpless, hopeless, pointless feeling he'd had after every interview for the last year and a half. And he knew he would. But these tedious phone calls had to be made. It was part of the rules. His sense of hope flickered like a candle in a gentle breeze. He clung to Frank's words about his strength as a candidate. On the other hand, every other time he had heard those words, the news had been bad in the end. Hope flickered. Hope flickered.

Impulsively, he turned to Theresa and told her, "Let's go out. I smell a second interview coming. I'll need a shirt." It wasn't true. He had no such instinct. He just wanted to get out of the depressing place where he lived and take Treese with him.

Chapter 30

Barb Baxter left the interview confident and happy. She knew she had done well, and she knew she looked good. It never hurt to be interviewed by a man when you look as good as she looked. It shouldn't be the criterion, of course. In theory, she'd like to be hired on her record. But it's dog-eat-dog in the job market. You use every single tool.

Feeling pretty good about things, she stopped at a shopping mall not far from the college. She thought she'd treat herself. Maybe a new scarf or purse. Perhaps a book of Isaac Watts charts from Hudson's Music. She'd seen such a book online with settings by Keith Kolander, a composer she admired. Maybe she'd have an early lunch with a glass of Pinot Noir. She had nothing to do until time to pick Dad up from work.

Dr. Glenn had suggested to her that she should think about a beginner's class she would like to teach on the genre of her choice. She could give that some thought; write herself some notes. Of course, given her druthers, Barb would certainly choose to teach liturgical form and history, but that wouldn't fly at this school. She would treasure the chance to teach Josquin who had obviously shaped all music, classical and otherwise, for centuries. But she had been duly appalled at every teaching post she'd worked, when she perceived the number of music majors who had never heard his name.

Glenn had hinted that he was looking to offer courses in more modern genres, more 20th century artists and composers. Barb dismissed this intent as a transparent effort to simply get more students to sign up.

The thought did not occur to her that recruiting students was fundamental to the job of a department director.

Similarly, Barb dismissed the director's question about the number of instruments she played. Surely piano and organ were enough, she thought. Why did he specifically ask about brass and woodwinds? Why would he care?

The mental dismissal of things that should have worried her allowed a cavalier self-satisfaction about the interview. Victory was at her fingertips.

Musing to herself, Barb went into the mall and trolled Macy's for a leather handbag that would go with her new Hush Puppies. She'd be hungry before long.

Chapter 31

"What are we going to shop for, Tim? What can we really afford? If you must have a dress shirt — and I agree you need shirts — let's go back to that thrift store and see what there is," Theresa said.

"I looked the other day. I couldn't find one that was dressy enough that didn't have something wrong with it."

"I guess you don't give a $30 shirt to a thrift store unless it has a problem. Remember way back in the day when we could pay $30 for a shirt for you?"

"That was then, and this is now. I just want to go to the mall, get lunch, and window shop. I know money's tight, but I think Cole is going to come through with some work for me. Did I tell you I talked to him this morning?"

"Cole again. No, you didn't tell me. Just keep me away from his house. It's all I ask."

Tim fell quiet. Theresa's attitude toward Shara mystified him, but he knew there was no sense exploring it. All in all, Theresa hadn't been herself for a long while. Her joyful optimism had long ago departed. Her feisty, funny, devil-may-care approach to life had followed on its heels, and had been replaced by that very haunted look Forbes Wilson had noticed.

This unexpected vitriol toward a woman who had only tried to help was new. Tim didn't understand it.

"I know you like them, and I know you like their music. I don't mean to be harsh," Theresa continued. She realized, at least, that her attitude was off. But why? "I'm just uncomfortable with the religious fanaticism."

"What fanaticism? All you told me was that she wanted to help because of Jesus Christ. What the hell is wrong with that?"

Theresa was quiet for a full sixty seconds, ruminating to herself, before she spoke.

"Okay, you want to know what it is? I'll tell you: Jesus Christ has done not one stinking thing for us! Jesus Christ has left us high and dry, and I don't know what we ever did to deserve any of this. We're good people. We pay our taxes, mow our lawn, give discarded clothing to the Salvation Army, and all we get is this hell we're living in! I don't owe Jesus Christ squat, and I don't want to hear about him or from him!"

Tim was shocked by the outburst. As long as he had known Theresa, she had seldom expressed any views about religion — for or against — but rather a somewhat patient tolerance for believers that she neither shared nor contemplated.

He took a breath. "I guess I just see this differently from the way you do. For me, the glass is still pretty half full."

"Half full of what? Bile? Tim, we're helpless. We live in that, that place; we can barely buy gas; I've taken a bag of somebody's used clothes that don't fit; and we have no clue when a paycheck of some kind will come in. What is half full about the glass?"

She was raising her voice. Her anger was growing, and Tim was unsure if it was directed at God or at him. Or both.

"Theresa, we had a beautiful home full of beautiful amenities. Now we don't. But it was a gift that we had those things to turn into cash when we needed to. It was a gift that we had money in the bank. Now we don't, but at the time it was a blessing. We lost the house, but we had a house to lose. We had friends who helped out, and we had family who felt our pain. Now, we have SNAP benefits, so if we're smart about them, we won't go hungry. Yes, we were homeless, but only for a day. We have made kind friends who will help us with a new life, and we met them at the most haphazard, unpredictable, improbable kind of way. They just happen to be musicians, so we have things in common. They may have some work for me that may fill in the space until this college job comes through. And I don't know about you," he paused for effect, "but meeting that deer changed something in me."

Theresa was quiet as the two drove toward the shopping center. At last, she said, "I know it did. It was a beautiful moment for you, and you could make a case that it was a gift from God. But it didn't really get us anything except a warm fuzzy."

"Yes, it did."

"What?"

"A promise that I am not worthless, old, and used up. It was a promise that I still have a contribution to make."

She sat in silence, looking straight ahead as Tim pulled into a parking place. As he turned off the engine, she spat back at him, "I wish I had that kind of promise. I wish I had anything at all to feel good about. This whole thing with job searching has eaten up my self-esteem, too. You're not alone."

"Let's get a bite of lunch, want to?"

Chapter 32

"So, what did you think of Ms. Baxter?" Lloyd Fuller asked Frank Glenn with his best crafted nonchalance. He was poking his head into the department head's office.

"She's got some chops, Lloyd, I admit. Her emphasis is on church music, as her resume indicates, and I give her credit for that. And she's strong on the history of the liturgical composers. My only fear is that her strengths are not as applicable to this department as, say, Shelton's or anyone else I've seen — "

"Frank," Lloyd interrupted. "The fact that she has strengths in the history of liturgy indicates a strong understanding of the mechanics of composition. It tells me that she would be highly adaptable to the needs of the department."

"Okay," Glenn reasoned, "I don't know that I agree with that, but if you're so sure about her and you know all of this, why didn't you sit in for the interview?"

Fuller panicked. He had been afraid to tip his hand during the interview and was now being questioned about skipping it. "I, um," (his mind went blank) "I didn't want to unduly influence you one way or the other." That was lame, he chided himself. He'd be lucky if Glenn wasn't suspicious.

"Dean, you've done nothing but try to influence me about this woman since we first got her CV."

"I just think she's a very strong candidate," Lloyd back-pedaled.

"Well, she is."

"Please just give it a couple of days and think about it before you hire her. I'd want you to be sure."

Frank appreciated the chiding pleasantness and good-natured presumptuousness he saw in his colleague.

"Should I tell Gabriela to call the Baxter woman back for a second interview?" Lloyd pressed.

"I think I know enough, Lloyd. Just have her called in Friday and I'll make her an offer. I sure hope she's as versatile as you appear to think."

"Yeah, sure," Lloyd agreed. His footsteps were light on his way out of Frank's office.

Chapter 33

Cole told Shara how he had circumvented the sound engineer issue at the convention center. He was proud of the work-around, but he didn't fool Shara.

"I'm glad it worked out, hon, but you can't take much credit. You might never have thought of using the sound guy on hand if Tim hadn't suggested it."

"That is very true," Cole admitted. "I knew somehow it would be a blessing to know that guy. Now, I've got to get him some work."

"Why don't you ask him to do Riverview Estates with you Wednesday?"

"Hey, that's a great idea. That way you won't have to leave work early."

"I have to tell you that Ms. Sutcliffe is getting tired of me leaving the office early to go do music. If you can work some jobs without me, that will settle her down," Shara said.

"Understood. I'd rather do jobs with you, but I'll ask Tim if he can go with me. It won't be much money, but it's better than nothing."

"That's what I think. Seventy-five bucks might be a fortune to him and Theresa right now."

"That's right, Shara, but it's seventy-five bucks we won't get to keep. Tim's coming over middle of the afternoon to work on material. If I press him, we might have enough to do a job Wednesday."

"Oh, I forgot to ask: What did the guy at the hotel say? Is he interested in booking us?"

"I never got there Sunday."

"Why?" she asked, already knowing the answer.

"Mama wanted to eat out and I didn't think it would be good to take her there . . ."

"Because she looks like a skilled nursing facility refugee."

Cole was silent for several seconds. He was standing in the kitchen in underwear heating up a pot pie in the microwave. He let the activity distract him until he could think of a way to change the subject.

"Anyway, I'll get back there Sunday for sure."

"Go see him before you go to your mother's."

Chapter 34

The Sheltons sat down in a booth inside a cute little bistro. It was themed with underwater decor. Murals on all the walls depicted hand-painted (not very well, Theresa thought) marine life as if the patron were viewing the ocean floor. A large, real aquarium in the center of the dining area sported sea horses, anemones, a variety of clownfish, tangs, and butterfly fish.

This place looks expensive, Theresa thought, but she didn't say anything. She stewed in silence. Once seated, she turned to her husband in a quiet, thoughtful tone. "Tim, I have friends, a number of them, who won't take my phone calls because they think I'll ask them for more money. I am so embarrassed by that."

"I know. I am, too. It bothers me a lot that Cole and Shara and Forbes and Quincy could smell the desperation on us. But I guess I'm glad they did or they wouldn't have helped us."

"Cole and Shara again. Do we have to discuss them?"

"Okay, what do you want to talk about?"

The waitress brought the couple water and they looked at the menu. Theresa ordered a bowl of chowder, hearty and warm. Tim asked for a fish sandwich. No fries, no slaw, no frills. When the server had gathered the menus, Tim tried again.

"For all we know, I'll get this job at the college, and our troubles will be over. A month or two in the apartment and we'll be able to move out and get something nicer."

"What do you honestly think are your chances?"

"My crystal ball is in the shop. When I called Dr. Glenn's office, the secretary, Gabriela, told me that he would have an answer on Friday. I'm supposed to call him back then."

"Okay. And have you formulated any theories on what happened with that guy, that Lloyd Fuller we had lunch with? I wonder why he turned on you like that. I thought he was a nice guy," she recalled.

"He wasn't. Something definitely changed between the first time I met him and the second," Tim agreed.

"What's going to happen if you don't get this job, Tim?" Theresa asked. The panic was rising in her again.

"What I said earlier about the crystal ball. I don't know, honey. We'll struggle and struggle until something good happens. We are not without resources — "

"Oh, Tim," she interrupted, "I think we are very much without resources. We're buying a five-dollar bowl of chowder and a fish sandwich in a restaurant and it's a major expenditure. We have 28 days to come up with $300 for our rent which seems like an impossible task, and we haven't even called the utility companies and gotten set up with light and heat. I'm so scared, Tim. I hope you get that music job because I'm just so scared." Theresa put her face into her hands and wept softly.

"Let's talk some more about the positives. Shara was very kind —"

"I know Shara was very kind. I just don't appreciate her rubbing her religion in my face —"

"She did no such thing."

"Fine, but I have no use for her Jesus Christ. He's done me no big favors, not any time lately."

"Have we given him any reason to do us any favors?"

"What?"

"I don't know. Maybe you have to believe first and then the prayers get answered. Or something. I'm no Bible scholar, but it seems like your anger and frustration, while understandable in some ways, may be doing you more harm than good."

Theresa thought about that statement until the food arrived.

Her corn chowder was very good, she admitted, and the fish sandwich Tim ordered went down just fine.

"What do you want to do this afternoon?" he asked her as he sipped his water. "I know you don't want to go with me over to Cole's."

"No, I do not. Drop me at the library and I'm going to get on the internet, check email, build myself a new resume and see if there are any jobs in Terre Haute for a washed up legal secretary with a 95 word per minute typing speed and only a moderately embarrassing habit of bursting into tears in restaurants."

"Let's pay for this and head out." The couple scooted out of the booth and made their way to the front to pay.

In the booth behind theirs, Barbara Fuller Baxter sat, slowly sipping wine and ruminating on every word she had overheard.

Chapter 35

Forbes Wilson was driving an overnight shift and was parked in front of the Greyhound bus station downtown. He was third cab back, so it surprised him greatly when a matronly older woman opened the back door and squeezed in. "Where to?" He started his engine and pulled away from the curb. The woman gazed at his face in his rear view mirror. Her hair was poofy and thick, salt and pepper gray. She wore a yellow house dress and an unpleasant face. She offered the address. "Is that across from Deveraux Park on the north side?" Forbes saw her disinterested nod in the mirror. As he turned toward the northbound highway, the woman opened a Bible from her tote bag. This would be a silent trip, Forbes noted. He was bored and sleepy after a singing job the night before. It was in his best interest, and the fare's, to stay alert. "Which part are you reading?" he offered.

"Which part? What?"

"You're reading scripture. I wonder what part of the Bible."

"Oh, uh, the story of Elijah leaving in a chariot of fire."

"You believe that?"

"You don't?"

"Hey, I grew up in church and sang in the choir. It's how I got started on music, which I still do."

"Oh," she said with sudden interest. "What choir do you sing in now?"

"Well, no choir. I sing with a singing group, The Cole Renshaw Trio. We do jazz, standards, some pop and r&b."

The woman's body language deflated. He had lost her attention. "You ever heard of us?"

"No, not at all. Have you ever heard of White Stone Missionary Baptist Church on Forsyth Street? It's near my house."

"That's the church I sang at growing up!" He grinned broadly in the mirror at the woman. Of course, it wasn't true. Forbes did sing in choir as a youngster, but not at the woman's church. He had never heard of it. But with fares, the truth didn't matter much. The idea is to keep a dialogue going. It was good for earning tips.

"My granddaughter sings in the choir now," she enthused. "She'll be leading worship Sunday morning. You ought to come. She is a beautiful soprano and the joy of my life."

Forbes's ears perked up. "She's a soprano? What does she, uh, I mean what does her voice sound like to you?"

"A soprano's voice. I just said that." The woman seemed bewildered and a little irritated.

"No, I mean, does she sound like Mahalia Jackson, Ella Fitzgerald, Dinah Washington, Sarah Vaughn — who?"

"Oh, I don't know. She just sounds beautiful. She's been on television singing, and on the internet. She's very good."

"Well, congratulations, then," Forbes said. "May I ask your name — so I know who to ask for when I visit your church?" he hastened to add.

"Ellen Bobo. And my granddaughter is Mary Jane Bobo. We call her MJ."

Chapter 36

"Hey, whaddup?" Tim said to Cole when the front door opened.

"You tryin' to sound black?" Cole retorted with an exaggerated dialect.

"Man, don't crack me up while I'm holding a piano, will you?" Tim, grinning, carried the keyboard into Cole's house as the latter held the door. He propped it against a wall as he and Cole went back to Tim's van to get the stand.

"You're in a good mood," Cole said. "Did anything good happen?"

"If it did, I'm unaware. I called the college and they're not deciding until Friday, so I'll call back then. If I'm in a good mood, it's just 'cause I'm going to play some good music for my new favorite singer, and he might even get me some work. I hope."

"Yeah, man, let's talk about that. . . "

"Oh, hey, did you get your issues straightened out with the convention center?"

"Yeah, I did, thanks. The sound engineer who works there is going to be on duty all weekend anyway, so it won't take much to run my equipment through his board."

"Glad to hear."

"But that's not what I want to talk about," Cole said.

"Okay." Tim's set the stand in place and the piano on it. He plugged the electric piano in and attached it to the nearby mixer.

"Can you work a job with me Wednesday? Shara may have trouble getting off work, and it would be a great trial run for you and me."

"Absolutely I can. What's the job?"

Cole explained that the Riverview Estates Senior Residence was right across town. It would only be an hour-long show as these seniors lacked stamina.

"The pay is not great, but it's actually not bad for just an hour's worth of work. I can give you seventy-five bucks. Sorry it's not more."

"Seventy-five bucks sounds like high cotton to me and Treese right now."

"That's what Shara said."

"Shara said, 'high cotton'?"

Cole chuckled. "Words to that effect."

"What words did she use, exactly?" Tim wanted to know.

"Uh, I think she said something about a little day job might sound good to you, or something like that. Why?" Cole was bewildered by Tim's abrupt change of mood.

"Nothing. Never mind. Sorry," Tim apologized.

"Thing is, I want 30 songs."

"You do? At three minutes a piece with no breaks between, that's 90 minutes of material. You won't need half that."

"See, some of the people will want to make requests. I'll have to answer them. If you don't know the material, well, I just want to maximize the chances that you will. I'd like 30 songs performance-ready."

"Cole, if you're worried about requests, I'm not the problem. You are. You are the one who needs a teleprompter. Most seniors are going to request songs from a musical era with which I am familiar. I'll follow you, but only if you know the words."

"I'll get them off my phone," Cole promised.

"Wow. Really? Okay. What do you want to work on?"

"I want to start with the number one most requested song in places like this."

"And that is?"

"Stardust."

"Of course, it is. I knew that."

Chapter 37

Theresa sat at a computer in the library not far from the apartment. The library was empty as the school day was in session. A few older people read magazines or played on the Internet. She and Tim had stopped on the way over and bought her a flash drive. She was glad to have it. The task of creating a new resume from memory was arduous, and with the flash drive, she hoped she'd only have to do it once.

The memory should be solid, she chided herself. Over the last year and a half, she had spent a great deal of time tinkering with the resume she had on a thumb drive in Columbus. That thumb drive was now gone, and she was on square one.

She wrote, re-wrote, and re-wrote again. Then she proofread the copy four times. When it was absolutely as perfect as she could make it, she saved it to the flash drive and opened the browser.

After a scant few minutes, Theresa drew the unhappy conclusion that jobs for her skills set were no more plentiful in Terre Haute than they had been in Columbus. She nevertheless plunged in and applied on line for several of them. She expected they would pay poorly. At this stage in her adventure, though, her expectations were the lowest they had been since she flipped hamburgers in high school. Anything she could get, she would take. Anything.

When she was finished applying, she checked her email. There was a reply from a job she had tried for two weeks earlier. It thanked her for her application, and went on to say, "Unfortunately, we have found a candidate whose skills and experience more directly answer our needs . . . ." She deleted the email.

She remembered that application. The job was a paralegal in a small firm in Columbus that centered its practice on intellectual property. Theresa doubted very much that the firm had found a candidate whose qualifications met the firm's needs better than hers did.

Some lawyer somewhere had written that verbiage to prevent age discrimination suits, she was sure. What had actually happened was that the firm had found a candidate who more directly answered its desire for a kid who would work on the cheap. With no grey hair. Or wrinkles. Or experience.

The taste of her anger came into her mouth. There was a bitter satisfaction in hitting that delete button.

Having not checked email for days, her Inbox was full. She deleted two offers for professional resume writing — only $100; four job alerts from websites of major Columbus firms, an invitation to get botox treatments to make her look younger, and a link to an article on why older women should not feel pressured to dye their hair. There was a litany of coupons for pizza delivery, Groupons, ads for jewelry from the animal-loving website that promises to feed shelter pets if you buy a ring, links to videos of cute kittens doing cute things, and a long article on what not to say in a job interview.

Tim's email was more fun. There were not one, but two rejection letters from jobs he had applied for, each containing nearly identical wording about how the winning candidate had qualifications more directly suited to the job, two ads for creams and pills to enlarge his manhood, and a notification from the college that they would like to reschedule his interview as the department head was out of town. She was amused by the last one. The email had been sent the day after the interview was originally scheduled. Gabriela, Theresa concluded, was not efficient. Yet she gets to have a job . . .

Theresa deleted the emails from Tim's Inbox and looked at her phone. Tim would pick her up in a half hour. That would be good timing as she had accomplished all she could.

She slid the phone into her pocket and resumed checking jobs, just in case she had missed anything.

Ten minutes before time to be picked up, Theresa removed her flash drive, put it in her purse, and went down the broad marble stairs to the lobby. Outside the large glass doors in the chilly November air, she realized the temperature had dropped. Her light jacket wasn't going to do all winter, she mused. She'd have to spend money for a thick winter coat. Another expense. Another worry.

With these thoughts, she set her purse down on the top outside step while she donned a scarf Shara had given her.

It only took a blink of an eye. Some kid in a hoodie, exiting the library behind her, scooped up her purse and made off with it, knocking into her with his shoulder. She stumbled down the concrete steps and landed on her face. She watched the kid run away. He turned left around the corner and was gone.

Immediately, a man was at her side. He helped her up. He was in his early twenties, with long dreadlocks and a frightened expression. His dark grey sweatshirt and sweatpants were stained and old. He smelled of pot. He wanted to know if she was all right.

She wasn't. Her cheek was badly cut on the edge of a step and blood was oozing. It began to run down her face. The young man produced a tissue from his pocket and gave it to her.

Pain and outrage overwhelmed Theresa. The helpless, hopeless weight of what had just happened came over her fast and hard, adding to the many burdens on her. Not just her brand-new flash drive was gone. Her driver's license, her SNAP card, and worst of all, her debit card had disappeared with that kid.

Her tears of rage and despair welled up like a hot geyser. The young man stood there, holding her by her elbows, as she sobbed.

Chapter 38

Shara answered the phone with her mind somewhere else. Just arriving home from work, it was ringing as she came in the door. It was Theresa on the phone and she sounded terrible.

"Theresa, what's wrong?"

"Is Tim over there? I was just robbed, and I'm bleeding, and . . ." Theresa dissolved into tears.

"I don't know, honey, I just got in — Cole!" At her call, Cole came into the main room and, seeing her on the phone, asked the question with his facial expression.

"It's Theresa. Is Tim here?"

"No. Tell her he left maybe fifteen minutes ago to go get her at the library."

"Theresa," Shara concluded, "Could you hear — ?"

"I heard," Theresa interrupted.

"What happened?" Shara asked.

"A guy pushed me down the stairs and grabbed my purse. I need that purse. Oh . . . " A stream of curse words came out of her mouth, many of which were unfamiliar to Shara.

"Theresa!" Shara interrupted, "What was in the purse?"

"My debit card, driver's license, SNAP card, library card, and that's about all. A hair brush and a lipstick. I can't do anything without those cards. I can't believe this!" Her wailing moan cut into Shara. Shara opened a drawer and fished out a phone book.

"Theresa! Theresa! Listen to me! What bank was the debit card connected to? Who is your account with? You have to call that bank and cancel the card. What is the bank?"

Theresa answered between sobs.

"Okay, I have the phone number to that bank. It's a toll-free number and you call it to straighten things out. Are you ready? I'm going to give it to you."

"No, don't bother. I don't have anything to write with, and I can't remember numbers right now."

"I understand. I want you to hold the line and I'm going to call your bank on three-way calling so you can talk to them before someone tries to use the card."

"Okay," Theresa whimpered.

Within minutes, the bank had canceled the card and made arrangements to issue a new one.

"Wait!" Theresa objected. I am living in a different city with a different address." The customer service agent took the new information and told her that a branch of the bank was not far from her home. "Can I come over there tomorrow and get a new debit card? I live on that debit card."

"So, I should not send you a new one, but wait for you to come in?"

"Please."

When the bank representative had hung up, Shara spoke to Theresa.

"Theresa, Cole has to leave here early to go to a job. But at 8:30, he'll come by and get you and Tim and take you to the family services office. You need to get your SNAP changed to Indiana anyway, so this will work out. What if he gets you at 8:30 and has you there by 9:00 when they open?"

"That would be very nice of Cole," Theresa agreed. "Shara, Tim just got here. I'm going to go. Thank you so much for helping me with this."

"My pleasure, Theresa. And I thank the Lord the robber didn't get your phone, too, and that you weren't hurt badly."

"Yeah, right. Thank the Lord." Theresa terminated the call.

Chapter 39

Tim found Theresa to be inconsolable about the mugging. Once at home, she went to bed and cried until she was cried out.

"Honey, it will be okay. They got the SNAP card, but we'll get a new one, and we just bought groceries, so we're good."

"After that shopping trip, there was only $4 left on the card anyway," she admitted.

"You already straightened out the bank, so that will be okay tomorrow, and you were hurt, but you could have been far more hurt or killed. This all could have been much worse."

"Tim, can I talk to you?"

"I thought that's what we were doing."

Theresa took a breath and wondered how to word her complex emotions. "Tim, I don't know, I just feel like I'm reaching my limit of things going wrong. I thought before I couldn't stand one more bad thing happening, and then this thug pushed me down those stairs . . . "

"So, what you're telling me is, you're stronger than you thought you were."

Tim was sitting on the edge of the mattress on the bedroom floor. His long legs were bent upward toward his chest and he was hugging them as he spoke to his wife who lay on the mattress, rubbing her puffy eyes.

"I hope this cut on my face doesn't leave a scar," she said. "I don't think we should go to the emergency room."

"No, I think they'd charge us $500 for a Band-Aid. But wait! It just so happens I have some peroxide and a much, much less expensive Band-Aid."

Tim retrieved the first-aid supplies he had bought on the way home from the library. He swabbed her cut with peroxide on toilet paper and applied the bandage.

As he did, she asked, "Did you notice that kid I was standing with when you pulled up to the library?"

"The dreadlocked kid with the dirty sweatshirt? I don't know why he wasn't freezing."

"He picked me up after I fell down the stairs and stayed with me until you got there. Do you know what he said to me when I was getting in the van?"

"I have no idea."

"He told me to have a blessed day!"

"The nerve of him!"

Chapter 40

Cole came out of the bedroom shortly after Shara got off the phone. "That was Theresa?" he asked.

"She was mugged. A guy pushed her down some steps, and took her purse," Shara reported. "She cut her face on the stair."

"We should pray for them," Cole decided.

"We should pray for them *more*," she corrected. "He got their SNAP card, and they need it. I told her that you will take them to the family services building downtown in the morning so they can apply for a replacement."

"Shara, I've got things to do in the morning. I wish you would talk to me before you schedule me for something."

"Can't you rearrange? I thought you just had to meet a guy about a music job."

"No, that wasn't it," he said tentatively. "Mamma has an appointment at the podiatrist."

Shara gave him her best you-gotta-be-kidding-me look.

"You need to be at Tim and Theresa's at 8:30 so you can get them there by 9:00."

"So, what — you want me to strand them there or wait for them to get finished. It could take hours to see an agent!"

"No, no, of course not. I want you to let them follow you in their own car. You'll be done before 9:00, depending on traffic. Tell your mother to cancel the appointment. This specialist du jour thing she's got going is on my last stinking nerve."

"You should have seen her Sunday. She could barely walk."

"She's had that bunion for years. Why is it suddenly emergent?"

"I don't know that it's the bunion that's bothering her," he said.

"You don't know that there's anything that's bothering her. She just wants you to waste half of your day pandering to her whims."

It was Cole's turn to look at his wife with an articulate facial expression. "Shara."

"What?"

"I can't help it if she's old and sick."

"Agreed. But you can help it that her self-absorption ruins a lot of your productivity. I wish you could just explain that your time is better used doing things that get us somewhere. . . "

"She'll never understand."

"She doesn't want to understand."

He then noticed Shara's waffle iron on the kitchen counter. "Look here," he said as he opened it up. "This is you and Mom," he said pointing to the top and bottom iron. "I'm the batter poured in." He closed the iron and set it back on the counter.

"I understand," she admitted. "It's not what I'm attempting to do, squeeze you between us. But I can't just do nothing when it costs you so much time and effort to deal with her three or four days a week."

"What do you want me to do?"

"Talk to her honestly and get her to understand that your work is important."

"And that her concerns aren't important. That's what she'll think. She won't understand."

"Then I'll talk to her," Shara said, voice rising."

"I don't want you to start a war. She loves you, and she won't understand why you're coming at her like that."

"Her failure to see past her own nose is at the heart of the problem, isn't it?" Shara reached for the telephone, but Cole reached out and took her by the wrist.

"Please don't," he begged. "Not today. Let me try one more time first."

Chapter 41

Wednesday at noon, Cole picked Tim up for the job, leaving Theresa with the car. The two drove straight out of the city, south, for 45 minutes to a one-story brick building off the highway in a residential section of some town Tim didn't know. He and Cole went inside the building where elderly folks of all levels of infirmity sat in wheelchairs, at tables, or moved about weakly in walkers.

It smelled a little like urine, Tim noted, and he wondered how often Cole played at these kinds of facilities.

Cole spoke to Mary DePeres, the white-haired activities director. She had a big smile and an ebullient laugh that Tim took as an affectation. Her hair was fashioned in an upswept style designed to make her look youthful. Her bright, laughing blue eyes belied her attitude toward what Tim assumed was her disliked job. A person couldn't really be very happy in such a depressing place, with that smell.

Mary was thrilled to see Cole, and she greeted Tim with graciousness when introduced. She spoke to a young woman wearing pink scrubs, and the task began of gathering the wheelchairs in a semi-circle around the staging area in the corner near the piano.

While that took place, Cole pulled the mixer and floor monitor out of the car. Tim lifted two small speakers onto their telescoping poles and set them at each side of the staging area.

"How did you know where to set those speakers?" Cole asked his new friend.

"Wave mechanics," Tim intoned.

"You know about wave mechanics?"

"Some. I certainly know that it's good that you have a floor monitor. Otherwise, where you plan to stand would be a dead zone. You wouldn't hear the music or yourself at all."

"Yeah, I hate when that happens," Cole chuckled.

When the two were ready, Cole stepped to the worn brown Baldwin upright where Tim was testing the sound. As he expected, the piano was significantly out of tune. He would have to do the best he could.

As Cole approached, Tim told him, "I figure this piano was new in the early 70s."

"And hasn't been tuned since the early 80s, right?"

Tim grinned

"Okay, Tim, look here. This is what's going to happen. We're going to play as much up-tempo as we can. If we do Nat King Cole, look to the "Straighten Up and Fly Right" more than the "Mona Lisa," get it? One of the tough things about these nursing homes is that they'll request ballads, but if you give them ballads, they'll complain afterward that the music was too slow and drippy. The activities directors, like Mary, want their patients stimulated, and that's where we come in."

"Well, if they request a song, won't we have to do that song?"

"Of course, and you can't speed a slow song up very much. But usually they don't request songs so much as they request artists. Doesn't matter. We'll choose most of the songs, and those that we worked on together are mostly swing. I've done this place a time or two, see?"

"Got it. I'm ready, are you?"

Mary introduced the duo as Cole and his friend. She labored visibly for a moment before saying Tim's name. As Cole stepped forward with his mic, there was polite applause. Five feet from Cole was the first row of wheelchairs. Front and center sat an overweight woman with grey, thinning hair pinned in a disheveled bun. She wore a blue print dress that came to just below her knees. Her legs were spread open immodestly. She didn't look at the stage, but seemed to be elsewhere, unfocused, almost catatonic. Tim, noticing her, remembered Cole's words about the need to provide stimulation.

Tim began playing "My Kind of Girl" in as fast a tempo as he dared. Cole, with his music stand up and his lyrics book open, glanced at it often as he sang. Tim was impressed at Cole's approach to his audience. As the song described the singer's ideal kind of girl, Cole looked around pointing at various responsive audience members. When the lyric "and her hair has a kind of curl," he waved at a curly-haired woman. When the lyric said, "her smile's like a kind of pearl," Cole waved right at a smiling woman. He made eye contact with everyone, Tim noted, with respect and just a little flirtation. Females dominated the audience, after all, and Cole winked and waved at them all.

Toward the end of the third song, Tim looked over at the woman in the blue dress. As if she saw him looking, her bladder released, and she sprayed urine on the floor at Cole's feet. Cole stepped back slightly and kept right on singing. Tim supposed this kind of thing happened a lot in places like this. His heart went out to the elderly and sick before him. There but for God's grace . . .

Promptly at the end of an hour and a quarter of singing, Cole announced the closing song, "I'll Be Seeing You." He signaled Tim non-verbally to pick the tempo up, even though the traditional tempo was slow. It worked well. The closing applause was satisfying to Tim even though the venue was far from what was familiar to him.

As caregivers began wheeling patients away, Cole nudged a worker's elbow and pointed to the puddle on the floor. She said to him, "I'll get a mop."

Then the two men packed the small amount of equipment in Cole's van, Cole excused himself to check on Mary. A moment later he came out of the facility again, sliding an envelope into the breast pocket of his suit coat.

"That was quite an experience," Tim told Cole when the latter slid into the driver's seat.

"In what way?"

"Do you frequently get urinated on in these places?"

"That was actually my first urination. There have been some occasions of vomiting, which I have tried not to take personally, and once a lady had a stroke while sitting in my audience. I tell myself to be kind. That may be me one day, if I'm fortunate to live long enough. And I don't mind these little shows. They're easy money, and I like it that these audiences like the music I like.

"I'm going to stop at the bank on the way back to your place and cash this check. Cash works for you, doesn't it?"

Chapter 42

Theresa spent a lot of her days at the library applying for jobs. Einstein's words about the insanity of doing the same thing repeatedly while expecting different results were not lost on her. She simply didn't know what else to do. Before the second week of her Terre Haute residency was concluded, Theresa had applied for thirty-five jobs, received twenty-two rejection form letters, and scheduled one interview.

The interview was with Biggs & Bean, an ad agency in the high-rent section of town. The agency provided web, print, and electronic ad support for some very well-heeled companies in western Indiana, she read on their website. They needed a secretary.

Tim and Theresa went back to the thrift store and found a grey wool suit that fit her, more or less, and a colorful scarf. The suit had two tiny holes on the shoulder. Clearly, moths had munched it. She hoped the damage was unnoticeable. But the ensemble was conservative and appropriate for the task at hand. She paired the outfit with a white blouse Shara had given her, and she was ready to doll up.

Thursday morning, Tim drove her to the loft where the company had its headquarters. Parking was expensive, and they both hoped she would get validation. From the garage, she rode the elevator to the seventh floor and stepped out into a surprising environment.

The vast window enclosed the offices and provided a view of Terre Haute's skyline and the Wabash River. Between the elevator and the window, the phrase, "business casual," was defined. Young men and women scurried about wearing jeans, tee shirts, overalls and sweat pants. There were sandals and baseball caps. One woman wore a tie-dyed broomstick skirt and a vintage 1960s fringed suede vest.

She was the only one who appeared to be a day over 30.

Right outside the elevator was apparently the company's break room. There was a full bar with a variety of liquors that made Theresa do a double-take. There was a microwave, full refrigerator and stove, kitchen cabinets and a pantry in which a variety of food was visible when a young woman with a ponytail pulled out a bag of chips. Tables and chairs were littered about haphazardly. She noticed the woman in the tie-dyed skirt open the refrigerator which was packed with food. She put a microwaveable dinner in the micro and nuked it.

Nice perks, Theresa thought to herself.

Glancing around, she saw no reception desk or other traditional place for a visitor to approach. She felt helpless for several minutes before a man with long, wavy blond hair and an arm covered in tattoos depicting Norse gods stopped and asked if he could help her.

"Yes, please. I am here for a job interview with Brandon Noble. Where can I find him?"

"Oh, I don't know. Just a sec." The man disappeared down a corridor. She heard him raise his voice to no one in particular, "Hey! Where's Brandon? There's a, um, somebody here to see him."

Theresa heard no response. Several other people passed her on their way somewhere or other. Some glanced up at her; many didn't, and her feeling of unease and inadequacy began to mount. She had never seen a business run like this. She was a fish out of water.

Then she heard her name spoken. The voice was just behind her head. She jumped, startled. It was a man with a full reddish-blond beard, shoulder-length hair, and a Metallica tee shirt. As she turned to greet him, he saw her face just as she saw his. At that moment, his warm smile faded into something negative that left a metallic taste in her mouth. She knew that this task was hopeless. She hadn't even spoken, and already, he had dismissed her as undesirable. The despair welled up in her, but she tamped it down as best she could.

"Hello, I'm Brandon. Please come this way." He turned and walked away from her without waiting for a reply. As he did, another man appeared in the hallway Brandon had darted down. When passing the other man, Brandon beckoned him with a curled finger. "Hey, Jason, sit in on this meeting with me, huh?"

Jason complied. He was a tall, heavy-set man with a bald head and a goatee. He wore a blue polo shirt and jeans. He exuded an air of comfort in his own skin that Theresa envied. She momentarily fantasized about Jason as an enormous blue juice box that she would like to plunge a straw into and suck out his confidence for herself.

Turning her attention back to Brandon, her discomfort level rose as her hands began to sweat. "I'm going to lead you to our conference room," he said over his shoulder. As he did, he ducked around a corner and through a doorway. Following, she entered a room lined with sofas and soft, upholstered chairs. No traditional conference table appeared. A coffee table held a tray of water bottles, and a pitcher of ice. Another tray displayed sliced bagels and a variety of single-serve flavored cream cheese containers.

The room, rife with potted flowers and Marc Chagall prints on the walls, had a window that looked out on the city, bringing in a sense of light and space. It bore no resemblance to any conference room Theresa had ever seen, and while the hospitality was clear from the bagels, her discomfort mounted again.

Brandon, watching her reaction, explained, "One of our clients is Quinn Farmer Bread Company. Their CEO is a buddy of mine. They send bagels and cream cheese every day."

"I see," she intoned, "Impressive."

"Have a seat and I'll get my materials and be right back."

What followed for Theresa was a seemingly endless droning monologue about what the company does, who its clients are and why it has such a grand market share. There were monotone anecdotes about other people, all men, who had held the position and their crimes that resulted in their discharge.

Following that came a barrage of questions about software and social media about which she knew nothing. Would she be able to use Twitter to start buzz on a client's newest software release? Does she know very much about posting videos to Facebook? Or even Youtube? Does she know how to make a website climb up to the top of a search engine? Under what name (since it obviously isn't under Theresa Shelton) can he find her Facebook page, her LinkedIn profile, or her personal web site?

During this, Jason said nothing. His interest in being there was feigned, she realized, because of his sweet, patient smile as he glanced around the room, his mind elsewhere.

By the third or fourth question, Theresa was assured that her chances of attaining this job were as slim as her willingness to cover her arms with tattoos like the man outside the elevator. She wondered why Brandon had kept her in the interview this long. She knew in her heart, but was unwilling to face the truth, that Brandon had written her off the moment he saw her face. And her age.

She answered each query, and followed each disclaimer with an assurance of her willingness to learn new things. Brandon responded by looking down at her resume. He had given up on making eye contact.

"All right, then," he was saying. "Let's look at some of the things you do have experience with, okay?"

It was then that a feeling of helpless despair enveloped Theresa. If she had a nickel for every time an interviewer had offered to look at some of the things she had experience with, she could buy Tim a steak dinner out on the town. The inevitable conclusion of this torture was clear, as it had been on many other interviews on many other occasions. Each time this had happened, she considered cutting her losses and dismissing the possibility that this interview would turn around at the eleventh hour and that there was some reason to complete it. She had always stuck it out till the end, hoping for that Hail Mary pass that never landed.

This time, she didn't.

"Let's not, Mr. Noble."

The interviewer looked up from his papers at her with surprise.

"Let's just call this a day and save my time, yours and Jason's. You don't want me. You want someone with 30 years of experience with software and marketing strategies that didn't exist 10 years ago, and you want her to be a hip, lovely, savvy 20-year-old whose left hand is soldered to her iPhone. We both know I'm not her. Have a good life."

Theresa stood and walked to the elevator, blinking away tears.

"How do you think it went?" Tim asked as soon as she got back in the car.

"Oh, it's a very young, very hip company with all the latest social media at their fingertips and software I've never heard of. Very modern, very youth-focused."

"So, not that great?"

"No. Not that great."

"What took so long, do you think? You were in there over an hour."

"Right. The interviewer was very careful to give me every question, every opportunity, even though he wrote me off the moment he saw me. He even invited a flunky in to chaperone the interview."

"Why all the detail if he wrote you off?"

"To make sure I have no cause of action for an age-discrimination suit. That's why he wanted a witness. He was C-Y-ing his A."

Chapter 43

Forbes Wilson had driven his cab to and from Hulman Field, the airport a few miles outside of Terre Haute, seven times the night before, and when Sunday morning arrived, he was ready to go home. One fare had gone to the north side of town; two others to the southern most parts of the suburbs, and with the lot of them, Forbes was at the end of a pretty good night. On the way home, he stopped at his new favorite breakfast place not far from his apartment. It was on a main drag. The storefront was ancient, probably built in the 30s, and the buildings around it, much newer, gave this little diner a blended sense of history and shabbiness. He stepped inside. A row of booths lined the wall on the right while a row of stools lined up in front of the counter on the left. Forbes sat at the counter and waited. A moment later, Ellen Bobo came out from a back room and took her place behind the counter. Seeing Forbes, she heaved and exasperated breath. Without greeting or ceremony, she asked, "Decaf?"

"Sure. Say, where's MJ?"

"Mary Jane is in Sunday School about this time on a Sunday morning. And it's where I'd be, too, if I didn't have to be here. What do you want with my girl?" Ellen's timbre, impatient and protective, was hard to mistake. She knew Forbes was sweet on MJ, and Ellen would be damned if she let her granddaughter date a cab driver thirty years her senior.

"She singing in church this morning?" Forbes ignored the attitude and remained pleasant.

"I believe she is. At Wednesday night's service, she's singing a solo. She has plenty of singing to do in church. She has no time for your silly nightclub singing."

"You don't know that, Ellen. I've invited you and her to several of our shows, but you can't see your way clear. So, you don't know how silly our shows are because you won't come. And, plus, I've been to church twice since we met. It's only fair she come and hear me sing."

"I know she don't have time for no nightclub devil's music. Are you gonna order?"

"Bacon and eggs. She's got a beautiful soprano voice, and you should rethink standing in the way of her using it."

"White or wheat toast?"

"Ellen, if you'd just stand aside for a minute and let me take her to an audition . . . "

"No. That's my word on the matter. And while we're at it, you can let go of that look in your eye. She's not for you. I have bigger dreams for my baby than hooking up with a cab driver."

"This cab driver might could put her in Hollywood. Then wouldn't you be sad you were the roadblock?"

"That'll be the day. Mary Jane don't have time for an old man anyway. Scrambled is what you're getting.'"

Chapter 44

"Hello. This is Tim Shelton. I'm calling for Dr. Glenn. Is he available?"

He recognized Gabriela's voice and smiled to himself about her SNAFU of inviting him to reschedule his interview after he had already had it.

"I believe he is available, Mr. Shelton. Please hold for just a moment." Gabriela's tone was sugary and artificial.

The music on hold was Rachmaninoff's "Rhapsody on a Theme of Paganini," and Tim took the opportunity to let the stirring, romantic piece carry him away — and his nervousness with it, he hoped. It was only in the back of his mind that he considered that it was taking a long time for Glenn to pick up the phone.

The phone finally clicked and Glenn's voice was audible. "Hey, Tim. Glad you called. Sorry you were on hold there for a while. What's going on?"

"Oh, no worries," Tim gushed too enthusiastically. "I was enjoying the Rachmaninoff. Hey, it's Friday, so I was calling to see if you've made a decision on the position we talked about."

Glenn's three-second pause before answering seemed like ten minutes to Tim, whose stomach was suddenly tight and sour.

"Well, as a matter of fact, I did make an offer this morning to a candidate, and she has accepted the position," was Glenn's perfunctory statement.

"I see. I can't tell you I'm not disappointed, Frank." The stomach acid was gushing now, and his extremities were going numb.

"Well, you were a great candidate, Tim. There was just one other who narrowly beat you out, and if another professorship comes up — although I doubt that it will very soon — I'll sure give you a call."

"May I ask what the other candidate had that I don't have?"

Frank paused nervously. Truth was, he couldn't think of a thing. But he could hardly tell Tim that he didn't get the job because Frank's own colleague bullied him into hiring the woman. "All I can tell you is that the winning candidate had qualifications that reflected the needs of the position just a little more closely than yours did."

Tim's stomach acid turned immediately to vitriol. "First of all, Frank, I seriously doubt that. I seriously doubt that your needs are for anything I can't directly, specifically, spectacularly deliver. Second, don't you think that as professors in this very proud discipline, you could afford me something other than a canned, clichéd answer from some lawyer's copy written disclaimer?"

Tim's heart was pounding and he felt light-headed. He hoped that when this phone call concluded, it would be cathartic rather than cataclysmic.

"All I can tell you is what I've told you, Tim. You've got great qualifications, my friend. I've no doubt you'll find work in a week or less. Hey, thanks for calling." With that, Glenn disconnected the call.

Tim knew instantly that his outburst was far from cathartic. If he had railed at Frank Glenn for an hour, screaming about how unfair it all was, then it might have been cathartic. But it would hardly be Glenn's fault. And it would do no good.

He sat down at the apartment's sole table and put his face in his hands. The panic and sorrow welled up in him, and he let it flow through him, over him. Let him process it completely and disarm it so that Theresa need never know how hard this news had hit him.

He could use a stiff drink.

Chapter 45

When Tim's phone rang, he was sorely tempted to not answer. He was in no mood. But habit compelled him. There was always the slim, absurd chance that it could be another hiring manager. Instead, it was Shara.

"How are you and Cole doing?" he asked tonelessly.

"Hey, we're great. Did you hear anything about the college job? Shara asked hopefully.

"I did. I didn't get it."

"Oh, no, that's awful. I'm very sorry. I guess you and Cole need to get some gigs, huh?" Shara said.

"Sure. That one yesterday was a big help. Four more just like it and we'll have the December rent."

"Why don't you go out tonight, hit some piano bars, see what's what?" she invited. "He'll pick you up."

Theresa was at the library again, and Tim was in no hurry to pick her up and tell her this bad news. "Here's my counter-proposal," he offered. "Why doesn't Cole meet me at the library on Fillmore Street, at, say, 5:30. Let me run in and give Treese the car keys, and then she can take herself home."

"Sounds good. Now, to what I called you for. Cole and I would like to invite you and Theresa over for Thanksgiving dinner. We don't have much family, just his mom, and you don't have any family in town, so it might just be great to share the holiday. Think?"

Shara's voice was warm, and Tim appreciated the offer. "That sounds great to me," he offered, "but let me run it by Treese before I answer. How soon do you have to know?"

When he was off the phone, Tim admitted to himself that his wife would probably rather be tortured with knives than have a holiday dinner with Shara. He shook his head with regret and wondered in passing how Treese had become so embittered about God, and he wondered if he himself had contributed to her anger.

Chapter 46

When Barbara got off the phone with Dr. Glenn early in the day, she knew that she should be enraptured by the opportunity. She'll be working with her father (although, on the "down-low"), she'll be teaching music that she favors, and the strong music department at the college will offer tremendous performance opportunities. She can form as many choirs as she would like, and if the voices she heard were strong enough within the student body, she could introduce to students the complex ore-Renaissance harmonies she dearly loved.

This will be a dream job. Why can't I feel good about it?

"Hey, Dad. Barb. How are you?" She hoped her telephone voice was happier than she felt.

"Hey, baby girl. I understand you accepted, and he wants you to start next week. I'm proud of you, baby."

"Yeah, thanks. I'll start after the holiday, actually, but I'll Start Monday planning my classes for the first of the year."

Her father had known her too long, and her efforts to be perky were for naught.

"You don't really sound that happy. Is something wrong?"

"Oh, I don't know. I certainly want the job. It's just that things aren't exactly as I had dreamed. I mean, it's a secular school, so I'll miss the liturgical content. . . ."

"You knew that going in."

"I did. Plus, I don't know. I've never had trouble getting work, so I wonder if I should, maybe, wait and hold out for something else. Let someone else have this opportunity."

"What in hell are you talking about?" her father demanded. "I did everything but jump through fiery hoops for you to get this. Now, what? Are you too special to work at a college?"

"No, of course not. It's just, I don't know. I'll feel better about it in the morning. Let's talk about Thanksgiving. I'll cook, okay?"

"Sure," he replied. "I still don't understand what you're doing with this job situation."

"I know. But, look, if I don't take the job, then you can let it be known that you and I are kin. No secrets. Wouldn't that be good? It would be more honest, at least."

"Don't even think about turning this down, Barbara. I'll have none of it. You beat out a couple of great candidates, so if you don't take it . . . it will be, well, disrespect. "

"I know. I get it. I'll see you when you get home." She hung up before he could say anything. She took a roast out of her dad's freezer and ran cool water on it to thaw. She couldn't get that couple in the restaurant out of her mind.

Chapter 47

"Really? Thanksgiving at Shara's? Do you think there is any place on the face of the earth I would not rather spend my holiday?" Theresa was livid. The nerve of her husband, asking her for this.

"I know you're upset. I understand that you don't want this. But, baby, you really need to understand that you're off on this. Shara has done nothing — nothing at all against you. She has been kind and thoughtful to a fare thee well." Tim's words struck Theresa as empty and beside the point. She was determined to vilify the dark-haired woman who had given of herself to be helpful to her. It wasn't a matter that Theresa couldn't see it. No. Theresa refused to see it. She did it with malice, Tim told his wife. It was ridiculous.

So, the timing was bad Wednesday morning when the phone rang. It was Shara, of all people, calling Theresa for a favor.

"Yeah, hi," Theresa said. She was gripping her impulses. While she didn't like this horsey, cheaply dyed hack, her reasons for doing so were internal. She must keep appearances.

"Hey, Treese. Can I call you Treese?" Shara asked.

"Tim calls me that. 'Theresa' is fine, if you don't mind.

"Um, okay," the other woman capitulated with some bewilderment. "I was thinking that, since you're coming over tomorrow for dinner, maybe you'd like to help me get ready. I need to clean and straighten. And, by that, I mean I need to remove cat hair from the furniture. I thought that, if you want to come help me today, you can use my washer and dryer while you're here, and it might save you a trip to the Laundromat."

Theresa, who had been washing out her panties nightly in the bathroom sink and hanging them to dry, saw the value of Shara's suggestion. All of their clothes were on the cusp of funky, and a good run through a washing machine would solve a lot of problems. Yet, stuck over there for a day, was she really willing to dispense with her dignity just to wash the clothes? She knew where the Laundromat was. It was in a terrible neighborhood where she didn't feel very safe. So, on the one occasion she had gone there, she had made Tim accompany her. People there were poor. They couldn't afford a washer and dryer either, she supposed. It wasn't a fun place to go.

Theresa thought it through. She could plan to spend the Wednesday at the library. But, having been through this last year, it was clear that hiring managers didn't do a lot of recruiting between Thanksgiving and the first of the year. Plus, Tim was going out for another of these little gigs with Cole, and it would make sense strategically to get dropped off at Shara's and let the men make a little money. For the life of her, Theresa could think of no plausible reason why it didn't make sense to truck over there with her laundry. She agreed to the plan.

At 10 a.m. Wednesday, she and Tim rang the bell at Cole and Shara's. Cole answered, dressed in a flashy performance suit, and the two men left with dispatch. Their job at 11:00, at a lunch place in the midtown section of Terre Haute, was a trial run. Cole was hoping to get a one-hour gig on Wednesdays on a regular basis, and the idea set well with Tim. Cole's two partners would be unavailable, and Tim and Cole could, thereby, split the little piece of money without Quincy whining about the dis. Plus, to Theresa's satisfaction, the gig was only two hours, so the men would be back in a relatively short time, and Theresa could be rescued from this incarceration at the home of her perceived nemesis.

"You want coffee?" Shara offered as Theresa stepped into the door. "It's a fresh pot."

Shara considered the large trash bag of dirty clothes Theresa was carrying. "Help yourself," she admonished, "And give me that bag. I'll put in a load."

Theresa admitted to herself that Shara was kind. She also owned the reality that she missed her coffee in the morning, but she had no Mr. Coffee machine at the apartment. Joe in the morning would be an extravagance, and a distant memory. She reached in the cabinet and poured herself a cup. As she did, Shara reappeared.

"So," Shara said, "Here's my plan. I need to scour this house for the gathering tomorrow, and I also need to plan this meal. I'd like to work on the living room and kitchen, washing the floors, dusting and whatnot, and I wish that you would slice up vegetables to make turkey stuffing. You with me?"

"I've been known to slice an onion or two," Theresa responded. The truth was, the feeling of being beholden to Shara was fairly acute, and Theresa would do nearly anything to minimize it. If she could scrub Shara's toilet, it would help her even out the balance sheet.

The two women set to work. Theresa sliced celery, onions, bell peppers, carrots, mushrooms, and scallions. She sautéed the giblets and toasted a loaf of bread for stuffing. Shara scrupulously cleaned the cat hair up, dusted and swept.

(When Shara had presented her with the loaf, Theresa realized that Shara wanted scratch-made stuffing instead of some processed package, and that pleased Theresa, she had to admit.)

"So, who all is coming tomorrow," Theresa asked.

"You, Tim, my mother-in-law, Cole and me."

"What can I bring with me?"

"Nothing, girl. And since I'm making way too much food, because it is my habit, I hope you'll abscond with leftovers."

"I guess I can do that," Theresa replied, thinking of her new, but depleted SNAP card. "What's your mother-in-law like?"

"Oh, um, she's fine. She's 83, so she has limitations. And she has issues. She's pretty needy, really."

"I'm not sure what you mean."

Shara was running a dust rag around the living room. She paused to look up at Theresa. "You know what they always say. If you can't say anything nice . . . "

"Don't say anything at all," Theresa finished her thought. "I'm guessing you are not the first woman ever to have issues with her mother-in-law."

"I'm thinking I'm not. But I think I have issues that other daughters in law don't have."

"Meaning?"

"I don't want to criticize the lady when she's not here to defend herself," Shara said. "But, since my husband is self-employed, the message that his mother gets is that he doesn't work. She believes that what he does has no value or meaning because it isn't a set job that he has to be at or that he has to stay at until 5 o'clock. So, in her mind, he should be free to do her favors for hours and hours every day. The myopia bothers me, I have to admit."

"Wow, okay," Theresa replied. She hated to admit it, but that chink in Shara's armor of sweetness was exculpatory to Theresa. Instead, she remarked, "Tim's parents have been gone for a lot of years, and I really never dealt with anything like this. Is she frail?"

"She thinks she is. She goes to the doctor ten times a month. That's an exaggeration, but because each doctor's appointment takes the whole day, Cole doesn't get things done the way I need him to. I shouldn't be telling you this. The truth is, I need help paying the bills, and while I am totally behind him and the music, I need another income into this house, and the time he wastes sitting in doctors' offices is something I can't afford."

"Shara, I am honestly uncomfortable talking about this. I don't even know this person." The truth was, Shara's objection to her mother in law was something Theresa found more understandable than she would like.

"You're right, and I shouldn't put it on you. Sorry. So, how are job prospects for you?"

"Dismal," she replied, thankful for the change in topic. "It seems like folks don't hire during the holidays."

"No, I don't think that they do. I took a vacation day today because there are so many at the hospital that are out to make a five-day weekend that's there's little point in my being there. So, that makes me think that hiring and interviewing is low on the priority list.

"You told me before that you have been a legal secretary?"

"That's right. The same firm for eighteen years."

Shara, who had been dusting off a lamp, straightened her back and looked at Theresa.

"This firm, what was its specialty?"

"We did a lot of IP."

"IP? You mean like internet addresses on a computer?"

"No. Intellectual property. Copyrights, and things like that."

"I see," Shara said. She continued to look at Theresa for a minute or two.

"What?" Theresa finally said with discomfort.

"I'm just thinking. At the hospital where I work, everything that is written has to be submitted to the Federal Trade Commission for approval to assure that the hospital doesn't make claims that it can't substantiate. For instance, we can't say that taking this drug will reduce your chances of getting cancer. We can only say that the drug MAY reduce your chances, or that it appears to have done so in test subjects. We have a team of lawyers going over all the marketing collateral for mistakes like that. They have secretaries.

"I'm going to need your resume and references," Shara concluded.

"I have the resume in my 'purse,'" Theresa said. "I'd be very thankful." Theresa meant it. With a sardonic demeanor, she fished a dollar-store sock out of her pocket — her new purse — and fished out of it her new thumb drive and apartment key.

"Oh, yeah, your purse," Shara commented. I've got a purse I never use. It's yours."

"What if I just get it stolen?"

"Let's cross that bridge later. Your resume is on here?"

The offer of help did not ameliorate Theresa's attitude or discomfort with Shara as a person, and it certainly did not mollify Theresa's dislike of Shara's religious fervor. But Theresa was not in a place to be choosy.

Shara set down her dust rag. "Come with me," she commanded.

A few minutes later, Theresa found herself in a spare bedroom with a computer and Shara reading the resume off of her flash drive. Shara saved the document to her own computer without asking for permission, Theresa noted.

"Have you applied for a lot of jobs?"

"Dozens. I have had one interview, and it was horrible," Theresa confessed. "A nightmare."

"Sorry. Let me hazard a guess, okay?" Shara said. "They won't cop to it, but they wished you were younger."

"Bulls-eye."

Shara dialed the phone on the desk. Shortly, she said, "Hey, Doug. Shara Renshaw," into the phone. "I've got a friend here who's a legal secretary, very experienced. She just relocated here and is looking for work. I'm going to forward you her resume, but I wish you'd just say hi to her for a minute. I don't know if you have any openings, but I'd like to introduce you over the phone. Okay? Thanks. And, happy Thanksgiving. Here she is. Her name is Theresa Shelton."

Shara handed off the phone.

Theresa, startled and unprepared stammered, "Hello."

In the next few minutes, she told Doug, the head of the legal department at the hospital, about her education, her background in Intellectual Property, contracts, and work her firm did for labor unions in Columbus. She hoped she didn't sound as stupid, unprepared or lame as she felt. Still, it was something, and she had no one but Shara to thank.

"Theresa, I don't have anything open in my department, but when your resume gets here, I'm going to send it on to Tom Dousman who runs our real estate department. Good luck with everything. Shara has my contact info."

When Theresa was off the phone, she thanked Shara. Now, she was more beholden to the woman than ever. She found herself unable to meet Shara's gaze, but rather looked at the floor.

Shara removed the flash drive from the computer and handed it back to Theresa who followed Shara back into the kitchen, muttering humbly, "I guess I'll caramelize the onions."

Chapter 48

"I want to talk about another — let's call it a — challenge," Cole told Tim on the way to the performance.

"Should I worry?"

"No. Here it is: Christmas." Tim simply looked at his friend, waiting.

"I mean, Christmas music. Starting Friday at this job at the convention center, we'll do a lot of holiday music, but you and I need to work up some of it too for these little gigs we're lining up."

"I didn't think about that," Tim confessed. "I know most of the popular tunes, but it would be smart to work them up with you."

"Maybe today after we get done?"

Tim dreaded telling Theresa that she was stuck at Shara's for even more hours after he went there to rescue her. He had left her the car so he could ride with Cole, but he nevertheless dreaded her reaction.

"Let me run that by Treese before I commit, okay? She may be ready to go home by then."

"I understand. Also, we have to talk about these little gigs`," Cole continued.

"Really? Okay."

"I know that until you find work, you're going to be counting on me. But, to be honest, these small little jobs are going to grind to a halt on December 26th."

"I didn't think about that, either."

"I've got the four of us working every weekend in December, but the two of us, you and I, are also booked for seven little shows — shows I would have done with Shara. But she is feeling heat from her job, so it's good I have you. However, for January, so far, I've got nothing for you and me."

"We talked before about going out in evenings and trying to line up some nightclubs. Whatever happened with that guy you told me about that you need a live musician for?"

"Oh, wow, I'm glad you said that. I need to go by there and see him. You want to do that with me right after this show?" Cole ventured.

"Uh, what I said earlier about getting back to Treese."

"Doesn't she have a car?"

"You're right. She does," Tim relented.

Cole smelled a problem, but he didn't want to interfere. "Why don't you call her and tell her you're going to be later?"

Tim hedged. Knowing his wife, she was already, back at Shara's, emotionally clawing at the door to get out of there. If he called her with this message, and made it more awkward for her to get away from Shara, it wouldn't set well. "Hey, look," Tim finally said. "This guy, on the eve of a major holiday, probably has plenty on his mind. Let's put off this meeting until, say, Monday and maybe we'll have more of his attention when we go to see him."

"You might be right," Cole acquiesced. "It gets tricky at the holidays."

"Solid."

Chapter 49

Shara was up at the crack of dawn to begin cooking. Company was expected in mid-afternoon, and she had devised a schedule of when to start various dishes and ready-making things to do beforehand. Generally, Shara liked to cook for holidays. She liked the whole family-gathering paradigm. But there had been so much loss in the last ten years that the usual huge gatherings with both sides of the family had been whittled down to just a few survivors.

Shara had lost her parents and her brother in a traffic accident six years ago. Cole had lost his treasured aunt to heart disease two Easters ago. Cole's father had succumbed to heart disease before she'd ever met him, and Shara's best friend had suffered a brain aneurysm last year. To Shara, therefore, holidays were a joy, but also a hallmark of the passage of time and the memories of those departed.

There had been aunts, uncles, and cousins who had passed for one reason or other and had reduced the number of folding chairs needed around the holiday dinner table accordingly.

She tried to stay positive.

One feature of each holiday that remained was the unusual dynamic she shared with her mother-in-law. Mom was admittedly a chore. Shara knew ahead of time that Mom's mastery of passive aggression, guilt-baiting, and manipulation of her son would be a highlight of the day. Always had been.

Shara began lubricating early. With three hours to go before the doorbell rang, Shara poured herself a nice vintage of Pinot Grigio and sipped it with relish. Cole never touched a drop, but on some subliminal level he recognized that meetings with his mother were a burden for Shara, and he wordlessly allowed her the indulgence.

This day, however, since new people were invited, he kept an eye on his wife, concerned she may overdo.

At 2:00, Cole kissed his wife. "The house smells great. I smell turkey and spices and it will be a great meal. I'm off to go pick up Mom. I'll be back in an hour or so."

"It's fifteen minutes there and fifteen home. Why will this take an hour?" Shara asked. She was already poised to be exasperated.

"I don't know, Shara. It just will. She'll not be ready, or she'll have forgotten something, or whatever. It's hard for her to move around and it just takes a long time. I'll get back to help you as soon as I can."

"Fine."

Tim and Theresa, in contrast, rang the bell at exactly 3 o'clock. Shara opened the door with a certain liquor-induced sparkle in her eye for which she made no apology. She took the couple's coats and offered them a variety of beverages she had on hand.

Theresa, with much the same strategy that Shara was using, agreed to the Pinot with gratitude.

Tim helped himself in the kitchen to a cranberry juice with just a splash of vodka. He hadn't taken a sip of liquor in months, and the treat tasted good in his mouth. He sat next to Treese and attempted to buffer the awkwardness he knew would emerge between the two women.

Shara stayed on small talk. "So, talk to me. Are you guys all set up with utilities and SNAP and everything in your apartment? I wonder if there are any household items you need that I might have in the morass of junk I have. You Know, Cole and I married late, and we both had stuff, so there is plenty of duplicate stuff I could maybe gift you with. What think?"

Theresa's eyes closed into slits. *Here we go again,* she thought, *with the unwanted benefactor,* but Tim stepped up.

"We've got nearly nothing. If you have a spare toaster or blender or any other small household appliance, I'm guessing we could give it a home."

"Small household appliances. Hmm," the other woman considered. "I'll look in the garage next week and see what I come up with. I'm pretty sure there's a hand mixer out there. We got two of them for wedding gifts."

"How long have you been married?" Tim ventured.

"Fifteen years this spring," Shara replied with confidence. "And I'm looking forward to the next fifteen."

"So, if you found a wedding present to give us, it would already be fifteen years old," Theresa commented with just a whiff of dissatisfaction.

"I don't think it's ever been out of the original box," Shara said. "Can you use it?"

"Sure," Theresa said, controlling her tone. "Uh, thanks."

"Oh, and Cole said your apartment has a shag rug. Is that right?"

"A shag rug that bears the fragrance of a sour dish rag," Theresa complained.

"It would be fantastic if I could send you home with the vacuum cleaner I don't need that takes up way too much space in the closet. Can I count on you?"

And so it went. As Shara poured more wine, her generosity grew. By the time the front door opened and Mrs. Renshaw hobbled into the house with Cole, Tim had caught on that there had been some beverages imbibed by Shara before the couple had arrived.

When he saw the elderly woman come into the house, Tim rose and introduced himself. He took Suzanne by the hand and led her to the most comfortable chair in the room while exchanging glances with Cole.

"This is my wife, Theresa," he told the woman.

Theresa, on her feet, stepped forward and shook the woman's hand.

"Oh, my, aren't you cute?" Suzanne proclaimed. "How is it that you know my son?"

"Oh, well, my husband plays keyboard and he and your son have been going out for music jobs while we search for full-time work," Theresa explained.

"I see. What kind of work are you looking for?"

The two were engaged. Suzanne and Theresa chatted about everything from household tips to Democratic Party politics. Shara stayed in the kitchen, charmed and relieved that her friend, Theresa, was assuming the burden of entertaining the self-absorbed wench who was the albatross around her neck.

Meanwhile, Cole and Tim took over the couch and talked music. Cole occasionally rose and went to the kitchen to ask Shara what he could do to help.

Shara bit her tongue and did not offer that keeping his mother busy was the most help in the world. But as she considered how to answer, a thought popped in her head. She dried her hands off and went into the other room.

"Excuse me. Mom, did you fill out that application Cole brought you?"

"What application, dear?" Suzanne asked innocently.

"The one for a home healthcare worker. We talked about this. The agency sends you someone a few days a week to help you shop, do your laundry, take you on appointments. Remember? We talked about this."

"Oh, no, dear. I didn't fill anything out. I guess I didn't know I was supposed to do that. I'll get to it."

"I remember telling you on the phone that the government pitches in and pays for the home caregiver. It's not out of your pocket. It's free."

"Okay, dear. I don't think I need all that," Suzanne said.

Shara went back into the kitchen. She slid the turkey out of the oven, sucked up meat juices, and basted the bird as she did a slow burn of her own. Then she poured another glass and took the bottle into the living room to fill up Theresa's glass.

Theresa followed her back in the kitchen. "Hey, I'm sorry I haven't helped in here. But your mother-in-law is so interesting that I sort of lost track of you being in here working."

"Not at all, Theresa," Shara said. "You have helped more than you can guess. I can't start to tell you how much you have helped. You have been a godsend. I'm so glad you and Tim came over."

"Oh, that's right. You and Cole's mother don't always see eye-to-eye, do you? I think she's delightful."

"Yes, well, she certainly can be when she wants to be. What have the two of you been chatting about all this time?"

"Criminal law. I don't know much about criminal; I mostly do civil documents. But, I learned that Cole's father was a criminal defense lawyer and she is quite knowledgeable."

"In Indianapolis. I never met my father in law. He died when Cole was a young man. But her house is full of law books from his practice. He was the go-to guy in Indianapolis for a long lot of years," Shara explained. "He was the first black man to join the Bar Association there in the history of the state."

"Impressive."

"It's an impressive family. It grieves me how many of them are gone now."

"Sorry."

Chapter 50

Sal closed the pawn shop early Wednesday night. The Christmas madness would start Friday, but traffic had dried up by 4 o'clock Wednesday, and he might just as well shut the doors. He had a good drive ahead of him to Indianapolis to his brother's house, and he should stop on the way and buy his sister in law a poinsettia or a package of dinner rolls, or something.

As he was counting out the cash drawer, he happened to look up and out the front window. There was an unfamiliar car parked in the space right in front, and a young woman was opening the door to get in. She was slender and tall, almost as tall as himself, with long dark hair that wrapped around her prepossessing face. Her eyes were large and expressive as she squinted slightly at the cold breeze. Her lithe movements were those of a goddess.

Sal was transfixed. To his great surprise, the woman reached into the car, grabbed her purse, fished something out and locked the purse in the car. She walked away from it and stepped up on the curb.

He went to the door as she walked down the frontage of the shops in the strip mall. He stepped out the door and watched her back as she stepped inside a store.

Without a coat, but in shirtsleeves, he locked the door to his place, leaving the cash drawer exposed, and followed the young woman into a dry cleaners four businesses down.

The woman was behind the counter and greeted him with a welcoming smile.

"Hi," he said, "You're probably getting ready to close. I own the pawn shop down the way here and I have a quick question. I'm about to tie up loose ends, too, but I wonder if you can help me with leather cleaning."

"Yes sir. It's nice to meet a neighbor," she replied. Her expressive eyes were dark and rimmed with long, lush lashes.

"So, this guy turned in a leather jacket a few days ago, and I can get good money for it, but it needs to be cleaned. Smells a little cigarette-y. What's that kind of cleaning job going to run me? If it's more than I can get for it, it won't be worthwhile."

"I understand, sir —"

"Call me Sal."

"I understand, Sal," she said, "But I would have to see the piece before I could say, and even then, my boss is the one to talk to about leather cleaning. We do have some spot leather cleaner you can buy for $5.95." She pointed to a shelf of cleaning products adjacent to the counter.

"Okay, thanks. Hey, you haven't worked here long, have you? I don't think I've seen you before."

"No, I'm new. I'm a student at the university working on my masters, and just picked this up to make ends meet until I graduate."

"Really. What are you taking in school?"

"I'm in theater over there, with emphasis on musical theater. I've got the lead in the winter production of 'Show Boat.' Maybe you'll come and see me."

"Maybe I will. I can see you in the part because you're kind of, you know, swarthy, so I guess you're right to play the mixed-race lady, right?"

"Exactly right. You know the show. I'm not mixed race, though, I'm Italian —"

"Hey, me, too! Salvadore Romano." He extended his hand to shake hers.

"Victoria Pappas," she grinned, grasping his hand, "Call me Tori."

"I certainly will. Can I buy you a cup of coffee to ring in the holiday? I'd like to know more about your theater work."

Chapter 51

Barb and Lloyd had a quiet Thanksgiving feast. She had brought home a large turkey breast and had roasted it with curry and a packaged stuffing mix. She had made cheesy garlic mashed potatoes and cream of mushroom green bean casserole.

Lloyd told her it was delicious. It certainly was, but as was the case with most holiday meals, both diners thought of their respective spouses who should have been at the table with them.

"Your mother used to make this green bean casserole," Lloyd noted.

"It's a popular holiday recipe. Almost ubiquitous."

"What will be your first task in your new office?"

"Interesting segue," Barb remarked. "I guess I need to get lesson plans together. I suppose I'll have access to the lesson plans of the previous professor, right?"

"There's no previous professor. It's a new position. You knew that, right? I'll help you, though."

"Oh, that's right. I'm sorry Dad. My mind is just not on this yet."

"So, I've noticed. What is your mind on, then?"

She looked at her father for several seconds, weighing the risks and benefits of coming clean with him about her concerns. At last she gave herself permission. In for a penny . . .

"I'm feeling guilty about taking this job, Dad, honestly. When I interviewed, I felt great about it, but then something happened that I never told you about, and I am starting to worry that the Lord is leading me away from the opportunity. I am committed to following His direction, and, well, something happened."

Her father's curiosity and need of an explanation was on his face.

"After the interview, I went and treated myself at the shopping center near the college. I sat in a restaurant, and a couple was seated next to me. I heard them talking."

Barb went on to describe the conversation she had overheard between the couple whose desperation and fear of not getting the job Barb had interviewed for was perspicaciously articulated.

As she relayed the conversation, Lloyd Fuller's face changed from one of curiosity to one of certainty and sadness.

"They said your name, Dad. They were talking about you. So, I know it was the job I've been offered. While I want the job, I don't need it the way those people do. I'm afraid I'll feel awful if I go through with it," she concluded.

Chapter 52

Seated around the dinner table, Cole held court. He sat at the short end, led the Thanksgiving prayer over the food, and reveled in the company.

"Oh, by the way," he told Tim, "tomorrow we start this weekend job at the convention center, and the contact there gave me a handful of free passes. You and Theresa are invited." Cole pulled a couple of passes out of his shirt pocket and handed them to Tim.

"What's the convention for?" Tim wanted to know.

"I think it's a home show. You can buy anything from a burglar alarm for your house to an in-ground pool to a fireplace to tax preparation help."

Tim demured. "We're not in the market for any of those things."

"Well, maybe not. But we'll be performing on stage and there'll be things to see and eat and drink. I just thought you might like a change of atmosphere. Some of the finer restaurants will be handing out samples of their cuisine."

Tim glanced at his wife expecting a dour expression of dismissal. To his surprise, her eyes were bright with anticipation.

"We'll be there. Thanks," Tim told his friend.

"And speaking of thanks," Shara interrupted. "While I'm pulling out the dinner rolls, let's go around the table and tell what we're thankful for on this day." She stepped toward the kitchen, but led the discourse. "I'm thankful for a wonderful husband who has made my amateur foray into the music industry a joy and privilege. Cole?"

"I'm thankful for the people who make my life rich. Not just Shara, but Quincy, Forbes, and now Theresa and Tim as well. And my mom, of course," he smiled at Suzanne. "Mom?"

Suzanne Renshaw returned her son's smile and effused, "Why I am so thankful this Thanksgiving Day for my cat, Sophia, who gives me such a smile every day. How about you, dear," she turned to Theresa.

Theresa squirmed in her seat briefly, considering her thoughts. After a moment of staring at her empty dinner plate, "I guess I'm thankful that when the sheriff put me out of my home a few weeks ago and scattered my lifetime's worth of belongings all over the ground and offered a field day of scavenging to the neighborhood teenagers, I wasn't there to see it or cry over it. That's all I've got right now."

Cole glanced around the table, noting everybody's discomfort. "You sure have had a time of it lately," he said. "I can't help believe, though, that you may have turned a corner. You've got a new city with new opportunities and the start of a new life.

"By the way, I was talking to someone recently who told me that the college where Tim interviewed has a pretty good law school and that many of the graduates just stay here and hang a shingle. Finding a job in your field may be easier here than in Columbus."

"Not so far," she murmured, embarrassed by her outburst.

"What about you, Tim?" Shara put in as she set a bowl of dinner rolls on the table. "What are you thankful for this holiday?"

"Oh, quite a lot," he said too cheerfully. "I'm thankful to have a home and a piece of income thanks to my bud, Cole here. I'm still alive and kicking, though I admit to also feeling a little kicked, like Treese does. But the glass is half full — more than half full. Shall I start passing around dishes?"

Shara, before sitting down, topped off her wine glass and Theresa's.

Theresa took a big helping of every delicacy that passed by her. The food was great, she admitted, and her herb stuffing was a highlight. She could take some satisfaction in that.

She regretted venting her outrage in front of strangers and the ugly way it must have made her look, especially to Cole's mother, whom she felt was just a doll. She had to reverse the negative image she had portrayed.

Tell me, Mrs. Renshaw — "

"Call me Suzanne."

"Okay, Suzanne, why don't you want to take Shara up on her offer to get you in-home care that the government would pay for? It sounds like a great idea."

Shara looked up from her meal with surprise and gratitude at Theresa.

"Oh, dear, I just don't think it's necessary. My son can take me to places I need to go." Suzanne looked at with pride.

Shara's fork banged loudly against her plate as she dropped it and scooted her chair to stand. "Mom," she spat between clenched teeth, "Why can you not understand that him helping you and taking you places every week is a huge burden, not just to him, but to me also? Why can't you understand it when it has been explained to you over and over?"

Suzanne, looking horrified, blurted, "I didn't mean to upset you — "

"Yes, you did. You absolutely did, and you do it routinely. I have said once for every hair on my head that I need Cole to work. Every day. I need him to earn money or else book himself to earn money.

"My savings are gone, my credit cards are maxed out, and I must have him make an income to help with expenses. And for the love of God — " her voice climbed in pitch and volume, "Cole has lost nine days of work so far this month taking you to doctors and grocery stores and restaurants. But when you're asked what your thankful for, it's your *damned cat!*"

With that, Shara stalked out of the room and down the hall, slamming the bedroom door behind her. Cole turned to the Sheltons. "I'm sorry, guys. I didn't want you to endure this. I don't think I knew she was under so much pressure."

"How much wine has she had?" Suzanne asked.

Chapter 53

By 7:30, the Sheltons were on their way home. Shara had reappeared, behaving as though nothing was amiss, but failed to make eye contact with Suzanne for the rest of the night.

Theresa couldn't help but enjoy the drama — drama that didn't involve herself.

"That's quite a lot of dysfunction in that family, don't you think?" she giggled to Tim.

"Yeah, well, every family has it. I've got it with Andy and Leah just as much as Shara has it with Suzanne."

"I don't know what her problem is. I thought Suzanne was wonderful. And she's quite knowledgeable about the law for someone who was mostly a housewife married to a lawyer. She's smart, funny, and well-educated. I don't see why Shara is so impatient."

"Really? You don't? I can see Shara's point. A huge burden could come off her if Suzanne would fill out a form, and she won't do it. That would upset me, too."

Theresa sat quietly in the van. Her lap was full of leftovers wrapped up in plastic, airtight containers, but she wasn't mentally thanking Shara for the two or three meals the gift would provide. Her thoughts were on the elderly woman.

"You know, if Shara won't or can't take care of Suzanne, maybe I should. I enjoyed the lady so much tonight that it wouldn't hurt to spend more time with her. From what she told me, I think she lives near us."

"Okay, well, I know you're bored at the library every day. Why don't you ask Shara when we see her tomorrow?"

Chapter 54

Friday morning, Lloyd and Barb went over to the college to look around. Barb asked her father good questions about the culture of the staff and student body, the location of the gym, the availability of music rooms, and the rigidity of Dr. Glenn's ideas on what to teach.

Lloyd had asked around in the facilities department to gather intelligence on which closed office would ultimately be Barb's, and got access to the room.

It didn't enthrall Barb. It was smaller than her office at the church in Rolla. There was no window in the room, and the drab beige paint job was reinforcement to her suspicion that she may not have made the right decision.

But she didn't reveal that to her father who gushed and effused about his little girl's pending academic career.

The room was musty and unventilated. The air-handling system was turned off, and even the light was dim. One of the florescent lights was out, and the other one buzzed in complaint, about to follow suit. All of these perceptions fueled Barb's distaste even while she knew they were superficial.

The truth is, she admitted to herself, her guilt was getting to her. She couldn't shake it. Something in her was rebelling against her taking this job. Something she couldn't name presented a dark abyss in front of her and the feeling grew worse by the moment. Yet, the disapproval of her father, if she turned down the job, also mounted pressure.

The rock, the hard place.

"Dad," she said, relenting, "If I don't take this job; if I kept looking, would Dr. Glenn call back that other guy he liked and hire him on the spot?"

"You'd have to ask Frank that question," Lloyd replied with a twinge of impatience. "But, why would you?"

"We had that discussion," she replied absently, her mind on the conversation she had overheard.

At that point, the office door opened, and a security guard stepped in. A tall, middle-aged man with thin grey hair, he was as startled as the others.

"May I ask what you're doing in here?" he asked. "This area should be locked." He fingered his side arm tentatively.

"We're sorry, officer," Barb said, stepping forward. "I'm a new hire for the music department and I was just checking out my new digs." She let her curves work the magic they usually worked.

"I need to see your employee ID," he stated. Clearly the officer was looking her up and down, figuring her out, but the enchantment she often invoked in awkward moments seemed to have no effect on the guard.

"I'm so new, honestly, that I don't have credentials yet. I'm sorry." Her smile was large and winning.

But not winning enough. "You'll need to follow me. I will take you to your car."

Then Lloyd spoke up. "I have my ID, officer. Here it is." He pulled out his wallet and offered the card. "I'm just showing this lady around, helping her get acquainted."

The guard looked at the card with suspicion and unease. Then gave it back. "Okay, Dr. Fuller, let's be on our way real soon, all right? Happy holiday." He gave Barbara one last look before he turned and went out.

"Well, that was as warm as any given crocodile," she commented.

"That's not all," Lloyd complained. "I hope it doesn't get back to anyone that you and I were here together on the down-low."

"Oh, for heaven's sake. You've got to get over this paranoia. What's Frank going to do? Bludgeon you with a plush velour teddy bear?"

"Don't take a tone, Barbie," her father scolded. "You've been talking non-stop about declining the offer of the job. There's no reason he couldn't change his mind about you if it came out that we're related. In-department nepotism is strictly against the rules, and our department helped make this rule."

"Non-stop? I have not."

"Don't reflect badly on me," he demanded. "It's all I'm asking.

Chapter 55

Friday morning, Shara woke up early. She looked ahead at the frenzied weekend she faced at the convention center. She called Quincy and Forbes to remind them to be early to help set up, knowing full well that they would trickle in at the last minute.

She advised them of which color-coordinated outfits to wear — the red three-piece suits for Christmastime — and she mentioned to Quincy in passing that for this big job, it would be beneficial if everyone could concentrate. He got her meaning. She knew he did.

Shara packed the car. It was light duty, due to the sound system at the venue, and she offered a prayer of thanks. Undoubtedly, Sunday night when the four were dead tired, it would be a blessing to have so little to pack back in the van. As was always the case, she hoped that this opportunity would lead to another, better one. It hardly ever happened, but hope springs eternal.

With a little time to kill, Shara's thoughts turned to the spat with Suzanne. She forced herself to think good thoughts and not let her anger boil over, but it was tough to do. She was embarrassed that Tim and Theresa had witnessed her meltdown, but it was Suzanne's behavior that was the most obnoxious. Surely Theresa would see that. Plus, Theresa had been less than positive, herself.

Theresa and Suzanne had hit it off, Shara noted. The former did not raise a peep when Suzanne made that ridiculous offer of gratitude for her cat. If she had someone like Theresa available to work for Suzanne . . .

The thought struck her. If she could line up Theresa to work for the government to care for her mother-in-law, well, she could kill all kinds of birds with one stone.

Shara jumped on the computer.

Within an hour, she had filled out the online application that Suzanne had failed to complete on paper. Now all she needed to do was talk Theresa into it. The website allowed applicants to nominate caregivers that the elderly person would prefer. She only needed Theresa to fill out the job app. Easy!

Having accomplished that, Shara felt good about the coming show. It would be exhausting, and she would have an early morning on Monday, but that was Monday's problem. She hoped she'd have some time during the show to tour the various vendors and do a little window-shopping of her own. Her dream of a gazebo for the back yard might just be in view. She said as much to Cole as he turned off the shower.

"What?" he replied quizzically. "Yesterday you were critical about the pressures on you to pay the bills and you blamed my mother for all of it. Now you want to buy a gazebo for God knows how many thousands of dollars? You are crackin' up!"

She could have taken offense, but his easy-going smile disarmed her. He was standing in the bathtub, dripping shower water, as he looked at her with affection and tenderness. Suddenly, he began to sing.

"You are so beautiful to me/You are so beautiful to me. . ."

As he rendered the Joe Cocker classic, Shara's heart warmed, glowed and rejoiced. Mother-in-law notwithstanding, she wouldn't ever want any other life but this one, with this singular man.

Chapter 56

Quincy picked up Forbes early to go to the convention center. The two men hung their performance suits in the back of Quincy's car and got inside.

"Hey, we're early," Quincy remarked as he started the engine. "I think I'll stop and get a little herb to take the edge off. This is going to be a long job."

"Yeah, man, it is," Forbes agreed, thinking of the first of the 12-hour days ahead. The paycheck at the end of it would be nice, though.

"You want a little herb, too?" Quincy asked.

"Hmm, what? No, man, I want to be straight so I can help Cole with all that equipment. I'd hate to be stoned and drop something, you know."

"Oh, man, didn't you hear him the other day? There's already a sound system at the center that we're going to tap into. There's nearly no set up to do. In a lot of ways this job will be easy."

"But it will be long," Forbes pointed out.

"That's why I wanna mellow out." Quincy pulled a joint out of his pocket and lit it with the car's cigarette lighter.

"All right, then." Forbes took the joint from Quincy and drew a long toke.

Chapter 57

Cole and Shara arrived at the convention center two hours before their show was to start. Though set-up would be minimal, Cole still wanted plenty of time to settle in and ask good questions, if they arose. They pulled around to the rear entrance and showed the security guard the contract with Simon Seloff's signature on it. The guard then propped the door open.

As they brought the dolly into the center, Simon promptly showed up. He shook hands with Cole as Shara stepped forward and introduced herself.

After the amenities, Cole asked Simon for Bob Norton, the sound engineer.

"Oh, yeah, you sure need Bob, don't you? I haven't seen him yet today. Let me ask around and see if any staff know where he is." Simon trotted away as Cole and Shara began setting equipment next to the sound booth at the back and to the side of the stage.

As the minutes passed, Cole became more and more thankful that he and Shara had left the house early. When 15 minutes was on the verge of becoming 20, Simon reappeared. He approached with palms up in an apologetic stance. "I swear, Cole, Bob has never been late to a show in 30 years. I'm going to go to my office and get his home number and call him. Be right back."

"No need," Cole said. "You gave me his number and I have it right here on my phone." He called the number. It rang several times before Bob's voicemail picked up. The man's gravelly, elderly voice rendered his voicemail greeting. Cole left a message explaining his identity. "Please call me back right away," he urged.

"Cole, I don't have a good feeling," Shara confided.

Simon, overhearing, agreed. "I don't either, Mrs. Renshaw. I'm going to send somebody over there. Meanwhile, my best guess is for you to set up here next to the sound office and leave it to Bob to interface your equipment with ours whenever he gets here.

"Hey! Rodney!" Simon hollered at a uniformed workman. "Do you know where Bob Norton lives?"

Cole and Shara set up their digital music generators with high hopes of Bob Norton's imminent appearance.

Cole noted that the doors were opened and people were filtering into the convention center. Vendor booths lined the huge room as well as makeshift stations throughout the center of the immense floor. A walking tour to see every vendor would take a person two hours, Cole estimated. As he scanned the crowd from his position on the stage, he saw two familiar faces. Tim and Theresa were strolling along one of the walkways created between vendor booths.

Shara also saw the couple and descended the stage stairs to greet them. Her greeting and hug startled Theresa. She squeezed Tim's elbow. "I'm so glad you came. I'd like to talk to you about something." She looked at Theresa.

"Funny, I want to talk to you about something, too."

"Where's Cole?" Tim asked Shara.

"He's at the top of the stage stairs. We're trying to set up, but management is having a hard time finding the sound engineer who should have been here by now."

Tim knit his brow quizzically as he climbed the stairs and greeted his friend.

"Okay, you go first."

"I want to help take care of Suzanne. I just really hit it off with her, and I wonder if I could find a way to be her in-home helper. I don't have much going on, and it seems like a good fit."

Shara cracked up laughing. "Great minds really do think alike. That's exactly what I was going to suggest to you. It would help me out in a lot of ways, and would help me bypass her objections if it was someone she knew already.

"I need you to go online and apply to the government. I'll give you the web address. I'll go back in to Suzanne's application which I completed this morning, and specify that you are the applicant she would prefer.

"The pay is not great, Theresa. It's minimum wage. But it's better than nothing."

"Understood." Theresa understood all too well. She had resisted taking low-paying jobs since her lay-off out of pride and discomfort with the venues involved: fast food, car washes, etc. But the last month had changed her. The sheriff's actions at her home had taken the last pinch of pride out of her.

This was a fairly perfect way to re-enter the workforce: helping a woman she really likes, ignominious as the job would be.

Meanwhile, Cole was explaining to Tim that the sound engineer was a no-show and a creepy, nagging fear was building inside the singer. He didn't know how he could execute this contract without Bob Norton.

As he was explaining, Quincy and Forbes arrived, holding their red holiday suits. Cole noted the time — only an hour later than Shara had asked them to arrive. This was unexpectedly cooperative of the two men.

As the four men discussed logistics: where to change clothes, where to put their street clothes, and so on, Simon Seloff turned up. His demeanor was changed. His face was gray with shock, and his hands were shaking.

Cole, noticing the change in the man, went to him. No question needed to be asked.

Simon took a deep breath. "Rodney went to Bob's. He couldn't raise anybody, though his truck was in his driveway. Rodney broke a window.

"When the paramedics got there, they said Bob had probably been dead since Thanksgiving morning. I don't know what to say."

Cole's stomach flip-flopped with panic. "Simon, I'm very sorry for your loss. I don't know how I can do this job, though. Your sound-board is way beyond my wife's capabilities. Can you get one of your other sound guys here?"

"I don't see how," Simon muttered, eyes on his shoes. "Troy Cutter is in Honolulu with his family, and John Strauss is at a conference with his church or something in Minnesota.

"I'm screwed. I've got to have sound this weekend. By the time I got a freelancer in here, the day would be shot. I don't know what to do." Simon's voice rose an octave as he spoke. His grief over the loss of his friend emerged, but he tightened his grip on his feelings.

Tim, Quincy, and Forbes watched this dialogue. The two singers feared the collapse of this good-paying gig. It was their habit to look to Cole to fix anything that went wrong, but neither man could imagine how he could fix this.

Tim stepped forward. "Excuse me, Mr. — "

"Seloff," Simon said distractedly. "Call me Simon."

"Okay, Simon," Tim continued. "What is your sound system? I mean, what kind is it?"

"It's a Bose Audio Pro. Why?"

"Well, um, I haven't operated one of those since I was in college, but I might be the best you've got."

The look on the faces of the four men, the look of astonishment and relief, was a treat to Tim.

"If you could operate it," Simon said with tentative appreciation, "That would be a godsend. Come with me. I'll show you."

Tim followed Simon to the sound booth adjacent to the stage. He opened the door and the two men stepped in with Cole and the others on their heels.

"Oh, this baby is an old panel. I used to use one just like it in Columbia."

"What did you do with it in Columbia?" Simon asked.

"Oh, I volunteered to run sound for the theater department at my college when I was a junior and senior. They put on musical stage shows, and I pitched in."

Tim hoped he didn't sound too proud or arrogant. But he could easily picture himself as the hero in this unfolding drama, and the sense of it was nearly intoxicating. He flashed a smile at the three singers that he hoped looked modest but confident.

"Okay, then," Simon concluded. "I'll leave you to it. And I'll have a check cut for you Sunday night."

Tim poked around the equipment for a few minutes, re-familiarizing himself. He took note of all the channels and which of them should house the digital music feed, which the microphones, and so forth.

With Cole's help, he connected everything and instructed the singers to test their mics. Shara set up her equipment, now linked to Tim's, and tested the sound. She would have preferred to test sound earlier when the convention center was less crowded, but she didn't complain. Her stomach was in knots.

A bullet was dodged, Cole told his singing partners.

When Simon came by to ask how things were going, Cole gave him a thumbs-up. "We're ready whenever you are," he told the manager.

And so, they were.

Chapter 58

By the time the gig was over, Theresa was exhausted. Proud of her man for stepping up in this unexpected disaster, she was nevertheless not thrilled. She had expected to come to the convention center, greet their friends, walk around for an hour and go home.

Who'd a thunk she'd end up being there for 12 hours with not a thing in the world to do?

She walked around the various booths, fantasized about the home and garden treats she might love to buy if she had a home or garden, ate greasy food from vendors attached to restaurants she could no longer afford, and did her best to kill time, waiting for Tim.

The thought that there would be two more days of this was daunting. She would certainly stay home during the Saturday and Sunday legs of the ordeal. It was serendipity, she realized, that Mr. Seloff would be cutting Tim a check. Her husband was a multi-talented man, she mused, and the fact that he had a leg up on the very equipment he needed to run this weekend was not lost on her. He was her hero.

Tim spent the day in deep concentration. He hadn't handled a Bose Audio Pro for a long lot of years, so the need was acute to both jog his memory and use logic.

After the first set, Quincy Garland popped in the booth to complain. "Hey, man, my mic is dry. I need more bass and reverb."

"No, it isn't. No, you don't," Tim stated without looking up from his controls. "Your mic is fine. It's your floor monitor that's dry, and I do that on purpose. Forces your tone."

Quincy opened his mouth to object, but out of the corner of his eye, he saw Shara watching him with one of her don't-you-dare expressions. He backed out of the booth and walked straight up to her.

"Hey, look," he began, "I can hear my mic is too dry. That guy won't amp my reverb. I can't stand this. Do something. Talk to him," he demanded.

"Quincy, no," she replied with strained patience. "First of all, your mic is exactly right. Your reverb is exactly right. Tim, apparently, subscribes to that school that says you dry the floor monitor. From where I sit, you sound fantastic. The guy knows what he's doing.

"Plus," she continued, "We'd be hung out to dry without him, so I suggest you be quiet and thank the good Lord he happened to come today. Gift horse. Mouth. Nuff said."

Cole had been doing exactly that. His silent prayers of thanks for Tim were inexpressible. He knew himself, and he knew Forbes and Quincy. He was completely certain that if Bob the sound guy had died and Tim hadn't been there, he would be blamed that the job couldn't be done, even though his culpability was zero.

Worse than that, Shara would be blamed because she had never seen this soundboard, and he'd be defending her to his partners for the rest of forever.

Oh, yeah, he told himself. It was a happy day when he met the Sheltons on a Terre Haute street corner.

At a quarter to midnight, Simon appeared and instructed Shara to close the show. Shara, exhausted, was happy to comply. She turned on her mic.

"Ladies and gentleman," she announced to the thinning crowd, "it's time for us to say good night. Let me introduce to you again Forbes Wilson, Quincy Garland, and Cole Renshaw. I'm Shara Renshaw, and we're the Cole Renshaw Trio." As she said each man's name, that man stepped forward and bowed slightly, then stepped back. With that, she cued the digital track for "Goodnight Sweetheart," and turned off her mic.

Chapter 59

The Saturday and Sunday shows went just as well as Shara could have expected, and she let herself indulge in a little fantasy about having someone like Tim with her all the time to make her job much easier. Balancing song selections, providing each singer an equal amount of solos, announcing each soloist, choosing not too many fast or too many slow songs in a row, communicating with the singers — all that was plenty to do. She didn't mind that Tim was handling the wave mechanics for her.

It was Sunday night at 11:15 when Simon told her to end the show. She was thrilled, but especially so when he pulled an envelope out of his jacket pocket and handed it to her. She noticed that he then stepped into the sound booth and offered a similar envelope to Tim. Good, she told herself. I hope the paycheck will ease their burden.

When Tim opened his pay envelope, his mouth came open as he stared. His worries about next month's rent evaporated, and possibly the month after that. He and Theresa wouldn't be cold, the lights would stay on, and he thought he might just buy her a little television for the apartment.

Among the thoughts flitting in and out, Tim realized that Cole's forecast of how business would drop off right after Christmas would not be the worry that it had been. The uncertainty of when another paycheck, or another *regular* paycheck would come in was still a source of worry, but not, at the moment, a source of panic.

Tim understood that Theresa was bored and had stayed at the apartment reading until he got home. He was excited to tell her that this job had turned into a huge, unexpected windfall.

In a perfect world, Tim would have been called in on such a gig, stated his desired pay, and then said yes or no to the job, depending on the variables. But this far-from-perfect world had changed him. If he had earned twenty bucks over the last three days, he would have been happy. His teetering self-esteem would have diminished all thoughts of entitlement.

This was quite a lot more than twenty bucks.

He helped Cole and Shara pack up their van. He didn't even care that Quincy was sitting on the side of the booth talking on the phone. Who in blazes is he talking to at a quarter to midnight? Tim asked himself. No one, came the answer in his head. Quincy's just lazy, and is probably faking the phone call. Tim adopted Cole's tolerance and assent.

Forbes had vanished entirely.

Just for fun, he approached Quincy and said, "Hey, Quincy, whenever you get off the phone, can I use it? I need to call my wife and have her come get me."

Quincy nodded, pretending to be distracted, as Tim picked up a case full of cords and loaded them onto the flatbed.

Across town, Theresa was unprepared to answer the phone. Earlier in the day, she had been sitting in her apartment with a library book until she verged on stir-crazy. The library was closed, so she couldn't play on the Internet, so she took herself window-shopping at the mall.

At 8 o'clock, the mall was closing up — Sunday hours — and she walked to her van. The Dodge Caravan was parked on the periphery of the parking lot, angled up. Traffic was dense leaving the mall since it was the first Sunday of the Christmas shopping season. She was humming a Christmas song in her head. The droning, repetitious "It's a Holly Jolly Christmas," she feared, would become an earworm and she'd be hearing it in her mind for days to come.

She climbed into the van and fastened her seatbelt. Four more hours until Tim would probably call her to come get him. Tick, tick, tick.

She started to back out of the space when a car full of shoppers blocked her way. It was a sedan full of children, and as nearly as she could see, they were misbehaving and the adult behind the wheel was leaning back into the back seat to issue commands.

This took a long time.

Theresa began to lose patience and looked around for an alternative. She could whip the wheel around and make a very tight turn out of the space, avoiding the sedan, but it meant backing directly onto the street with a blind corner. Better not. Oh, but wait. She could see the street clearly from the opposite way, and if she pulled out onto the street pointed in the wrong direction of home, she'd be okay. She'd just have to turn around.

Chapter 60

Donna Umberger was livid when she left her apartment. Her boyfriend, Truman, had come home stoned and had announced to her that he was going over to his sister's to party for the rest of the night. Donna and Lucy did not get along at all, so Donna wasn't invited to go with.

A fight had broken out between the couple. Donna had bellowed that Truman obviously didn't need any more party, and Truman had bellowed that she was wrong because her stupid, selfish temper was killing his buzz anyway.

Donna responded by taking the last cold beer out of the fridge and guzzling it in front of Truman.

The 22-year-old Donna had lived with the 32-year-old window washer for three years and their fights were frequent and loud. Neighbors had called 911 seven different times, and on one occasion, the police had found Donna bleeding from her nose as her battered eye was swelling shut. The police had dragged Truman off over night, but she declined to press charges the next day. The jail released him, and life continued as usual.

Donna, it seemed, was at high risk for domestic abuse. She had dropped out of high school, had no marketable skills, and relied on Truman to pay the rent in the studio apartment they shared. Sure, she reasoned, he could be scary when he's drunk or stoned, but what else could she do? She hadn't told him yet, but she'd missed her last two periods. Her job at a Mickey D only gave her 18 hours a week, and until she got something better, enduring his temper tantrums was better than being homeless.

Plus, Donna realized, she was small. Not even 110 pounds, she was perfect prey for an abuser, and on more than one occasion, Truman had given her what-for. Her appearance didn't help. Her thin, dishwater blonde hair hung unkempt around her shoulders, and her gaunt, long face and small features could only be described as "mousey." She had been bullied by one guy or other most of her life and had resigned herself to never having experienced anything that could raise the bar.

This day, the beer Donna was chugging was not her first, and had escalated the argument.

The Strattons next door were out buying an artificial Christmas tree and weren't there to call the police.

Accusations were made against Donna because she had once described her co-worker, Dale, as "cute." Accusations against Truman took the form of complaints that he seldom came home when expected anymore and she had prepared and then thrown away more than one hot meal.

She had been told at that point that what Truman did with his time was not her business.

"It isn't? Aren't we a couple?" At that moment, Donna realized that they weren't. The unexplained absences and wasted Hamburger

Helpers all fell into place. Thurman had met somebody. He wasn't going to see his sister; he was going out to tomcat. His silent gaze at the floor confirmed her epiphany.

Donna screamed, "I guess we're not!" She picked her coat up from a pile on the floor, grabbed the car keys and slammed the door behind her.

She stopped at a filling station on her way into town and picked up a cold six-pack of beer that she knew Truman didn't like. She popped one in the car as she drove away. The fact she was buzzed was not lost on her and she wished vaguely that she could drink as well as some of her friends who had quite a few pounds on her.

Her anger fueled her misjudgment as much as the beer, and as she came around a blind corner adjacent to the mall, she crossed over the center line at just the wrong moment for a Dodge Caravan to back out of the lot. Donna swerved, over-corrected, and swerved back into the oncoming lane. She tee-boned the Caravan.

Theresa saw the oncoming car way too late. There was no chance to process the information, let alone respond. Brakes screeching in her ears, she saw the rusty red sports car come across into her lane. She barely had time to open her mouth in surprise before it plowed into her. Theresa felt the impact as the car smashed her side panel. It should have knocked her into the passenger seat, but her seatbelt held her in place. A snapping noise, and a sharp pain indicated the fracture of her left femur. A ragged slice of the car door stabbed her mid-section. The airbag deployed in her face, and the windshield and side window shattered, spraying her face with glass. A large piece of the windshield sliced into her scalp, and blood gushed. That's the last thing she would later remember.

The woman driving the car full of disruptive kids saw the whole thing. She reached for her phone and called the police. An ambulance was dispatched, and when it arrived, Theresa Shelton was loaded into it. Her injuries were numerous, the loss of blood, perilous.

Donna stepped out of her car and walked away from it. Her airbag had deployed and saved her from serious injury. Her glasses were broken and had cut her eyelid, and she may have sprained her wrist, but she waved off the paramedics, fearful of medical attention that would include a blood alcohol test.

She didn't fool Officer Pasternak, however, who handcuffed her on the spot after spying her open container, now emptying itself onto her shabby upholstery.

Chapter 61

Tiffany Pasternak, a ten-year veteran of Terre Haute's police department, took Mrs. Shelton's purse out of her mangled minivan and set it in the ambulance moments before the paramedics loaded Mrs. Shelton's gurney. She called two tow trucks and took a statement from the young mother with the rowdy passengers.

Her partner, Phil Mueller, suggested she ride with the victim to the hospital, so Pasternak climbed into the ambulance and sat down on the other gurney.

The woman, Shelton, was out cold, and soaking in her own blood. The gore was such that Pasternak, whose history with the department was so jaded she thought nothing could get her sick, reconsidered. A paramedic had bound the victim's wounds, sterilized her scalp wound, wiping off blood, so Pasternak could see her face. Mid 40's, white, and petite, she noted. She picked up the purse on the floor, fished out the cell phone and called the last number dialed.

It went to voicemail. She spoke, "Hello. This is Officer Pasternak from the Terre Haute police department. I have a woman here identified as Theresa Shelton. She's been in a traffic accident, and her ambulance is on the way to Terre Haute Regional Hospital on South Seventh St."

With nothing else useful to say that wouldn't violate patient privacy, she turned off the phone and returned it to Theresa's purse.

At the convention center, Tim thought it very odd that Theresa wasn't answering her phone.

Quincy had relinquished his for Tim's use, thus forcing him to help pack the car. And if that wasn't annoying enough, Tim kept calling and calling with no answer. Did Tim not realize Quincy paid by the minute? Quincy scarcely concealed his disgruntlement.

When the car was packed and ready at a quarter after midnight, Shara, exhausted, offered to drive Tim back to his apartment.

"I'll let you have my phone overnight so you can figure out what's going on. Maybe Theresa will call my number because she can't call you."

"Good thinking," Tim murmured gratefully as he climbed into the back seat.

Shara got in beside Cole and took her phone from her pocket to hand it over. "Oh, look, Tim! She called already and I missed the call. Hang on."

Shara dialed into her voicemail and caught the four-hour-old message from Officer Pasternak. She became very still, listening.

"Cole, hold on. Don't drive. Tim, Theresa's at the hospital. She's been in an accident."

"Which hospital?" Cole demanded."

"Regional, on South Seventh."

As Cole pulled out into traffic, Tim, in the back seat, felt cold.

Chapter 62

The minivan packed with sound equipment had not pulled to a complete stop in front of Regional's emergency room when Tim opened the door and hopped out. He rushed into the waiting room full of patients and approached the desk.

"I'm Tim Shelton. I got a message that you have my wife, Theresa here. Something about a traffic accident."

Tiffany was at a nearby desk filling out paperwork. She overheard the frantic man, so she stood and approached. She introduced herself and gave Tim a brief outline of what had happened at the mall. As she did, Cole and Shara walked up behind their friend.

"I want to see her."

"She's in post-op right now," Tiffany explained. "She was in surgery for a long time."

Tim turned back to the desk with a brief, grateful nod to Tiffany "When can I get in to see my wife, please?"

The young man at the computer wearing sea foam green scrubs and a tired expression told Tim, "I'm going to call a doctor to come out and talk to you. Why don't you have a seat?"

Tim's mind raced with panic and assorted objections to the suggestion. He'd been sitting for twelve hours. He was hungry, tired, and freaking out. He wanted answers, not another chair.

Shara, meanwhile, was filled with dread, not just because of Theresa, but also because of her job. She envisioned that, by the time this was over and she got home, she'd be just in time to get dressed and go to work. And if she didn't, her boss would be treated to another call-in because of her music career. Already on thin ice, Shara would have to go to work.

As if reading her thoughts, Cole told his wife, "Come on, I'm going to take you home. Then I'll come back and wait with Tim."

"Go on," Tim agreed. "In fact, you both go on home. If you're as tired as I am, you want to. I've got Shara's phone. I'll call Cole's if I need to."

Shara stepped closer to Tim and wrapped an arm around his waist. She leaned into his shoulder, and prayed, "Father in heaven, we thank you for Theresa, and we ask, in Jesus' name, that you heal her and restore her to us swiftly. Amen."

As she stepped away, she squeezed Tim's hand. Cole nodded at his friend with hopefulness and concern as he followed his wife out of the building.

Tim stared after them, unsure what to do or to say. He felt like he was being strangled by his mounting fear. He was hearing his wife's words in his head, complaining about Shara's ludicrous faith and its farcical ineptitude in the face of the reality Theresa was living. Perhaps her chronic blasphemy was coming home to roost and she was being punished. All at once, his loneliness closed around him like a dark, narrow canyon. He shuddered, and blinked back tears.

Chapter 63

The Sunday morning following Thanksgiving was a joyful one for Barbara Baxter. She tried on a new church and it appeared that it might fit her just fine. Faithful to the Word of God and her own faith, Grace Community Church distinguished itself with a fine choir and a music director whose understanding of the place music has in worship mirrored her own. She felt comfortable as soon as the opening hymn rang out.

She vowed to herself to show up for choir practice on Wednesday night, and, what do you know? The church actually has a grief management support group that meets in the fellowship hall on Tuesdays. Maybe she'd go, and if it suited her, maybe she'd bring Dad.

The thought of Dad and his grief inevitably returned her to her own. She thought of Bill, and a deluge of memory fragments, snippets of things he had said and done, flitted through her head. Bill, sweaty and smiling, kicking her tail on the tennis court. Bill, greasy and filthy, fixing her car. Bill, grinning, handing her the flowers he'd brought home for her as she wrapped her hands around the stems and sniffed. Bill, mowing the grass, pausing to toss a stray basketball back across the street to the yard where it had originated. Bill, holding her as she wept at her mother's funeral. The memories were random and disconnected, depicting both significant and mundane events with only Bill himself as their common thread. The ache in her gut began again and she fought the memories off.

This was a new life, she scolded herself, and it's time to look forward. There was a limitless universe out there of potential new friends and maybe even a new man to love. Why, then, did she feel so dragged back? There was some inexplicable coefficient of inertia in her heart. Something was whispering at her that she didn't deserve happiness, a new life, a new church, or any of it.

Ridiculous, she reasoned. After Bill's death, she was uniquely deserving of something good happening.

Really? The voice in her head whispered. Is that what grace means?

No, she admitted. Grace means we receive from God the good we don't deserve.

Same question. What have I done that makes me feel so immobilized and sad? Why am I struggling to make peace with myself?

Chapter 64

Officer Pasternak was scheduled to end her tour at midnight, but was delayed at the hospital by the two-car accident involving Theresa Shelton. When she finally got to the precinct at a quarter after 1:00, turned in her paperwork and clocked out, she wasn't tired. Rather, the adrenaline was still with her from the crash scene. Her heart went out to the injured woman, and, to tell the truth, it went out just a little to the young woman who caused the accident. Umberger's life would be irreparably changed by this DUI charge, and vehicular homicide charges would follow if the Shelton woman succumbed to her injuries.

Tiffany told herself with a sardonic wisdom that when she found herself on the scene of her one-millionth traffic accident that involved alcohol, confetti and ticker tape would magically fall from the sky, a marching band would appear, and a parade would spontaneously form to play, "She's a Jolly Good Fella."

That should happen next week sometime.

It's really not that much trouble to avoid drinking and driving. If a person could see what Tiffany had seen in the last ten years, it would be even easier.

As she headed out of the precinct and got into her blue VW Jetta, she decided to demonstrate to no one in particular how easy this is to do. She stopped at an all-night grocery on the way home and bought a bottle of cinnamon whiskey and a bag of ice. She had a dvr full of prime time and a microwaveable burrito waiting for her. She'd be in bed in a couple of hours, drunk on her tail, but causing no one any harm.

Lots of cops drink, she told herself. How many of them drink alone, holed up in a messy apartment, with a fish tank full of African cichlids and one lone angelfish for company? She couldn't answer that question.

Chapter 65

"Are you going to the hospital today?" Shara asked Cole early in the morning. "Cause I want to go tonight when I get off work."

"I'm going to pick up Tim at the hospital, take him home to shower and change, and then take him right back. The doctor told him she's nowhere near waking up, so he's got time."

"What about you? Do you have time?"

"What do you mean?"

"Don't you have a doctor appointment at 10 for your mother?"

"Oh, nuts! I forgot all about that. Thanks for reminding me. I'll have to call Tim at the hospital and tell him I can't make it until later."

"I have a better idea." With that, Shara picked up the phone and dialed. Cole watched her curiously.

"Hello, this is Shara, Mrs. Renshaw's daughter-in-law. Mrs. Renshaw won't be able to keep her appointment today and will have to reschedule. She'd like the first opening you have in January or February. Valentine's Day? That sounds great. Oh, wait. That won't work. We'll be booked that day." The last sentence she muttered to herself. "The twenty-second, then, at nine in the morning. I'm writing it down. Thank you so much."

The cheery timbre to her voice as she concluded the call to Suzanne's doctor rendered Cole aghast. "What did you do that for? She can't wait three months to see that doctor, and you know she can't get up that early."

"Yes, she can, and yes, she can," Shara countered.

"Helping Tim and Theresa is more important, and now you are free to do that," she concluded.

"Shara," Cole pleaded quietly, "Is it such a crime that my mother loves me enough to want to spend time with me?"

"Cole, she doesn't even appreciate the things you do for her. She appreciates her cat! I still can't believe she said that at Thanksgiving dinner. Makes my blood boil!" Shara's voice was shrill with rage.

"I believe you have expressed that several times, but there may be a clue here you are missing."

Shara defiantly plopped her hand on her hip and demanded, "Okay, fine. What am I missing?"

"You gave her the cat, Shara. When she says she's thankful for the cat, it's her way of honoring you, of telling you she loves you."

Shara stared at him slack-jawed. The thought had simply never occurred to her and the disclosure caught her off guard. To make it worse, she was flooded with a wave of guilt. She grappled within herself to recoup her dignity for several seconds before the way out came to her. Suzanne was the queen — the absolute queen of bestowing guilt. Her passive aggression made guilt her gift to the world. Shara wasn't going to buy it.

"How do you know that's what she's saying, Cole? Did she tell you that?"

"No, of course not. But I've known her my whole life, and that's what she does. She's indirect. It's a face-saving thing with her. She doesn't want to owe anybody, so she kind of comes at it sideways."

"I see," Shara spat. "She certainly doesn't mind owing you. The time you throw away on her is to your credit, I guess, but, baby, I need you, too. You have to lay it out to her plainly."

"I'm her son, so it's different. She'll never understand."

"I need you to make her understand. I think she does it deliberately. I think she *does* understand, but her selfishness won't let her own it.

"By the way, Theresa agreed to take care of your mother, but I guess that ship has sailed."

"She wouldn't be happy with Theresa taking her to appointments anyway. Only I can. There's more to this than you realize."

"What don't I realize?"

"Nothing. Never mind."

Chapter 66

MJ Bobo sat at the Missionary Baptist church that served as her second home on Monday night following the holiday, waiting for the pianist. Rev. Shim, the recent seminary grad from Lafayette Seminary, was asked to accompany MJ Sunday for a rousing piece she intended to teach to the worshippers. "Wonderful Grace of Jesus" was a song by an early 20th century composer named Haldor Lillenas, and featured a descant for women that made every toe tap. But Rev.

Shim wasn't here, and the wait was nibbling at MJ's patience. When her phone rang, she grabbed it swiftly, certain it was the young minister. But it wasn't.

"Hello, MJ. This is Forbes Wilson."

"Oh, hi."

"Don't sound so disappointed."

"Oh, no, I didn't mean to. I'm at church waiting for the piano player to rehearse with me. I thought you might be him."

Forbes invited MJ to tell him all about the rehearsal, the material, and her plans for afterward.

"I'm going home afterward. Why?"

"Well, I wondered if you'd like to go to a piano bar with me this evening and see if we can get the pianist to let you do a number. Or, I could do a number with you. I told you I'm looking for a soprano to sing with, and I'd still like it to be you."

MJ took a breath. Where to begin. "Forbes, in the first place, I would get murdered at home if I went to a place where liquor is served. Second, I want to polish this song and my accompanist isn't here, so if this goes late, I won't have time. Third, and I can't stress this enough, I don't want to be your soprano. I'm not interested in your music. And you're just too . . ." She stopped herself from saying "too old," but her meaning wasn't lost on Forbes.

"MJ, do you want me to just leave you alone from now on? If I do, it'll be your loss. I could maybe make you famous, though, so think it through.""

"Yes, please go," she answered immediately, and hung up. Forbes held the phone to his hear for a good half minute weighing what he could have said to convince her. MJ was young, naive, and talented, but the whisper in his ear said she would, at best, be a great singer — in church. But for the level of celebrity Forbes craved, there were better sopranos. And this insane notion that liquor comprises sin would be hard to get around. What would it get him to mold a soprano into something if she refuses three quarters of the gigs? He turned the phone off.

Chapter 67

When Theresa opened her eyes in the ICU, three days had passed. It took a few seconds to form a theory about where she was and why. As she drew conclusions, she looked around the room, and there was Tim sitting in a plastic chair.

He looked like hell, she thought, and his disheveled appearance was another clue to her situation. She moved a little, and Tim sprang out of the chair and came to her.

He stank of sweat and tension, she noted. She wondered vaguely about how much time had gone by. Plenty, she concluded. He hadn't shaved or washed in days, and he'd hardly slept, it looked like.

Theresa's head ached. It was probably the worst headache of her life. Another clue.

"How do you feel, baby?" he was saying to her.

She tried to answer, but words didn't form. She abruptly became aware of pain in her midsection. It was a dull ache that stretched out over much of her body.

As if reading her mind, he began to explain. "You were in a car accident. Drunk driver, a woman, hit you. The van is totaled, but you're going to be okay. It will just take some time.

"The doctors operated, took out your spleen and appendix, and sewed some other parts of you back together. A piece of jagged metal from the van tried to slice you in two, but my girl held her ground." He attempted a reassuring smile. His breath on her cheek was stale.

"I am in big trouble" was her last thought before she lost consciousness again.

Chapter 68

Forbes and Quincy stopped by Marietta's on the way to rehearsal. Marietta's home was on the south side of Terre Haute in a gated community. Her late husband had been a gynecologist before his death a few years before. Dr. James Washington had been a respected and well-known leader of Terre Haute's black community, writing a weekly column for the black newspaper in town on topics relating to women's health. During his lifetime, Marietta had used his income wisely and invested in real estate. Her rental properties provided a sustainable income that kept the widow comfortable.

This morning, Marietta opened the door for her brother and his friend, welcoming Forbes with a kiss on his cheek.

"I'm so glad you men came by. Can I get you two to help me get some paint cans down out of the garage? I need to get the light cream cans so I can paint the apartment on Brennan Street before new tenants move in the first of the month."

Forbes and Quincy looked at each other knowingly. "Sure," Quincy promised. "Forbes and I have a rehearsal over at Cole's in a couple of hours, though."

"This won't take but a couple of minutes," Marietta promised. "I'm just kind of wobbly on that step stool and I'd like you to get the cans down off the top shelf.

The two nodded in knowing affirmation. What they knew, in fact, was that, since James' death, Marietta had let her weight balloon. She'd spent her life as a fitness fanatic, at the gym daily, fearful that she'd lose her good man if she didn't stay trim and lovely. But when she lost him anyway, there was really no point, and at this configuration, the use of a step stool was not only uncomfortable, it was dangerous.

Quincy led the way to the garage, arriving just as Marietta, inside the house, opened the overhead door with a remote.

Forbes chuckled. "Nice try, Quince. You think she's not going to make you paint the apartment?"

"No, I'll end up painting it, but not today. Cole seemed to think we need a load of new songs. I wonder why."

"His helper is out of commission because of that car accident, so Cole's not running off with him and booking jobs without us so much now," Forbes explained with just a pinch of vitriol. "It's a good thing he's getting us any work at all with that guy around."

"Shara said something to me the other day on the phone about Tin Pan Sally's calling us back. That right?"

"Yeah, this weekend."

"Hand me that step stool over there, will you?" Quincy opened the door to a wide storage cabinet against the wall, revealing more than a dozen half-used cans of paint, each carefully labeled and dated. He took the stool from Forbes, opened it and stepped up, retrieving the oldest cans labeled "off white" and handed them down to Forbes.

"I don't like it, Quince," Forbes continued. "I don't like getting cheated out of work just because Cole has a pianist in his hip pocket."

"I know, man, but the jobs he's doing with Tim don't pay enough for all four of us. Besides, he's just doing jobs during the day when you and I are working and so is Shara. I don't see any harm in it."

"I gotta admit that guy being around to run the sound was kind of a lucky break," Forbes said almost to himself. "Still, though, if we're going to hire someone, we need a soprano more than we need a pianist."

"No, man. If we don't have Tim, then jobs like Thanksgiving go undone. And jobs that Shara can't work will go undone."

"We need a soprano," Forbes repeated. "Think of all the material we could do: all the Gladys Knight, Ruby and the Romantics, Platters, and all that."

"Really? As far as I know, no one at any show I've worked has ever requested Ruby and the Romantics. I don't think we get much call for Platters or Pips either."

"I want a soprano. If Cole won't get one, I'll get her myself. Here comes Marietta. Is that all the off-white?"

Chapter 69

It was fortuitous, or it wasn't, that Forbes stopped in later that day to drop off his red tuxedo at the dry cleaners. A young woman he hadn't seen before was clerking the front counter. She was beautiful. Long black hair curled around a perfect oval face. Her caramel skin was flawless and her eyes were huge and sultry.

May she help him?

The woman was 25 at the oldest, and Forbes, at 53, began forming a pipe dream. Her magenta Christmas sweater clung to her thin frame, and the V-neck plunged at just the right angle. The memories of a long ago past came flying into the front of Forbes's mind. How he would so like to . . . "Uh, hi. I want to drop off this for cleaning, and I wonder if you are able to repair this cigarette burn on the inside left sleeve."

The woman picked up the sleeve and gave the burn a look. "Hmm, we could patch the burn using a piece of material from some part of the garment that isn't seen, but that's the best — "

"It's okay. Never mind. You look very familiar. Have I seen you before?" The woman was looking down at the sleeve, so she felt free to roll her eyes at the clichéd come-on from this old man. Sheesh, she thought. It's the one bad thing about a part-time job where you meet the public.

Changing the topic, she asked, "This is an unusual color for a tuxedo. Where do you wear this kind of thing?" "Oh, I'm an entertainer. I sing baritone with the Cole Renshaw Trio. Have you heard of us? Probably not. Our music is way too old for a young lady like yourself." "Standards," she replied. "You sing standards. I heard you at a street fair I was at last summer. Very memorable. I'd love to get a gig like that."

"Really?" Forbes emoted with sincere astonishment. "Do you sing?"

"I do. I'm a theater major at the university, and I've been cast for 'Show Boat' early next year."

"Okay, so do you sing, or do you *sing*?" His intent was clear to her despite his ambiguity.

"I really *sing*."

"I don't believe you," he teased. His tone was playful, facetious, not challenging.

It turns out, she could sing. The woman launched into "Make Believe." She was dead center of the note, clear, toneful and quite strong. Forbes's heart sped up. This could be just the thing he was looking for.

"Wow. You sound hot — I mean good!" I wonder if you would like to meet my partners and sing a song or two for them."

"Really? Really? Oh, I would love that. Just tell me where to come and when. I'll be there. Here," she offered, grabbing a piece of paper and pen, "Take my cell number. My name is Tori Pappas. What's yours? I so hope you'll call."

"Let's not go too fast," Forbes back pedaled. "Call me Forbes. I'd like to hear more of you myself before I include my partners. You think you could get a cup of coffee with me tonight after you get off work?"

Chapter 70

"She's not out of the woods yet," Tim explained to Cole on the way back to the apartment. "She woke up for just a minute, and I got real excited, but the doctor said, basically, to curb my enthusiasm."

"She did wake up?"

"Just for a minute. I told her what happened, but I don't know if she understood me."

"The doctor didn't actually say to 'curb your enthusiasm' did he?"

"Oh, no. They've all been very decent at this hospital, but it doesn't do me much good to have decent doctors when there are so many unknowns."

"Like what?"

"Like how these hospital bills are going to get paid. And how much I can work with you while she's in there. And, oh, that reminds me. I never did deposit the check from the Thanksgiving job. Do you think we can run through my bank on the way back?"

"No problem. I think, though, that the other driver's insurance ought to pick up all the hospital bills along with whatever rehab and physical therapy will be necessary down the road."

"Yeah, well that's another problem," Tim complained. "The woman has disappeared. Her boyfriend doesn't know where she's staying and the insurance company that the cops wrote down for her has never heard of Donna Umberger. The insurance people won't adjust the claim and bills are piling up."

"Oh, nuts," Cole said sympathetically. "If she can't be found, will your insurance pick it up on their uninsured driver clause?"

"I don't know. That's a good question. But if they do, my rates will go sky high and we are barely able to pay the premium as it is. She may need a quarter-million dollars in care, and the company won't be happy."

"I understand. Hey, you need a break. Why don't you come to the show Saturday night? I'm doing it with Shara and the guys, but come, have a drink, relax. I'll pick you up and take you home."

"I don't know, Cole. Thanks, but what if the hospital needs me?"

"Then you'll take our car. In fact, we'll take both our cars so you can drive Shara's if that happens."

"Wow, Cole. You have been really good to me since we met you. I can't tell you . . ."

"You've been pretty good to me, too, man. I couldn't have gotten through Thanksgiving without you." Cole reached out and fist-bumped Tim.

When the two men had finished their bank chore and went in to Tim's apartment, Tim excused himself to the bathroom. When Cole heard the shower running, he called Shara.

"What up, love of my life?" she answered.

Cole briefly explained the problem with the car insurance company, concluding with "What can you do?"

Shara said simply, "I'm on it," and summarily hung up.

Chapter 71

"Momma, I just can't take you to the doctor so often." Cole was at his mother's house after dropping Tim off.

"I have an appointment today," Suzanne complained. "You're not taking me?"

"No, Shara canceled the appointment."

Suzanne looked wounded. "She canceled my appointment? Why would she do that?"

Cole squirmed. His last intention would be to tell the truth, that Shara doesn't believe these appointments are needful, or that Cole has more pressing duties.

"She rescheduled for some time in February," he offered.

"Oh." Her voice was helpless and small. After a moment, she recovered. "Well, then, that leaves me time to make an appointment with the ophthalmologist. I want Dr. Gunther to find out if this cataract has grown . . . "

"Is your vision worse?"

"No, not really. But I want to keep an eye on it, so to speak."

"No, Mom."

"What do you mean 'no'?"

"You've got to understand that the doctor appointments are too many. It's every single week, and it takes up the whole day. I need to run our business and the appointments are crowding me."

"You mean your little singing group is more important than your own mother's health?" Suzanne's voice climbed to near-hysterics. It was sudden and unexpected. Cole dreaded what was coming next. "You're siding with Shara now. She's got you ganging up on me!"

"She has legitimate concerns, Mom. She wants me to take a job at a record store, but I'm not doing it — for you. But you have to understand . . .

"How about I take you for lunch?" he segued. It was an awkward segue, but the best he could do for the moment. At least that would take less time than the doctor, and he might be able to hit a venue and talk to a manager before getting back home to meet Forbes and Quincy.

"Certainly not. You obviously, obviously don't have time! You can go, now, if that's what you call gratitude. I'm alone and don't have my husband to take me, remember. Remember? Leave!"

Cole went to his car and called his wife at her office. She picked up the phone on the first ring. Rather than greeting him, she said, "Donnatella."

"Um, what?"

"Donnatella Renee Umberger is the full name of the woman who hit Theresa. There's an insurance company out of Maine that holds her policy. She has full coverage, and while we're on the topic, this is not her first DUI accident. The first one was a year ago and it was just a fender bender. Anyway, I found her."

"Really? That's great. What's next?"

When the couple disconnected, Cole phoned Tim and told him the toll-free number to reach the insurance company. Tim seemed to actually relax for the first time in as long as Cole had known him.

He offered Tim the policy number for Donnatella Umberger's insurance, and Tim scribbled it down. "This is terrific news, Cole. Thanks a million."

"Okay. No problem. Let me get off here and call Shara back."

When Cole had his wife on the phone again, he explained that his mother was very upset about Shara's refusal to allow the appointment.

She listened silently, and when he had portrayed the unfortunate conversation with Suzanne, Shara could only say, "So what's the rest of your day look like? I'd like you to take a nap."

"Why do I have to take a nap?"

"Because you'll be at the hospital all night."

"What in blazes are you talking about?"

"You argued with your mother. Therefore, you'll be in the hospital all night."

"Make sense, woman."

"Haven't you ever noticed that whenever you have a fight with her, in the wee hours of the following morning, she calls for the ambulance. There is some crisis. Chest pains, or she can't breathe, or her blood sugar is high, or her blood sugar is low or something. It's like clockwork. Then you and I go to the hospital and sit there and sit there for hours until some rare doctor with stones informs her that nothing at all is wrong. That's your punishment for disagreeing with her."

"You are kidding me."

Shara made her case. She had evidently written everything down and was reading to Cole over the phone about the last three emergency room trips. The doctor had been unable to isolate a cause for Suzanne's complaints, and the date coincided with an argument the patient had with her son.

"Except for the last time," Shara concluded, "when your mother did have something wrong. Her blood sugar was through the roof — 700 as I recall — because she had swigged a half gallon of orange juice to drive it up so she could then call the ambulance. It was deliberate. It's always deliberate. Take a nap. You're going to need it."

Cole was silent, not knowing what to say.

Chapter 72

Cole laid down as Shara had suggested, but he couldn't fall asleep. He got up and straightened up the living room, then took the vacuum cleaner to the sofa that was particularly rife with cat hair. The cat in question fled the room when the vacuum came on and Cole smiled to himself, thinking of Shara. He wanted so much to be strong for her because she was so strong. Cole recognized that the placating of his mother made him look weak, but he was simply afraid to tell Shara everything about his relationship with Mom. It was too ignominious for his taste. So, instead, Cole allowed Shara to be upset about the time he wasted at Suzanne's. It was the lesser of evils.

As he turned off the vacuum, the doorbell rang. When he opened the door, Forbes was standing there with a cross look on his face. "Man, you know we're coming over. Don't run that machine, will ya? We've been ringing the bell for ten minutes!"

"No, you haven't," Cole shot back, fatigued already with Forbes's demands. "I scarcely had it on two minutes."

"Doesn't matter, man," Quincy complained while he followed Forbes inside. "The dust it turns up bothers my allergies. I can hardly sing when you do that."

"Nope, I don't buy that either," Cole teased. "You could sing while I drown you in an aquarium." He revealed a good-natured smile.

Forbes, noticing the smile, recognized how Cole was so good at derailing people, knocking down their defenses, making the best peace. Forbes was both envious and annoyed.

The three men took their seats, and Cole presented his nominations for a handful of songs he would like to have performance-ready for Tin Pan Sally's Friday and Saturday.

"Okay," Quincy nodded, "but another song we really need is 'Birth of the Blues.'"

"We sure do," Cole agreed, "and I've looked, but the digital music for that isn't out there. There's an arrangement by the Mcguire Sisters, but the music is too feminine, too fluffy. Too many strings and xylophones. Soulless. I can't find a Sammy Davis arrangement. And I count five requests for it in the last month, and we couldn't answer them. Plus, one of them was at Tin Pan Sally's the last time we played there."

"That's a crock," Forbes put in. "I love that song. Sammy's has a ton of brass. It rocks, man. Hey, you know another thing we need: a soprano."

Quincy noticeably rolled his eyes while Cole looked at Forbes and considered the irrelevancy of bringing this up now.

"What?"

"A soprano. There's a lot of music we can't do without a female lead."

"No, there isn't. Most of it we can do fine if we just change the pronouns in the text. Lighten up, Forbes. You're the one who's always jealous of the size of each person's cut. Why do you want to make it smaller with another singer? Can we get started on some Christmas music?"

Forbes objected, but Quincy slowed him down. "Let's take this up next week after we're through this show." Then, turning to Cole, he said, "What about 'Baby, It's Cold Outside'?"

"Exactly!" Forbes burst out. "How in blazes are you going to do that song without a woman?"

"You know, Frank Loesser wrote that for his wife," Cole segued, "and when they sang it together at parties at their house, Frank told the guests that he was the evil of two Loessers."

Quincy and Cole chuckled at the anecdote, but Forbes didn't crack a smile. He again recognized Cole's attempt to smooth over a conflict. Then Cole applied the track for "Have Yourself a Merry Little Christmas" to the cdg player and handed the men each a microphone. "Forbes, you take the lead," he suggested. "Quince and I will follow on the third and fifth."

The truth was, Cole didn't really want to give the lead to Forbes; he wanted to take it himself. But he could see Forbes was agitated and he hoped the offer of a lead would settle his friend down. Shara, he reminded himself, was forever critical of the sacrifices he made to mollify his two partners. Cole pursed his lips slightly at the thought, hoping his friends didn't notice.

Quincy did. "This song is from 'Meet Me in St. Louis.' Judy Garland sang it. Did you know that these aren't the original lyrics? The way it was first written, it wasn't happy. The original lyrics were kind of depressing, really."

Both men recognized Quincy's attempt to change the subject, and they were thankful.

"No, man, I didn't know that. Where do you get this?"

"I don't know. Judy Garland didn't like the lyrics, and MGM studios asked the guy to write new words."

"Cole, cue it again, will you? Quincy talked through the opening. So, here I go singing a song for a soprano. This is exactly what I'm talking about."

"No, it isn't, Forbes. It's exactly what *I'm* talking about. Let's drop it for now," Cole concluded.

Chapter 73

Maeve Baumgardner had practiced medicine at the Regional Hospital for 27 years. Her specialty was traumatic surgery, and Theresa Shelton was on her mind these days. Mrs. Shelton was not bound for a merry Christmas, and the conversation Dr. Baumgardner was set to have with Mr. Shelton would not be merry either. She stepped into the telemetry room where Theresa's monitors beeped and chirped continuously. As expected, Tim sat with a magazine, staring at a photo of a lion with teeth bared. The image Maeve observed over the man's shoulder was both beautiful and unsettling.

"There's a beautiful cat," she commented as she took a seat in a plastic chair near Tim's. "How are you feeling?"

"Better than Theresa, I'd wager," Tim said glumly. "Give me some good news, Dr. Baumgardner."

"All right, then, I will." The doctor pulled the chart out from under her arm and browsed through the top few pages. "I have decided that we may want to wake her up artificially. She's in less pain while she's asleep, but at the same time, we can't really tell much about how she's doing without talking to her, and hopefully getting her to talk back.

"I'm going to stimulate her brain and pull her out of the coma. X-rays indicate that the pressure is off her brain and her concussion is healing, so my worries about permanent brain damage are reduced."

Tim rubbed his face with both hands. "That's good. That's really good," he said mostly to himself. "What about, you know, the rest of her?"

"It's just going to take some time, and quite a lot of therapy. As soon as she's awake, we'll start moving her muscles and helping her get back some muscular strength. We've got hydraulics on her legs now to prevent blood clots, but the sooner she can get on her feet, the better."

"This is the first time I've heard you talking about getting her on her feet. This sounds good." Tim was daring to hope for the first time since the accident. He clenched the doctor's words.

"We are a long way from the edge of the woods, Mr. Shelton. But, based on brain wave activity and her blood work, I think there is reason for guarded optimism. But, again, it will take time."

"Doctor, I just got word that the driver of the car who hit my wife has been identified and I have talked to the insurance company. The coverage will be in place for all of her care . . ."

"I'm sure that's a load off your mind, Mr. Shelton, but I advise you to not worry about money right now. It shouldn't be your first concern, and it's definitely not mine." Maeve ventured a reassuring smile.

"So, when will you wake her up?"

"I'm thinking late tomorrow afternoon."

"Okay. I'll be here."

She looked at Tim thoughtfully for a moment. Then, "What do you do for a living, Mr. Shelton?"

Tim started to say he was a professor of music as he had said to that question for years, but the words froze in his mouth. "I'm a musician. I play backup for a nightclub singer."

"Oh. I see."

Clearly, Tim thought, *she is not very impressed. Well,* he told himself, *I'm not either.*

"Keyboard?"

"Yes."

"What genre do you play?"

"All of them." If that doesn't impress her, nothing will.

Instead, she offered a snort of derision. "That's quite a statement, Mr. Shelton. With a resume like that, I'd expect you . . . "

"To have a much better job?" he interrupted.

Maeve told herself the man was more than just a little defensive. But he was within his rights. He'd been through a lot. "I'd like to hear you play sometime," she offered.

"Sure."

Chapter 74

It was 2 a.m. when the phone rang. Immediately, Shara awoke and said a prayer of thanks that Suzanne had let her sleep a full four hours before calling from the emergency room. Cole answered the phone on the night stand, and groggily said, "Hello."

"Is this Cole Renshaw?"

"Yes, who's calling?" he added "as if I don't know," in his head but didn't say it.

"This is Jaimie Sunter at Regional Hospital emergency services. I have Suzanne Renshaw here, and she's taken a fall. She'd like you to come to the emergency room." "What kind of fall?" he looked at Shara whose eyes were still closed. "I understand that Mrs. Renshaw took a tumble down her back stairs, landed on concrete, and has some minor injuries. She's been treated, and she'd like you to take her home." Nurse Sunter waited curiously at the silence on the phone. "This is her son, right?"

"Yeah. Okay. I'll be there." Cole disconnected.

"What is it this time?" Shara said. "What did she fall off of?"

"She fell down the back stairs."

"I bet you a dollar she didn't. Go back to sleep. Please. You have a big day tomorrow and a show tomorrow night." Shara was relieved when Cole turned out the light and settled back into bed. But in 15 minutes, the light came on again. He silently dressed and ducked out the door.

Chapter 75

"Hi, Tim. This is Shara Renshaw. I'm just calling to find out how things are going at the hospital."

"Hello, Shara. I do have some news. They've moved her out of ICU and into telemetry, so visiting is easier. Plus, they are going to wake her up tomorrow afternoon." Tim was sitting in the hospital cafeteria. His coffee and bagel had that bland, institutionalized flavor that was to be expected, but since he was virtually living at the hospital, he'd grown accustomed. He glanced around him. The pale, dusty blue walls were designed to be calming, he realized, and the matching upholstered plastic chairs were designed to be comfortable, but not too much so. Eat and be gone — that was their message.

Shara was saying something about prayer.

"What? I'm sorry. Say that again, please."

"I said I'm praying for Theresa daily," Shara repeated.

"Oh, thanks. Well, we'll know tomorrow afternoon if he's been listening."

"I promise you, He's been listening. I'm sure you are praying, too, about your whole situation. I want to remind you that He doesn't give us anything we can't handle."

"'Handling' is a relative term, I think. What Treese and I have faced the last few months would break a bull elephant in half. But I'm still alive, so I guess you can argue that I am handling. But I don't feel like I am."

"It's been my experience that God does the most for us when we're weak. People who think they're strong are, well, they're wrong, but also their rigidity stands in God's way."

"Okay, well, thanks for that, Shara. I'm going to go back to the room, and if anything else happens, I'll let you know." He disconnected the phone before she had a chance to reply. As he put his Styrofoam plate in the trash and secured a lid on his coffee cup, the thought occurred to him that he hadn't really prayed since all of this began. Was it because he had given up on prayer during the months since he and Treese had been unemployed? Maybe. But if there was a time to pray, this was it. He'd have to give that some thought.

Chapter 76

In the evening, Cole invited Shara to go with him to meet a club owner in Midtown. The two dressed just a little nicer than usual and took her car, which was less rusty.

The club was on a corner in an upscale neighborhood. The sidewalk in front was wide, and abandoned tables were set inside a wrought iron fence that was ornate, rendered like branches with leaves. This must be a nice setting, Shara mused, when the weather was nice, to dine outdoors. All a person would need would be live music. She smiled to herself.

Inside, the appointments were elegant. A row of booths lined one wall. The Naugahyde was deep forest green, and it surrounded dark wood tables. The tables in the center of the room had matching cushioned seats. Over each table or booth, a Tiffany-styled lamp hung from a chain.

Across from the booths, a large bar lined the opposite wall. The mirrored glass shelving behind the bar sported what Shara guessed were dozens of bottles of liquor of every description. The bar itself was of a similar dark wood, varnished and shiny. More Tiffany-styled lamps hung over it from the ceiling, and a prominent tip jar was poised on each end.

Behind the bar, a young bartender with a mustache designed, Shara guessed, to make him look older, lifted his chin to greet the couple and gestured that they were welcome to the table or booth of their choice.

Cole took the booth nearest the bar, though other booths, farther away, would be more romantic. Romance later, he told Shara with his eyes. He helped Shara off with her coat and settled in across from her, stuffing their outerwear on the seat next to him.

Rising, he went to the bartender who said, "What can I get you, sir?" Cole noted the impeccable manners. He saw no sign of vitriol as he occasionally did in these situations. Some places know they're supposed to be welcoming to everyone, but they honestly don't want black people in their place. They know it's wrong, but they feel the way they feel. Cole didn't get a scent off of this kid. Yet.

"My wife would like a glass of house Pinot Grigio, and I'd like the house Noir. I'd also like to see Christine Berthold, if she's available."

"Yes, sir. Is she expecting you? Let me get your wine, and I'll let her know you're here."

"Thank you. Cole Renshaw with the Cole Renshaw Trio. Are there dinner menus? She and I would like a to get dinner."

Before leaving the bar, Cole took care to be noticed when he dropped a five dollar bill in the tip jar. Seed money, he hoped.

It was a good fifteen minutes before Christine Berthold made an appearance. She was 50-ish, gray, and significantly overweight. Shara generously attributed the woman's weight to the luscious-looking menu. But she kept that to herself.

Christine was happy to meet the couple. Could she bring them an appetizer? No? Were they ready to order? She wrote nothing down, but promised to put the order in and be right back. When she returned, another ten minutes had passed, but Shara was feeling her Pinot Grigio and didn't really mind.

Cole began his sales pitch. It was upbeat and confident. He can fill this room within a couple of weeks, he claimed. His group was so popular, had such a draw, and so on, that she could not help but be pleased. If she would like to book the group for five weeks to start out, she would only be charged . . .

Shara, glancing around, only then noticed the small staging area to the left of the front door. It wasn't big enough to hold her sound board, and the three singers. This could be a problem.

She interrupted. "You should know, though, Christine, that my husband also acts, in smaller venues, as a solo performer, and specializes in the popular standards of the 30s, 40s, and 50s. Do you have a clientele that might appreciate a repertoire like that?"

Christine perked up immediately, and Shara was unsure if her sudden enthusiasm was in response to the idea of singing popular standards, or if it was in response to the suggestion that fewer singers would cost less.

"Oh," Christine said cheerfully, "What instrument do you play? As you see, the stage is small and I believe the popular standards often call for quite a lot of strings and brass, which I can't handle. But if you're good with a synthesizer, you can get over." Christine grinned knowingly. Her obvious intent was to let it be known that she was experienced in handling music acts.

"Well, actually, we use something even better. We use digital accompaniment which simulates the 30-piece orchestra that you hear on many standards, but takes up, obviously, far less space." He tried to appear triumphant in the disclosure.

"Canned music? No. I don't think so."

Here we go again, Shara thought. These club owners whining about the digital music were making this business harder and harder to manage. And harder for themselves. If we were in Vegas, she mused, where everybody uses it, she and Cole wouldn't be getting this grief.

"Christine, I promise you, your audience won't notice that the music is 'canned.' All they'll notice is that the music sounds like they remember. It makes for wonderful memories. Tell you what, let me do one evening with just Shara and me, and if you aren't pleased with the digital accompaniment, I'll concede to your greater wisdom. But give me a chance."

It was at that moment that the young bartender appeared with two plates of food. *Timing is everything,* Shara thought. *Doesn't the kid know we're trying to close a sale?*

Christine, grateful for the interruption that Shara resented, demurred. "Let me let you enjoy your dinner. Our veal piccata, you know, was on the front page of the Terre Haute Cuisine magazine last month. Enjoy!"

She stepped away without waiting for a response.

Shara squinted her eyes closed, uttered a prayer of thanksgiving, and dug into her veal whether she was really grateful or not. That had been the lesson lately: stay grateful, even when things go wrong.

Cole speared a ravioli dripping in marinara and took a bite. "Umm. Not bad." Looking over at his wife, he noticed her body language, and, knowing her as he did, sought to reassure her. "I'm going to get her, Shara. Just hold still and enjoy your meal."

When the two had finished, Cole got up and went back to the bartender. "Hey, what's your name?"

"Ted," came the reply.

"Nice to meet you, Ted. My wife and I would like another glass of wine and the check. Hey, what happened to Christine?"

"Oh, okay, sorry," Ted apologized. "I think she's on the phone. I'll go tell her you're about ready to go." He poured two more glasses of wine and set them on the bar for Cole before turning back and going in the kitchen.

When Ted came to the table with the check, Christine was right behind him. She slid into the booth next to Shara as if they were old friends. "Here's what I'll do. I'm going to start Sunday brunch here this coming Sunday. I'll hire one singer for two hours. Can you sing from 11:00 to 1:00 this coming Sunday? I'll pay a hundred dollars. That's my offer. I am sending out an email blast to our regulars announcing brunch. If this works out well, we'll talk about another engagement."

"That should work, Christine. We have another engagement Sunday evening, but there's no reason we can't play your brunch. Thanks so much."

Cole reached in the pocket of his sports coat and lifted out a folded contract. He wrote the specifics on the form, signed it, and offered it to Christine.

"All right," she said, signing. "I'll see you Sunday at 11:00."

"You'll see us earlier than that. We'll have some set up to do. Can we get here at 10?" Cole asked. He looked at Shara, victory sparkling in his eyes.

Chapter 77

Tim opened his mail and was surprised to find a check from Donna Umberger's insurance company. The adjuster had called yesterday to say he was on the way to the car lot where Tim's van had been towed, and that a check would be forthcoming, but Tim was amazed at the quick service. This was the first good thing to happen for a while. And from the looks of this check, if he scaled down to a compact, less expensive car, he could bank some of this money. He called Cole. After a quick explanation to his friend about the check, Cole agreed to take Tim to the bank the next day and then help him go to a used car lot.

"But I've got a job that night, remember, so I can't take all day," Cole concluded.

"Understood. This is the Tin Pan Sally's job, isn't it?"

"Yeah. Are you going to drop by and show off your new wheels?"

"Depends on Treese. They're gonna wake her up in the afternoon, and I want to be there, so if we can do this early in the morning, that will work out for the best for both of us."

"I'll pick you up at 9 in the morning." As it turned out, the used car lot, no different from any others of its kind, had a sedan that interested Tim. It was nine years old and had some miles on it, but if Tim had learned anything in the last two years, it was to limit his expectations. He may never, at this rate, buy another new car. He may never buy a used car from a dealership with a high overhead. His personal paradigm had shifted from the period when he owned a home in the suburbs, and it was up to him to embrace the new reality. He mentioned to Cole that this perfectly acceptable red Toyota Camry, unquestionably bought at auction by the owner of this corner lot, was priced so as to allow some extra money from the insurance settlement. He accepted that it had probably been in an accident and then refurbished. There was a scant suggestion of rust. The power windows were not reliable. It smelled faintly like cigarettes. Cole sat in the driver's seat and showed Tim how to bang on the inside of the door with a fist while holding the down button to make the window mechanism cooperate. But the oil was clean, and there was a miraculously provided folder of maintenance records. The tires had plenty of tread going into the worst part of winter. This would do, Tim told Cole, and then he told the salesman to start the paperwork.

When Cole left his friend at the dealership, he headed for Christine's Bar and Grill. It wasn't quite open yet, but Cole waited for Ted, the young bartender, to unlock the door at 11:00 sharp. He exchanged pleasantries and then took a fresh look at the space where he would be performing on Sunday. He stood up on the stage and gauged how much of the room he could see from there. Making eye contact with an audience was important. Then he considered where to place speakers. The room was sized so that his smaller sound system would work fine.

"Hey, um, Cole?" Ted called out from behind the bar. Cole jumped down from the stage and approached the bar. He wondered momentarily if he should order something just to garner warm feelings from the bartender. Too early, he told himself. "Yeah, what's up, Ted?"

"Christine said you were going to use karaoke music. How does that work? I am not in favor of half-drunk caterwauling idiots in my bar, so she says you're playing here Sunday, and I'm off, but I still think it's a cruddy idea. Talk me out of it."

"Oh, Ted, no. I promise, no caterwauling whether you're here or not. No, I'll do the singing. No guest singers from the audience. You'd enjoy if you stop by." Ted looked skeptical. "I've never seen Christine go for this kind of music, not in four years I've been here. You want to know why she hired you with the canned music?"

"Yes, I do. Why?"

"You're cheap."

"Yeah, well, I'd have to charge a whole lot more if I brought a 30-piece orchestra with me, wouldn't I?"

"Fair point. You want a drink of something?"

"Coke."

Chapter 78

When Theresa opened her eyes, she saw immediately a room full of medical personnel in seafoam green scrubs. One of them was taking her blood pressure, and another was adjusting the devices on her legs that squeezed and unsqueezed her calf muscles. Yet another seafoam-clad technician was on a laptop at her bedside, typing furiously. In a far corner, anxiety riddling his face, was Tim. He was wearing a white shirt she had never seen before, and his jacket. She smiled at him weakly and he took two swift steps to her bedside.

"Hey, Treese, long time no see." His smile was toothy, but his eyes were crinkled up more with worry than mirth.

"How long?" she murmured.

"Almost two weeks. You've been out cold, except for a couple of minutes you probably don't remember. You were in a car accident. You were badly injured, and you're going to be here for a while. But you're going to be okay eventually. I'm so happy to have you back." He kissed her lightly on her lips. Her breath was awful, but he hardly cared.

"I vaguely remember . . . a small red car that T-boned me," she muttered. "Did I wreck the van?"

"Yes, but we have a new car. New to us. We won't worry about that now. We will worry about getting you better."

Before Theresa could respond, Dr. Baumgardner appeared behind Tim and softly asked him to join her outside. In the hallway, Baumgardner got to the point. "Mr. Shelton, your wife is stable. Our next challenge is to get her on her feet. Since her femur was shattered, that will be no mean trick, but pneumonia is a worry. We also need to evacuate her bowels which haven't moved."

"Why has she not, you know?"

"Because the pain drugs she's on tend clog the plumbing, as it were. I can't be sure my work was successful until her bowels move. Her injuries are nowhere near healed. She was almost cut in two . . ."

"Yes, I know. Go on."

"In a small way, it's a blessing. Did I talk to you about the volvulus?"

"The what? No, I don't think so. What is a volvulus?" "Mr. Shelton, your wife had a place in her intestine that was twisted *before* the accident. The CT scan we did revealed it. It would have been life-threatening, with or without the accident. That section of her intestine's tissue was dying and was about to go gangrenous. We're lucky we found it." Dr. Baumgardner used her hands to describe for Tim how the intestine had flipped over in one section twisting itself into an obstruction. "If she hadn't been in this accident, it could have gone much worse for her. That's an irony."

Tim, somewhat astonished, absorbed this news. "Are you telling me she would have died if she hadn't been in that accident?"

"No, no, not at all. She would probably have been in quite a lot of pain for a while before the situation reached a critical stage,"

"What kind of pain?"

"Usually it manifests as a low backache."

"She'd complained of a backache for days. We thought it was this old mattress we've been sleeping on. We got some Tylenol and we're making the best of it."

"And the Tylenol didn't do much, I'm guessing, and a crisis was creeping up on her, and you didn't know."

"Oh, God!"

Chapter 79

Barbara had spent the better part of two weeks studying the syllabuses of her colleagues in the Music Department. A few ideas had come to her about the courses she was set to teach. Over time, she hoped to convince Frank Glenn to let her teach a course in a discipline closer to her heart, but for now, she would teach what she'd been hired to teach. To bolster her low enthusiasm, she thought about her new church.

Barb took great pleasure on a Sunday morning, to get dressed in her most fashionable ensemble, with a Christmas theme, or at least a Christmasy piece of jewelry, and settle into her pew to expect the best blessing. She really liked this young pastor whose take on the Christian life included social justice, fairness, equality, brotherhood, and grace. But Barb's appreciation of those values was abstract. She didn't let them touch very closely to her own life. Jesus had told the rich young man to get rid of everything he owned, give it to the poor, and follow Jesus. Barb didn't think about that very personally. Even when it was the sermon topic, she glanced away. A voice deep within her was whispering that this chasm between her faith and her actions might be at the heart of her unease about the job at the university. Then on Monday morning, she returned to the Music Department and imagined that everything would shake out in the end. The still small voice, in the midst of Christmas bustle and new job tensions, was easy to ignore.

Chapter 80

Cole and Shara arrived at Tin Pan Sally's at 6 o'clock for their 8 p.m. show. They set up quickly. Set ups were easier the second time you do them. For one thing, you know where all the electricity is. Having finished, the two ordered sandwiches. Cole ate light. He didn't want a heavy stomach when he had to sing. Shara ordered a heavy meatball sandwich even though she hadn't slept well. The sandwich might make her lethargic on the job, but the experts say that if you don't sleep well, eat well, and vice versa. She had tossed and turned after Cole had left for the emergency room to take Suzanne home. She was just a little aggravated with her husband. Cole had lost sleep too, of course, but he didn't have to get up so early. This night, the two were surprised to see Tim Shelton stroll into the nightclub as they were finishing their sandwiches. Shara noticed the lightness in his step. It was new, and she offered silent thanks.

"Is she awake?" she asked before even greeting him.

"She was, and she was talking a little, but now she's asleep again. But it's just sleep, not a coma she's in, so, I'm relieved.

"I'm also relieved about something else I learned." Tim took a seat at the Renshaw's table and welcomed the glass of water a server placed before him. "Turns out Treese was already sick when the accident happened. She had a volvulus." He smiled at the expected bewildered expressions on their faces. "Her intestines were twisted and she could have died. She'd complained of a backache, and we thought it was the mattress. But it was serious." Tim went on to explain all that Dr. Baumgardner had told him.

"So, let me get this straight," Shara put in at the conclusion of Tim's narrative. "She might have died if she hadn't almost died in this accident?"

"Correct."

"And if it was vital to take her to the ER with this volvulus, and you didn't have any healthcare insurance, you would have been on the hook for thousands of dollars. But since she was in this accident, the insurance will pick it up. Is that right?"

"Wow. I didn't even think about that," Tim answered, his eyes wide with surprise.

"Jehovah Jireh," she advised, winking at him, "God provides."

"Yeah. When are the guys arriving?"

"Ten minutes before show time, probably. That's how they usually do things." Cole's answer was tinged with sarcasm.

Tim nodded.

"Hey, Tim. You hungry?" Cole said, changing the topic.

"Yeah, I guess."

"Look here," Cole said, pushing his plate toward Tim, "Finish my sandwich, will you? I don't want to eat too much before a show." The half sandwich was of roast beef and Swiss cheese piled high on a Kaiser roll. Cole had left behind his dill pickle spear as well. It all looked delicious.

"Uh, okay, thanks." The other two left him to his meal. It was time to warm up and check sound.

"I thought you were going to eat your sandwich," Shara remarked quietly as the two stepped up on their stage.

"It was great, but I really don't want to sing on the whole sandwich, and, look, Shara. I'm getting to know the guy. I bet you a buck he hasn't eaten all day at that hospital."

Quincy Garland arrived at Tin Pan Sally's fifteen minutes prior to the start of the show. This irritated Shara greatly.

As was his custom, Quincy didn't care to take part in the set up. It was beneath him, and beneath his massive ego, she recognized, and the prima donna attitude burned her. He did this routinely. She became so annoyed that she didn't even realize that Forbes, who was usually on time, wasn't there either. It wasn't until Cole approached her at her sound board and told her to call Forbes that she realized she was one singer down. Her call went to voicemail and at show time there was still no Forbes. Shara programmed duets and solos for Cole and Quincy as she muttered quiet prayers under her breath.

Sure, Cole and Quincy could do the show alone. The two of them had plenty of material. But the contract she had signed with Tin Pan Sally's called for three singers. It was a good 35 minutes into the show when Forbes finally came in wearing jeans and an incongruous dress shirt. He came up behind her on the stage and whispered that he thought the show started at 8:30. "It never has before. It's always started at 8:00, and by the way, it's 8:35, so you're late no matter what. Get dressed."

"Okay. Sorry. Where's my tux. I thought we were wearing red tuxes, but the guys have on green." "Your green tux is in my car. Go out the back door."

It was four songs later when Forbes finally returned, dressed and ready to sing. He had that smell on him that Shara disliked. He'd been smoking and the message was clear to Shara. His tardiness had nothing to do with misunderstanding the time. He was stoned. And there was little she could do about it as long as her husband wouldn't enforce rules.

Truth be told, she loved them, both of them. She loved their friendship, their warmth, and their long history with her husband. The good times they had all shared far outnumbered the bad. It was like all relationships, she told herself. You love the whole person, and swallow the less savory attributes, praying that the other person will swallow yours.

But their lack of professionalism, their fondness for bud, and the resulting extra responsibility that landed on Cole — well, that made her grind her teeth. Shara let "Makin' Whoopee" end, and then she got on her microphone. "And now, folks, joining us from God-knows-where, is Mr. Versatility, Forbes Wilson." Cole shot his wife a disapproving look as Forbes took the stage. She cued an up-tempo song for him as the others joined her at the sound board.

"Did he say why he's late?" Cole asked his wife.

"He's stoned."

Quincy stared at Shara, aghast. Truth was, Quincy never perceived that Shara ever guessed his fondness for "herb," as he called it. He had always imagined that his wholly innocent drug use was a mystery to her. That not being the case, he would need to act cautiously. Before he could say anything, an elderly man approached the three at the sound board. Quincy took two steps toward the man and asked how he could help.

"Can you do 'Birth of the Blues'?"

"Uh, I don't know, man. Lemme find out. Hang on." Quincy turned on his heel and strode two steps back to Cole with accusation and blame splashed across his face.

"Okay, man, it's just like I told you earlier. We've got a request for 'Birth of the Blues,' and we can't answer it." Cole took a deep breath and let it out slowly. Quincy's remark was an accusation and an indictment and it didn't matter at all that Cole hadn't bought the music for the Ray Henderson standard because it didn't exist. Somehow, Forbes and Quincy held him in contempt for this failure to produce, but this wasn't the time or place for an argument. He looked out over the crowd and wondered what to say. He could apologize to the white-haired man in the grey sports jacket at the foot of the stage steps, or he could . . .. His eyes fell on Tim who was sitting at his table nursing a PBR.

Cole stepped down from the stage just as Forbes reached the bridge of "That's Life." He spoke to the grey sports jacket,

"Excuse me. Let me see what I can do for you." Then he stepped around the man and strode swiftly toward Tim.

"Tim, can you play 'Birth of the Blues'?"

"Sure."

"I'll have to mic the piano."

"Sure."

"We got a request . . .."

"I figured."

"Can you play it in C minor."

"Who's singing it?"

"Quince."

"Okay. Sure." Tim rose and followed Cole. Reaching the side of the stage, he raised the lid of the black lacquered piano and took the mic that Cole handed down from the stage. He set the mic inside the piano near the strings and hoped for the best.

Cole, on the stage, stepped toward Quincy and said, "I hope you know this song as well as you think you do." With that, he took his mic and walked out to Forbes to relieve him.

"Mr. Forbes Wilson, show him your love." As the audience clapped, Forbes dutifully walked off stage as Cole segued.

"We have a request here for a 1941 standard we seldom get to do because the orchestration is not available. But The Cole Renshaw Trio, in league with Tin Pan Sally's, strives to answer every request. So, here's 'The Birth of the Blues,' brought to you by Quincy Garland, with special guest artist Tim Shelton on piano."

With that, Tim began fingering the intro with a light, energetic riff that allowed Quincy time to gather himself and step to the front of the stage.

Chapter 81

Shara wasn't happy to answer the three curtain calls the Tin Pan Sally's audience insisted upon. At 11:15, she was ready to pack it in and go home. She had promised her boss another Saturday to make up for a work day she'd missed. A local magazine, geared toward seniors, had hosted a special event last October and had paid Cole well to bring his entire act. Fine, she had agreed. Now the bill was due, and another chance to sleep in on a weekend was sacrificed.

She had already given up all hope of attending her church. She'd missed every Sunday for months because of one music-related interruption or other. But it was the price of doing business, literally, and she'd buy more concealer for the bags under her eyes.

So, this night, when the show had finally ended, Shara began the task of pulling wires out of devices, wrapping them up on spools, and putting them in cases. She did this mostly alone as the three men were called to sign a few autographs and listen to anecdotes brought by audience members about where they were the first time they heard a certain song, or the specific memories a song brought with it. The singers, having grown used to an audience's need to share, would nod and smile and say how wonderful it all was. They invited spectators to the next show, shook hands with great sincerity, and passed out business cards.

Shara didn't mind. The celebrity her husband enjoyed was equally enjoyable to her and she reveled in his success. At one point, however, when she had secured all of the tangentials in their cases, she tapped Cole on the shoulder and whispered, "I'll pull the van around. Give me your keys."

Cole stroked both of his thighs feeling for his keys. "I don't have 'em, honey. I thought you had 'em."

Shara's eyes got big. She went back to the table she had used to steady her sound board and found her purse. She searched it fully, but Cole's keys weren't there. She dumped it out on the table. Nothing. Her own keys were in the purse, but they were not complete. At a show in October, a would-be thief had put a screw driver in the door locks, trying to break in. Cole had replaced the door locks, and Shara had a spare key for that, but she had no ignition key.

As if she weren't tired enough, she thought, she would have to walk all of this equipment across the parking lot to the van rather than pull up behind the back door. Eventually, the keys would be found, but this mystery made a hard night harder.

She carried two cases to the van, opened the back hatch and began loading the car. Within moments, Cole joined her, his arms loaded with cases.

She told him she couldn't find his keys. Cole's eyes widened also. This meant he couldn't get into his mother's house, her garage, or the padlock she kept on her backyard gate, let alone drive them home.

As the couple was discussing the problem, Forbes appeared. "Hey, man," he said as he approached Cole, "Do you think you can drop me off at home?"

"Uh, I guess. Where's your car?"

"Oh, I left it and took a bus over."

"That why you were late?"

"Oh, yeah, man. I didn't. . . . I, uh, didn't feel like driving."

"Sure. Problem is, I can't find my car keys. Just in case Shara dropped them somewhere, will you and Quincy look around the stage?"

"Man, I've got a date tonight. I need to get home."

"I got that, Forbes. I can't leave without my keys. I'm happy to drive you, but I've got to find them." Cole began to bristle at his partner's attitude. "You could speed things up if you would look around inside. Maybe she left them in the bathroom. Get a woman to look in there. Ask the kitchen crew. See if anybody turned them in to the bartender. Get Quince to help you."

Cole marched back inside the building to pick up a speaker and bring it outside.

Forbes did a slow burn. The dark-haired woman from the dry cleaners had agreed to meet him for a drink at midnight. She said she'd be at a tavern not far from Forbes's apartment and have a quick one with him to talk about his music career and how he might help her with her own. She seemed real interested, and this potential delay could force Forbes to stand her up.

His intention was to schmooze and charm, to regale her with his heroic exploits — most of which were Cole's — and for which he intended to take credit. He was going to be as large and in-her-face as he had to be to get her. Down the road, the triumph would come when he would not only get her in the group as his own ally and co-conspirator against the powerful team of Cole and Shara, but he would also get *her*, and that would be the real triumph. As he thought of the potential, saliva filled his mouth.

But this delay in leaving the club would only delay his plans, and his anger at Cole, which regularly blossomed with little provocation, was quickly turning into a white-hot rage.

"Hey, man," Forbes said to Quincy as he met him at the door. Cole can't find his keys, and I need to get home. Can I get a ride with you?"

Quincy, aware that Forbes hadn't been in shape to drive, replied, "No, man. I've got an early shift in the morning, and you're way on the other side of town. I gots to leave right now, man. I've got to get up in five hours." Quincy's own hypocrisy was not lost on himself. He fully knew how many times he'd been too polluted to drive a car and had called on Forbes to pick him up. But the disclaimer about his short night of sleep was truthful. It would reduce his rest by an additional hour if he hauled Forbes' carcass home.

"All right, man, thanks anyway. I'm gonna go in there and look for these damned keys. Give me a hand?"

"No, man, I just said. I'm going home."

Forbes re-entered the nightclub and glanced around on the stage. No keys. As he lazily put forth the minimum effort, his anger against Cole returned. Stupid mother couldn't even keep track of his keys and I'm trusting him to run a singing group, Forbes reveled in his exasperation.

Plus, Forbes called to mind. This was not the first, but the second time in a few weeks Cole had misplaced his keys. What a bone head! Forbes looked past the fact that Cole's mother had sat on the keys, and resumed laying culpability on his friend and partner.

The two men had been friends for decades, and there was a natural tendency to take each other for granted, Forbes knew. But the anger and exasperation suited him at the moment.

He picked up the chair Shara had occupied as if to look beneath it. He climbed down off the stage and gazed under the piano and the chairs surrounding cabaret tables. The clean-up crew was wiping off tables and putting the chairs up on them. One young brother was running a vacuum cleaner. Forbes signaled the kid to turn it off, and then he asked him if any keys had been found.

Not that he knew of.

Forbes gave up and went outside. There he found the Renshaws packing cases into the van. "Hey, man, I thought you packed all that already."

"We did," Shara replied with some acrimony. "Now we are *un*-packing, shaking each case, listening for keys. Where's Quincy? Did he help you look around?"

"No, man, he left. He's got an early shift in the morning and had to rack out."

"I heard that," Shara assented. "I've got an early shift, too, and I'd like to get home."

"Yeah." Forbes looked at the sky overhead. It was a starless night, overcast and grey. The wind was carrying the clouds along, and as he stared into space, enjoying his buzz, a thin spot in the clouds allowed a full moon to peek through. That was sufficient to assist Forbes in losing concentration and forgetting the task at hand.

He thought of the young woman at the dry cleaner. Torino, he thought, was her name. Or is that the name of a car? Torindra? Tortilla? Tornado? He smiled to himself. He was coming down off his high, but not too fast. He glanced at his watch. It was a quarter after 12 already. He'd missed his date with Tornado. He recited expletives in his mind. The anger in him surged.

Shara, piling cases and machines back into her van, noted Forbes' lack of helpfulness. She pushed aside her anger and dissatisfaction, and mentally traced her steps across the course of the evening. She had spent most of it sitting at the sound board. She had set up her station on time. She had started the show on time. She had done three duets and two solos with Quincy and Cole. Forbes had been late . . .

Forbes had been late!

She had sent him to get dressed! The epiphany hit her abruptly.

"Forbes!" she exclaimed, voice raised. "Are the keys in your pocket?"

Forbes, jarred by her outburst, stuck his hands in his pockets. "Oh, yeah, man. I got 'em. Sorry."

Chapter 82

Tim went home from Tin Pan Sally's and fell into bed. The bed was empty and lonesome. He reached over to where his wife should have been and thought of her. He hoped she was sleeping well through the night. He saw her face in his mind's eye, smiling at him and laughing at one of his jokes.

He recalled a time several years ago when she climbed a step stool in the kitchen pantry at their house in Columbus. She shifted her weight awkwardly and the stool tipped forward and pinned her legs against one of the pantry shelves. She was trapped and couldn't move. She called his name, and hearing her from the basement, he raced upstairs to rescue her.

After he extracted her from the trap, he held her in his arms. Her shins were badly gashed and bleeding. He picked her up, carried her to a kitchen chair and applied bandages. Theresa cried more from embarrassment, he thought, than pain. As the sun shone through the kitchen window, it caught her strawberry blonde hair and danced off of it. She was beautiful, he remembered, even when she was a mess. Once the bandages were on, he kneeled between her legs, hugged her and kissed her face.

If God would just let him rescue her now . . .. If she would just be okay . . ..

Tim stared at the bedroom ceiling, sleep evading him. Out of nowhere, his earlier conversation with Shara Renshaw came back to him. She had encouraged him to pray, and he had admitted, but only to himself, that this situation warranted prayer if anything did.

But he couldn't make himself do it. It just wasn't in him. Was he mad at God? Certainly. Had he done anything to earn God's wrath? Probably. So, if anyone in this crisis is to blame, is it God, or is it himself? He didn't really care. He neither knew how to talk to God or had any interest in doing so. He just hoped God was above punishing Theresa. Quietly, he muttered, "Don't hurt Theresa, please. Leave her alone." He shut his eyes hard and fought back a jumble of emotions.

Chapter 83

Shara got up early on Sunday morning, even though she was skipping church again. She let Cole sleep in while she packed the van alone. This job at Christine's On The Green pleased her from the start. Having dealt with the resistance to digital music for years, she felt proud and gratified by the way Cole — who could sell the proverbial ice cubes to Eskimos — had convinced Christine Berthold to give him a chance.

The place looked classy when she visited it. She would take pictures of Cole performing, and maybe use the photos for publicity. She was, as yet, unfamiliar with the kind of crowd the place would draw. But as Shara had been collecting email addresses off of request slips from her audiences, she guessed that some who came to Christine's following Shara's email blast would be lovers of Cole's music. The venue itself was impressive, and Shara had a good feeling about this show. It was in a wealthier section of town, and quite often the tip jar would reflect the audiences' status. The contract for only one singer pleased Shara as well. She had yet to convince Cole that he didn't need the others, and every job without them added fuel to her fire. Forbes and Quincy were far more trouble than they were worth, she felt, owing to their laziness and fondness for being late and stoned.

It was regrettable, in some ways, that she was as fond of the two men as she was. They had provided more than a share of laughter and fun through the years she'd known them. Quincy, for example, had a huge, generous heart. He didn't have anything to give, but he gave generously of himself, his time, and his knowledge. Forbes clearly loved her husband, despite taking him for granted. The stories she had heard of their long friendship, adventures, and mischief were funny and engaging. Their closeness was palpable, she acknowledged, almost to a fault. She realized that if Cole ever stepped between Forbes and something Forbes wanted, he would hurt her husband without a moment's regret. Then he would assume forgiveness, and Cole would offer it. It's that way with friendships of long duration. It's that way with unconditional love.

A voice spoke in her head: "Forgive us our sins as we forgive those who sin against us." Well, okay. Cole was head and shoulders above her in that department. Still in all, those two singers could be a pill. As she considered her conflicted heart, she recalled a time last summer she was walking across a parking lot with her three men, coming from a job in a bar. She could see it in her mind's eye. Her sense of camaraderie and partnership with these three men warmed her like few other moments ever had. She told herself she is a member of the Cole Renshaw Trio, and that meant something in Terre Haute. It meant something to her, too.

Shara was interested in developing Cole's friendship with Tim Shelton. Not only did he provide excellent accompaniment on small jobs, he may well save her marketing career which was on thin ice owing to her frequent absences.

When Shara heard the shower running, she knew Cole was up. She set out to provide him a sturdy breakfast. Not too heavy, though, and not too rich. When he joined her in the kitchen, she confirmed that the van was already loaded.

"How do you feel this morning?" she asked her husband.

"Fine. Why?"

"Do you wanna go heavy on the Sinatra, or are you up for some of the tougher Sammy Davis songs?"

"I'm fine. I'll do both."

"We should leave early. Makes a better impression."

"There's no sense in leaving too early, Shara. There won't be anyone there until 9:30. I got there early the last time and had to wait."

"I'm just anxious."

"I know."

When the pair left the house, it was a little after 9. Cole, at the wheel, got onto the interstate to go east to the Ohio Boulevard area. When he exited the highway, onto a major artery, it was clear the couple was driving through a high-rent district. The charming older homes smelled from a distance of money. Shara fantasized momentarily about owning such a home someday, but she kept her thoughts to herself.

Two miles from the highway, Cole glanced in his rear view and noticed a police cruiser behind him flashing its lights. He pulled over and leaned against the steering wheel to retrieve his wallet from his back pocket.

"What'd you do?" his wife asked.

"No idea."

The officer was young. He wore a tightly trimmed mustache and impeccably trimmed blonde hair. His name tag said "Mueller."

"What's the trouble, officer?"

"Yes, sir," the officer said. "May I see your driver's license please?"

Cole, already holding his wallet, dug out the license and handed it over. He smiled at the officer, as disarming and genuine as he could manage. "What's the trouble, officer?" he repeated.

"When I ran your license plate through my computer, it didn't have your car registered or properly licensed."

"The car is licensed, officer," Shara put in. "The tags are up to date. Why did you put the plates through your computer when the tags are fine?"

"Ma'am, the computer said the car is not licensed. I'd like to search the back, if that's okay."

"Really, officer?" Shara continued. "We're on our way to a job, and the tags have a current date. I don't understand why you would put the license plate into your computer to start off with when the plates are up to date."

"What's the job?"

"I'm a singer, officer, and she and I are performing at Christine's On the Green for their Sunday brunch." Cole continued to smile as with a warmth that was starting to border on the ludicrous. His voice stayed friendly and non-threatening.

"Christine's doesn't have a brunch," Mueller commented suspiciously. "Wait right here. Don't exit the vehicle."

Mueller returned to his car and sat down next to Tiffany Pasternak. "Here, put this through." He handed Cole's driver's license to his partner.

"What are we doing this for?" Pasternak complained. "His plates aren't expired."

"That's what the passenger said."

"Why did you stop them?"

"They look suspicious."

"In what way? Because there's a little rust on the van?"

"It's not the color of the rust."

"Oh, I see." She glared at Mueller. "Were we not lectured at length about this kind of thing at the station a couple of weeks ago? Americans are far less tolerant of profiling than they once were, and that's all this is about. Is that your driver?" She pointed at the on-board computer monitor which displayed an image of Cole. The attached information confirmed that both the license and the car's plates were up to date. There were no outstanding warrants, and Cole Renshaw's criminal record was clean.

"Does this look like the hood to you?" Mueller demanded. "What's he doing here?"

"Did you ask him that? You have no reason to stop this man," Pasternak snapped.

Mueller returned her glare for a moment, then replied, "Yes I did. And he lied to me." He snatched the driver's license from her, got out of the car, and went back to the Renshaw's van.

"It appears that your license checks out," he told Cole. "But I would still like to have a look in the back. What is all that equipment?"

"As I said earlier," Cole said, still using his disarming smile, "I'm a singer, and that is music equipment I use to do live shows."

"Officer, I still want to know, of all the cars on this busy street, why you chose ours to put into your computer," Shara interrupted.

The young Mueller's face changed. Since the license had checked out, his bluff had been called. He looked caught, trapped. The clichéd "deer in headlights" metaphor came to Shara's mind.

"I told you that your vehicle's license did not appear to be in order in my computer the first time I put it through."

"I understand that, officer," Shara said too quietly. Her patience was thin. Her next words were spoken slowly, condescendingly, as if she were talking to a dim child: "Why did you put our license plate number into the computer *in the first place?* I mean, what is it, *specifically*, about my husband, *himself*, that inspired you to pull us over? I'd really like to know." Her perspicacity allowed no misinterpretation. Mueller had been nailed. His face showed at once anger and fear.

"Wait here," he said. He handed Cole his license and went back to the patrol car.

When he was out of earshot, Cole turned to his wife. "Shara, please. I want to get to this job and do it and get paid. Will you please *shut up?*"

"Cole, he pulled you over because you're black!"

"Of course he did. Let's just get through this so we can get going."

"You're not bothered by this?"

"I don't have time to be bothered."

"Cole!" Shara's outrage was complete. Her face flushed red, but as she thought the situation through, she chided herself. Cole had been black all his life. It occurred to her that this was not his first "driving while black" offense. It was new to her, and she wanted to take a stand against the unfairness, the injustice, the sheer rage she felt. But deep inside her was knowledge. This kind of treatment is commonplace to black folks in every city. She should trust her husband to handle it.

Cole, watching the patrol car in his rear view mirror, told her, "Here comes another one." He saw that the cop had a partner, a woman, and both were now approaching his car.

Mueller got to the window a step ahead of Pasternak. "Sir, I'd like you to unlock the hatch to this van so that we may examine your cargo — "

"That won't be necessary," Pasternak interrupted. "You folks are fine. You may be on your way. Have a great rest of your weekend." She tugged at Mueller's elbow as she returned to her patrol car.

As Cole pulled back out into traffic, Shara asked, "Did you recognize the other cop?"

"No. Should I have?"

"That was the cop who was at the hospital when we took Tim there after Theresa's accident."

"Really? You sure?"

Shara remained silent for several minutes until she reached over and squeezed Cole's hand. "I'm sorry," she said.

"For what?"

"Not trusting you."

Chapter 84

Tiffany was aware that in her fairly small Midwestern town, the culture inside a lot of police stations was less than progressive. She considered herself a member of a minority, albeit a different one from the Cole Renshaw that her partner had profiled.

She was impatient with the whole process, but may well be alone in her views within the department. Even her fellow cops who were black were as likely as Mueller to pull over someone on a bogus suspicion if their hue was off-putting. But you've got to go by something, she allowed, and this could be a dangerous job. It was a crap shoot.

Tiffany was alone in the world. No family to speak of, few friends, and a job she endured more than she liked. The sense of comradeship she should have enjoyed within the department had been ruined.

The last hookup was four years behind her, and had ended with a screaming fight. Her companion, Debbie, had been up half that night worrying that Tiff wouldn't come home alive. Tiff had stopped off at a bar that sold packaged liquor, stayed for one beer and a dart game, and headed on home. But it was a last straw for Debbie whose evenings were, more often than not, spent glued to the evening news watching for an officer-involved gunfight. Something on TV had spooked Debbie that night, so when Tiff came into the apartment, the screaming had started.

A neighbor placed the 911 call.

Tiff's colleagues had responded, and in a stroke of irony that made her laugh as well as cry, the domestic disturbance revealed the secret she had guarded about her preferences to the very colleagues she was guarding it from.

It was hard enough, she complained inside her head, to meet someone to love when she was different. But condoning the mistreatment of other folks who differed from white bread, "normal" middle America, well, that she would not do.

The loneliness stung, she admitted. She was blocked from the man-centric police department by her gender, her preference, and her refusal to join in the pejorative regard with which many colleagues viewed the black community. She took it on the chin, though, reminding herself of her strength. Her strength was all she had. That, and whiskey.

Chapter 85

To Forbes' relief, Tori Pappas forgave him for standing her up on the weekend, and enthusiastically agreed to see him for a drink. To Forbes, this was a date, and he prepared accordingly. Whether Ms. Pappas regarded it as such was yet to be determined. He hoped the years between them wouldn't matter. They did have music in common, he reasoned, and that could cover a multitude of sins.

He showered and shaved Sunday afternoon at 4, though he wasn't scheduled to get her until 6. When Cole arrived to bring Forbes his Tim Pan Sally's pay, it was not lost on him that the quantity of English Leather Forbes had applied was an overwrought cry for attention.

"Man, wow, I smelled you coming up the sidewalk. You got a date? Cause that much smelly-smelly isn't a seduction. It's more of an air-quality alert."

"Yeah, all right. You know all about it. Whether I've got a date or not is on you."

"How in blazes is it on me?"

"I want us to audition this woman, man. I think she'll be good, and we need a soprano, man. I keep telling you that."

"This again. Forbes, no one wants a soprano except you, and I keep getting the sense that you don't really want a soprano either, or the smaller paycheck it would bring. I think you just want . . . "

"What, man? What do I want, since you know so much?" The defensiveness was clear. Cole had edged too close.

Cole considered his friend for several seconds. The dynamics over the last 40 years of the relationship had become complex, had grown over time. Forbes was a lonely older man with a taste for young women, and as such, had put himself in a trick. Cole expected the solitude to continue until Forbes met someone he could love who was his own age. Plus, there was the competition over leadership in the music business. Forbes wanted to use the celebrity to get girls, but, truth be told, he had neither the leadership skills nor the salesmanship to run the business.

Shara resented the drug use of both Forbes and Quincy. It didn't seem to impact their performance, but because they were often stoned at gigs, neither Cole nor she trusted them lifting the heavy equipment. Thus, that doubled the work for the couple. Shara had once compared Cole's management of this singing group to climbing the Matterhorn using a clothesline with Forbes strapped to his back.

But Cole claimed he couldn't do it without Forbes. Forbes' ear for harmony, his versatility, his precision with his notes, and his ideas about vocal arrangements were something Cole found invaluable.

These musings flitted through Cole's mind. When he spoke, his words were borne of both his personal insecurities and his fear of losing a friend he had esteemed since he was an adolescent. "Forbes, man, I don't know what you want, and I *sure* don't understand why you seem hell-bent on making this music group as difficult for me as it can be. Can you give me a stinking break once, man?"

Forbes answered with a sweetness Cole regarded as both manipulative and grandiose. "Sure, man. No problem. Hey, thanks for running the cash by here. But, look, I'm gonna get going in a minute, so I'll see you later."

Chapter 86

Pasternak's tour Sunday had her getting off work at 8 in the evening. Okay, fine. The change in schedule on the weekends was part of the job, and she'd lose a little sleep with the short break between shifts, but she'd live. Her only qualm about the tour was her partnership with Phil Mueller. Mueller was a good cop, sure, but that incident with the black motorist — motorist — not suspect — had left a taste in Pasternak's mouth that she didn't appreciate.

As a cop, she wasn't supposed to be political. She was supposed to follow the policies and procedures mandated by her department, and the department wasn't supposed to be political either. But Pasternak was still a human. All of the drama in Baltimore, Chicago, St. Louis, Charleston, and the west coast in the last few years had changed her view a little. She was still a cop, and was very aware of the dangers attached to her job. She knew that every traffic stop a cop made could be her last, and that she never knew who was in a car before she approached it. It was a tense, dangerous job, and the last life partner she thought she'd ever have had left simply because the woman couldn't handle the thought that Tiffany might get herself dead one day by pulling over the wrong burned out taillight.

But this thing earlier with Mueller was the other extreme. There was *no* reason to hassle this man other than his race. It wasn't even close, Tiffany reasoned. There was no gray area in this traffic stop. Phil was just wrong.

She drove her squad car silently. Phil, just as uncomfortable as he doubtlessly battled his conscience, rattled on about fictional statistical probabilities of a crime in progress, a contraband payload, or some sort of malfeasance whenever a black is pulled over.

"'A black?'" Tiffany interrupted. "Don't you mean a black *person*?"

"Whatever."

Yep, she mused silently. This is going to be a long tour of duty. Mueller continued defensively making a fragile case for profiling, saying nothing that hadn't been said before, and Tiffany tuned him out.

Chapter 87

"Hey, baby, what you doing?" Sal hummed into the phone when Tori answered.

"Hey, Sal. I'm a little rushed. What's up?"

"I thought I'd bring over a pizza tonight and we could watch the fight."

"What?"

"The fight. Bull 'Pound-Pound' Esposito faces Bruno 'The Hammer' De Luca for the lightweight title in Vegas. It's on TNT. I told you about this."

Tori was still in the early stages of this love affair and was unwilling to reveal that she would prefer to snip off her big toe with a kitchen scissors than sit through a prize fight.

"Sal, I have plans tonight."

"What do you mean?"

"That guy I told you about, Forbes Wilson, the one who lives not far from me, invited me to sit in at a piano bar where he knows the musician. He's working on getting me a paying gig at the place. It's a good opportunity."

Silence.

Then, "Tori, this guy isn't going to get you paying jobs. He's after your pants. No one is going to get you singing jobs while you're so beautiful. They all want your pants."

"That is insulting and wrong. You don't know Forbes. He's older than my dad, and he sings with the Cole Renshaw Trio. There's no sex here, Sal. There's just a nice guy wanting to help me in music. What is the problem?"

"The problem is that you're going out with another man."

"I am physically going out of my house, yes, but this is a long way from a date. He's got 30 years on me!"

"Is he good looking?"

Tori had to think about that question. No, Forbes was not an attractive man, but at least his face was symmetrical, while Sal's had that nose thing going on. "He's got 30 years on me."

"Tori, you are my woman, and it's my job to protect you. I don't like this guy and I don't like you going out with him. I am coming over with a pizza, and I expect you to be there."

"Sal, you've just told me loud and clear that you don't believe in my singing career. That's really all I need to know. Enjoy your cold pizza on my front stoop." She disconnected.

If Tori Pappas had been a few years older and a tad less naïve, she might have seen through the fog to the man she was really dating. But instead, she was charmed by Sal's assertion that she was his woman. She liked that idea and myopically didn't see a problem with it. Admittedly, his lack of faith in her bothered her, but he hadn't heard her sing yet, really. He'd come around once he grasped that she has a gift. She'd make up with him tomorrow. Right now, she needed to find her red sequined top.

Chapter 88

Tim got to the hospital mid-day and got a surprise. Theresa was sitting up in a wheelchair. A nurse was pushing her down the hall with one hand while rolling the IV pole with the other. "Need some help?" he asked the nurse. He slid in next to her and took over pushing as the nurse followed, tugging the pole along.

"Where're we going?"

"The cafeteria," Theresa answered. Her voice was gravelly and weak, enervated by the ordeal and the weeks of intubation.

"You hungry?" Tim thought of the $3 and change in his pocket.

"No, huh uh," she croaked. "I just want to look at something different."

He leaned down to hear her inaudible response.

"I see." He then turned to the nurse and offered a smile to acknowledge her. The three rode the elevator and got out next to the cafeteria. The hallway was crowded with staff, and the ambient noise, Tim realized, would make hearing Treese even more difficult.

As they entered the dining area, Theresa pointed to a window on the far wall. Tim headed for it. When they arrived and Theresa could see the view of a few denuded trees and the parking lot, the nurse stepped around and locked the wheels on the chair. She told Tim she'd leave them alone and be back after a while to help push her back upstairs.

Tim seriously doubted that she would return at all, but he didn't care. He pulled a chair away from a table and sat next to his wife. She took his hand.

"How are you feeling today."

"I'm a little better. The pain is going down some. Dr. Baumgardner thinks the big problem now is getting a . . . "

"What, honey? I can hardly hear you?"

"I need to go to the bathroom."

"You need to go *right now*?"

"No. Not now. I need to go soon so they can see if the vol —"

"The volvulus surgery was effective. She told me the same thing. And I understand that the pain drugs are causing the problem, but you have to have them."

She nodded.

"Oh, hang on. Somebody's calling."

Tim took the cell phone out of his pocket. He didn't recognize the caller's number before he answered.

"This is Tim Shelton."

"Okay, good, Tim," a strange voice said. "This is Simon Seloff at the Terre Haute Convention Center. You helped out with my home and garden show Thanksgiving weekend, and I wanted to give you a call."

"Yes, Simon. Good to hear from you. What's going on?"

"Well, as you know, my sound engineer, Bob, passed, and I've got an opening for another show and don't have sound coverage. My main guy is taking off between Christmas and New Year's, and his back up just called me and said he's leaving town. Can I get you to sub for them, and while we're on that topic, I wonder if you have any interest in filling in permanently on a part-time basis?"

Tim's mind went in a hundred directions. "Uh, yeah, Bob, I have an interest. About how many hours a week do you mean for a part-time position?"

"That's what's hard about filling this job, Tim. I have no way to predict. We book shows and events sometimes years in advance, but if somebody wants to come in at the last minute and rent the facility, well, we're not turning down the money. Now I'm down a sound guy, and I'm under some pressure. I've got a convention of — you won't believe this — darts enthusiasts, and they want the center for December 26. Can I count on you?"

"Well, yeah, sure. Did you say darts enthusiasts?" Tim chuckled. "Happy to help. I can't believe there's such a thing as a convention for darts. You mean darts like you play in a bar?"

"Exactly. I can't believe it either." Simon snorted a laugh.

Tim and Simon worked out details of the hours and the specifics of the job while Theresa stared out the window. She gathered the gist of the conversation and was both pleased with the potential income, and concerned that Tim would be leaving her alone. But they needed the money. She nodded to herself.

When Tim disconnected, a nagging vague memory gnawed at him. Something had been said at some point about December 26. What was it? Oh, yeah. Cole had mentioned that these little hundred-dollar jobs they'd been doing together would abruptly end on December 26. What a co-inky-dink. What a stroke of luck. Almost weird.

Chapter 89

Forbes had given a ridiculous amount of thought and planning to his meeting with Tori Pappas. The woman was stunning, and it was incumbent on him to impress and seduce her. Not in a sexual way, no, not yet. He just wanted to make a huge impact on her because, God knows, guys probably hit on her all the time — guys with far, far more chops than he had at his age.

His beginning strategy would be to present himself and be very helpful with his guidance in music. He must be a perfect gentleman, a mentor, a friend, a man of extraordinary talents and abilities who could help her succeed in the field where he had, himself, garnered such great success. Then later, perhaps, there could be a more personal connection. After he had engendered trust, after he had worn the white hat a few times, only then he'd make a move.

Forbes turned a blind mental eye to the truth: that the lion's share of his musical success had been on the coattails of his best friend. He wouldn't mention Cole at this meeting. TMI. Plus, he'd go to the date straight. No need to reveal his fondness for bud. More TMI.

He borrowed his mother's car to pick Tori up. Driving his rusty cab with the missing door handle to her home in Terre Haute's nearby Italian Holy Rosary neighborhood would not be conducive.

"Thanks for picking me up at home, Forbes," Tori said as they stepped down off of her stoop. I can't take long, though. I've got a paper due tomorrow and I'm not quite ready to turn it in. I may have to ask for an extension."

"Oh, that's right. You're at the university. What's your major?"

She smiled. "My field of study is theater. But I'm doing my master's thesis on how physical disability influences musicality, with emphasis on Art Tatum and Chick Webb.

Forbes, not knowing what she was talking about, had to put on a face. "Oh, yes, he agreed. Art Tatum. He played . . . " He pretended to be grasping for a term.

"Piano," she filled in.

She realized that Forbes was lost and faking it. It was cute.

"Arguably the greatest pianist of the era," she continued. "And nearly completely blind," she added. "But one of my main interests is in singing jazz. I wonder what you have for me on that."

"Well, let's talk about that over dinner. How's that sound?"

"Whatever, Forbes. Hey, how'd you get a name like 'Forbes.'"

"I guess my mother thought if she named me after a magazine for rich people that it would help me get rich and successful."

"How's that working out?"

"That's what I'm trying to show you."

Forbes drove to a jazz club in the middle of town with a piano bar. It was the right setting, and he knew the owner. Forbes had two or three little places where he took ladies to sing.

"Hey, Price," he waved to the barkeep as he strolled in with the beautiful ingénue. "Do you have anyone playing tonight? I'd like to hear this young lady sing. This is Tori, she studies at the university, and wants to be a jazz artist. Can she sit in with anyone?"

Price drew a mug of Bud Lite and put it on the bar for Forbes. "What'll it be?" he asked the young woman.

Tori ordered a seven and seven and took a seat at the bar.

"Tom Bartolino is playing 8 to 11 tonight. You're too early," Price told them. He looked down at his hands and rolled his eyes. This was the third woman Forbes had brought in here in the last two months, and the old man's failure rate had become a source of amusement for all the musicians who play there.

"Not so," Forbes assured him. "We'll need dinner menus. What's the special tonight?"

After an hour, a dish of lobster ravioli, and a second cocktail, Tori had developed a sense of Forbes Wilson. He was certainly a nice man. Respectful, and smart, and he knew what he was talking about where local jazz is concerned. He knew most of the major venue holders, she grasped, and knew a lot about harmony. Perhaps she had been hasty, misinterpreting what she had thought was a cheesy come-on line. Maybe he did know things that could give her a leg up. Not knowing much about Art Tatum was not an indictment. He'd died, after all, in 1956, and a lot of music has happened since.

Forbes reminded her of her father. Both men were warm (when they wanted to be), stocky, not very tall, and pedantic. Certainly their nationalities were far different, and while Forbes was balding, Giovanni Pappas still had a full head of wavy black hair. But the two both listened to her well, considered her viewpoint, and offered guidance. Suddenly Tori felt that she could confide in Forbes.

When Tom Bartolino entered the place, he went directly to the piano and sat down. Tori noticed he had no paperwork with him; no charts. That impressed her. He plays by ear, she assumed, and plays from memory.

Forbes coaxed her to her feet and made introductions. Forbes explained his intent to help this young woman succeed in Terre Haute music, and Bartolino regretted coming to work.

How many young female singers does this make? Tom thought *This one, at least, was good looking. But he had seen several with Forbes, all young, and with varying degrees of talent. This need to bring in young-sters and use Tom to find out if they can sing — all of it smelled like desperation and Forbes' driving urge to make himself larger than he was.* Tom knew Forbes well. He knew Cole Renshaw, too, and knew Cole's vocal group had a good thing going. He didn't understand why Forbes was always trying to play one-upmanship. *Didn't matter*, Tom told himself. *Not my business.*

"What do you want to sing?" he asked the young woman.

"Anything by Adele."

"I'm not familiar," Tom stated with finality.

"Toni Braxton?"

"I thought you wanted to sing jazz," Forbes objected.

"I do. I just don't know, I mean, what jazz do you know?" Tori asked the pianist.

Bartolino set aside his pejorative regard for Forbes who had brought in yet another clueless newbie so he could hum on her all night. Tom hated being used like this, and hoped Forbes would be decent and leave a large bill in the tip jar.

Forbes, sensing Tori's insecurities, went first.

"Tom, give me a little Hoagy to get us started. Concert key."

Tom began a flowery opening riff, and when Forbes took the mic from the piano and began singing "Stardust," Tori's eyes grew wide with wonder.

"Wow, I knew you were good, but I had no idea . . ." she announced at the song's conclusion.

"Now, you," Forbes told her, handing over the mic. He noticed the girl still looked bewildered and indecisive. He glanced at Tom, asking for help.

Tom began playing "My Funny Valentine," hitting the melody well to guide the young woman. He picked the tempo up, and added some jazz riffs.

Tori listened to it all the way through before raising the mic to her lips to begin.

The young woman had a nice voice. It wasn't a lightning strike, and Forbes noted plenty of rookie mistakes — but that's what he wanted. He reveled in the guidance and advice he would offer to fix those bad habits.

Her breathing was way off, for one thing. She gulped air in the middle of a phrase instead of at its beginning. She rushed the end of her phrases so as to jump to the next phrase, thus, not really completing the first phrase. This is easy stuff to fix, Forbes recognized, *and this young woman could be a great find.*

Forbes was looking at the big picture, he told himself. He would get her included in the Cole Renshaw Trio, soon to be the Cole Renshaw Quartet, and then he would begin the task of convincing Cole and Shara that Quincy wasn't really necessary. He would exemplify Quincy's practice of being stoned all the time, didn't help out, and showed up late. Most importantly, he would play up how a soprano is better than a baritone. Eventually, Quincy, Forbes' friend of many years, could be pushed out and the group would return to being a trio. And if not, well, by then, Forbes would be ready to take her away and form a duo, just him and her. The "just him and her" part set well with Forbes. As he thought of it, his mouth filled with saliva, and his conscience became a small whisper.

Tori sang "All Right, Okay, You Win," and Jobim's "Quiet Nights of Quiet Stars" before she complained that it was time to go home.

The patrons offered mild applause, as the two went back to their table and put on their coats. Forbes was careful to help Tori on with hers, as a gentleman would, and as he guided her to the door, his hand in the small of her back, he glanced back over his shoulder and threw a thankful look at Tom.

Tom, Forbes noticed, had his lip curled up in a scowl with no attempt made to conceal it.

Crap! "Hold on just a sec," he said to Tori. He turned back and stuffed a twenty in the tip jar, melting Tom's scowl.

"Do you ever sing karaoke?" he asked Tori as they reached the door.

"No, I haven't. Should I?"

"Oh, yeah. Tuesday night is karaoke night at this little place south of town. I'll pick you up around 7 and we'll head down there. But I gotta tell you ahead of time: you won't win the karaoke contest."

"Oh, really. I'm not strong enough to win in a bar?" She was indignant, just as Forbes intended.

"No, that's not it. The winner of a karaoke contest in a bar isn't the best singer. It's the singer who sells the most beer. Usually it's someone with a horrible voice, but who brought all the friends in the world to get stupid and cheer. But it's great practice to compete. *And*, they'll probably have a karaoke track on every Adele song ever recorded." He smiled at her gently. "Seven okay with you?"

"Well, I had something planned that night. But I'll change it."

"What'd you have planned?"

"A concert. With my boyfriend."

"Oh, I didn't realize you had a boyfriend. I think you should go with him. We can do karaoke another night. Does he, uh, know about me?"

"Sure. I told him all about you."

"Is he okay with, uh, everything?"

"What everything, Forbes? He wants me to succeed in music, and so do you, right?"

"Well, you know, not all guys take kindly to other men hanging out with their women."

"Well, right, he is kind of the jealous type. But I explained all about you and how much, um, how experienced you are, and he was fine."

"Experienced in what way?"

"In music. What other way would there be? Anyway, Sal works a lot of evenings. He owns a pawn shop in midtown. So when he gets a night off and schedules something, I'd like to go with him. So let's do karaoke the following Tuesday, okay?"

"Okay, I'll hold you to that," he grinned. But his heart felt a blow. This wouldn't be as easy as he had hoped.

Chapter 90

Tori was scheduled to open the dry cleaner at nine, but she had agreed to have a very early breakfast with Sal. She might be a few minutes late getting the door open and the cash register readied, but it was Christmas, and her boss was out of town.

She expected the two would drive through a fast food place, get egg sandwiches, and call it a morning, but Sal would have none of that. He made grandiose promises about a brunch in midtown that served prime rib and mimosas for the holiday. He could really be a sweetie, she thought, always going the extra mile. They had gotten up at 6 after very early morning lovemaking. While dozing before the alarm, Tori heard Salvadore suddenly say, "I think I should move in here with you."

"Why would you do that when your place is so much nicer than mine?"

"Then, you move in with me?"

"Why, Sal? We're fine the way we are. What's the rush?"

"I need to keep you safe."

"Safe from what? Nothing is threatening me."

"Threats are only threats when you don't see them coming."

"What do *you* see coming at me?"

"Tori." Sal had rolled onto his back and was examining the ceiling fan overhead. "I want you to stop seeing Forbes. I mean, at all."

"I will not!" Tori sat up in bed and swung her legs over the side. "Forbes says I could be the next Whitney Houston. He believes in me, and if you want me to stop seeing him, that just proves that you don't!"

"I do, baby, but this cat you're fooling with can't be trusted." Sal got up and walked around to her side of the bed. He scooped her up in his arms and carried her into the bathroom.

She clung to his neck. "What are you doing?"

"Look there," he commanded, turning her toward the mirror in the medicine chest. "Do you see that? The most beautiful woman in the world, and any man would want to be with you. This cab driver you're fooling with is no exception. Drop him before he starts something he can't finish."

"Like what?"

"Like forcing your boyfriend to step in."

Tori wiggled her legs until he set her down on her feet. Sal pressed his hands on her bare shoulders and faced her toward the mirror, looking over her shoulder at her slender, perfect, naked body. "Any man would want you, Tori. All men do, even old, ugly cab drivers who dream about you while they wet their sheets. But you're *mine!*" The last was blurted with such ferocity that Tori jumped, startled.

She stared at him for several seconds, unsure whether to be flattered or alarmed, seduced as much by the danger as the flattery. Then she reached into the tub, turned on the shower water, and stepped in. "Coming?" was all she said.

Chapter 91

"Shara, I just can't. I don't have the range. I don't have the ear. That song is impossible for me." Cole was appealing to Shara to not force him to learn Andrew Lloyd Weber's "Music of the Night."

"I think you do. I know it's got some jumps, but if you would just practice it, I think you can push your range. Look, when we started this music company, you didn't have much range, but your voice box is a muscle. You work it and you strengthen it. You're the one who taught me that. Believe in yourself!" Shara's winning smile, designed to seduce Cole, provoked a smile in return.

Cole's repeated objections to the song grew weaker and weaker as Shara put the music into the cdg player and keyed it lower for her husband's baritone. She handed him a microphone.

"Just try it." The couple was in their living room where the cdg rested when not in use at a job. The cat reclined on the sofa, curling and uncurling his tail, but not in time with the music. He watched the couple with a feline's signature disinterest.

"See, there? Even your cat doesn't think I can do this. Look Shara, if we develop this song at all, Forbes should sing it. He's much closer to a tenor than I am. The song is traditionally done by a tenor."

"Never once in the history of this trio has anyone ever cared what register a song was originally recorded in. This is why we have a pitch changer. Why are we discussing this? Sing the song."

"You're cute when you're bossy."

"I happen to know that I am not."

"Shara, why are you pressing me to learn this song? I mean, why are you *really* pressing me?"

Shara's head fell forward as she gazed at the carpet. Her shoulders slouched in a posture of defeat — almost as if to say, "Okay, fine, you caught me."

"I'll tell you, but please *hear* me, Cole. You're not going to like this."

They gazed at each other for a moment while Shara collected her thoughts.

"I talked to Quincy yesterday. He told me Forbes found his soprano. He's going to bring her in and use you and our equipment to train her. Then he plans to force Quincy out, and, when that doesn't work, he'll take her and leave to form a duo."

"Really." Cole intoned. "What will he use for instrumentation? Where will he get bookings? He can't sell water in a drought."

"I don't think I said he would succeed. Dollars to donuts this is far more about Forbes getting his rocks off than anything. He told Quince the girl is hot."

"By 'girl' I take it he meant 'girl.'"

"Yeah, she's very young and pretty."

"He'll get his heart broken."

Cole considered his wife. "So, answer the question. What does Forbes have to do with me learning this song?"

"You don't have to learn it, honey. I just want you to embrace the fact that you may have to let Forbes go."

Cole embraced what she was telling him. A fear rushed him. "I can't do this without Forbes."

"So you've said a hundred times. I want you to see that you can. If he takes off, you won't have a choice. Two-part harmony will have to do."

"It will change the music without him."

"Yes."

"Start the song again."

Chapter 92

The discomfort was becoming unendurable. Barbara Baxter had poured through class schedules and curricula from other music teachers at the university, and as she did, it became clear that she didn't belong.

Most of her fellow professors had written their theses based on beliefs she did not share. One of them had even had the gall to write a thesis on the value of country music in shaping the popular culture. *Oh, yeah,* she thought. *That's great. Let's meld into our culture a love of pickup trucks, Confederate flags, and beer-guzzling. That's the contribution.*

She knew going in that this was a secular campus. That's okay. She wasn't inclined to force her very conservative fundamentalist beliefs on others. But at the same time, did she belong in a department that offered more courses on Wagner than Bach? She didn't think so.

She would have to get out of it. She didn't want the job. And to make matters much more difficult, George Winter, the affable music director at her new church, was leaving to follow his wife to a great job in Silicon Valley. His job would be open soon, and she would love it more than life, but she feared upsetting her father.

She thought about it a lot. She was qualified to direct the choir to unparalleled levels. One soprano, an 84-year-old from the old school, could nail a high C and make it possible for Barb to perform a soaring composition of her own based on a Bach piece she loved.

But how would she present her wishes to her dad who had, let's admit, put himself out quite a lot to get her the one she had.

This was so aggravating. Barb stewed on this the week before Christmas. She now felt, after much rumination, that she was being called, by God of all people, to take the job at the church. It paid less, but she would be deliriously happy in it. She considered the Bible which admonished her to "be not conformed to this world but be transformed by the renewing of her mind."

Well, certainly, working at this university would be regarded as being conformed to this world. Being in church, instead, would be tantamount to "renewing her mind." That was all there was to it, then, she reasoned. She would have to quit the job. The tough part would be telling her father what her plans were.

It was almost Christmas week, and she didn't want to hurt him. She would look for just the right moment to break the news. There it was, her decision. No further class preparation was warranted for a job she was giving up.

She left work early and went to the mall.

Chapter 93

When Tori went inside her house after leaving Forbes, she fully intended to concentrate on her paper. But with the option in mind of asking for an extension — which she had never done before — she called Sal instead.

"Yeah, babe, I've been calling you," were his first words when he answered. "Where you been so late?" His second-generation Italian accent amused her. His own parents, of whom she was fond, had just about let their accents morph into a Midwestern twang, but Salvador Romano had adopted his, practiced it, and deployed it for charming women and for interacting with the first- and second-generation customers who came to him from the neighborhood for short-term loans.

"I told you I was going out with that guy, Forbes, who's a singer and wants to help me with my voice."

"Oh, yeah, right. Where'd you go?"

"Oh, we had dinner and drinks at a piano bar and he got me a chance to sing."

"Dinner and drinks? He didn't touch you, did he?"

"He was a gentleman. And Sal, he's my dad's age. Take a pill." Even as she spoke, she remembered Forbes's touch on her waist as she had headed toward the door. It was sort of personal, she recalled. But it meant nothing, she was sure.

"Don't be tellin' me to take a pill," Sal objected. "You still don't know how beautiful you are. Any man would be after you. All men would be."

"Sal, it's sweet that you're so possessive. I'm charmed and flattered. I am. But you have got to understand that I think working with Forbes is my best chance for succeeding in music. You've got to let me do this and don't be so . . . driven . . . to separate me from my best chance. Don't be so jealous."

"It's not so much jealousy, and even if it were, don't I have a right?"

"We've been going out three weeks. Give me some space."

"Space to do what? Cheat on me?"

"Sal, no. Jesus. This is about business. Why can't you understand that?"

"Because I'm a man and I know how men think. This isn't right. He touched you, didn't he?"'

"There was no sexual contact."

"What kind of contact was there?"

Tori was silent, thinking of the touch Forbes had made to her waist. No, she shook it off. That was nothing. Or was it? Sal's assurances that Forbes was after her body weighed on her. What did she really believe about Forbes? She couldn't be sure.

"I'm going to look out for you," Sal promised.

Chapter 94

As soon as she heard that Theresa was up and about, so to speak, Shara Renshaw showed up at the hospital to pay her friend a visit. She took along a small, pink teddy bear that presented with its plush velour arms wrapped around a tiny flower pot full of violets. She came into Theresa's telemetry room and found Theresa enjoying an unappetizing lunch of processed turkey, frozen peas and instant mashed potatoes.

Shara spoke first, observing the meal. "Well, the first thing I'm going to bring you is a decent meal. How do you feel about a fish filet sandwich from McDonalds and some large fries?"

"Not as good as I feel about a Burger King Whopper with extra mayonnaise and a side order of onion rings with catchup," Theresa replied.

"Done. Anything else? Clean panties? Listerine? A bottle of Pinot Grigio?

Theresa laughed, and the laugh sounded good to Shara. For a moment, Theresa's personality was back. It was a cause to celebrate. "Seriously, what can I bring you? And when are they letting you out of here?"

"Oh, Shara, don't rush the drama. Really. I've got months ahead of me of rehab and recovery. This was a bad thing. I'll be stuck here through Christmas and a long time after that. But your optimism is a nice thing to have."

"I see," Shara said soberly. "If all of that is the case, then I submit this idea for your approval. We'll have Christmas dinner here. You, me, Tim and Cole and whoever else you want to invite. I'll bring in the food, and we'll have a real meal right here in your room, and it will be the best we can do for a Christmas in a place like this."

Theresa, stunned, was filled with raging, complex thoughts. She never thought she would spend this holiday in a hospital hundreds of miles from her real home with people she regarded as little more than strangers, and an ordeal in front of her capable of taking all hope out of her. This offer was an act of kindness she could never repay. She kept piling up debts to Shara, and for once, she was willing to accept the kindness. The circumstances were such that the balance sheet was skewed.

To make it worse, Shara seemed to suddenly have something come to her. "Oh, I forgot to tell you. I have a message. That guy I know from my job who works in the legal department just got an opening. A secretary quit, and you are now on the short list to take the job. It pays a good salary, Theresa, with full medical, dental, vision, and a nice vacation. Full bennies for Tim, too."

Theresa stared at her, miserable. This could have been a dream job. It could have been the answer to her direst hope. It could have been a reservoir in a parched desert. This was so depressing.

"Shara, I just told you this. It will be months before I can work. I would love to take the job, but I can't. I am simply too messed up right now." The tears welled up before she could stop them. She looked at her lap and blinked quick to diffuse and hide them from Shara.

"I know, Theresa. I was just telling you because, I guess, I wanted you to know that you are *not* unemployable. You have terrific value to employers, but we have to get your health squared away."

"Really? This was helping?" Theresa's voice started to tense. A seed of anger was sprouting in her mind. She had been through the mill, and the physical and emotional pain had been extraordinary. Now here was this so-called friend making it much worse. "Shara, thank you, I guess, for *trying* to help. But, honestly, this help is not helpful. I wish you'd never told me about the job. And while we're at it, my friend, since you're so religious and such a fan of Jesus Christ, would you mind telling me just what in the hell he *wants* from me." Theresa's voice was raspy and hollow, but the anger in it was clear to the other woman.

"I'm not good at reading His mind," Shara confessed, "but if I had to guess, I'd say He wants your attention." Shara tried valiantly to use hushed tones. No good would come of upsetting Theresa further.

"Yeah, right," Theresa spat. "Doesn't he know that I am *too poor* to pay attention? People like you irk me. You really do."

"I irk you?"

"Sure. It's all about praise, honor and glory to Jesus Christ who has not done one stinking thing. I've lost everything I ever had except Tim, and Jesus Christ wants to be thanked. I'll take a rain check."

"Oh, Theresa," the other woman lamented, "I had no idea you felt this way. I don't see your situation like this at all. You lost your jobs and your home, but you had friends to reach out to. What I see is God's mercy in spite of your rage."

"I have every right and reason to be enraged, Shara. I didn't do anything to deserve this."

"Theresa, none of us deserves anything. God is holy, and we're not. But He loves us enough to take on a cross for us so that He can forgive us, free, for the asking. We have everything to thank Him for. He didn't have to do jack."

"In my view, he didn't do jack. I'm done talking." Theresa took her call button and pressed it to get a nurse. "I'm going to use the toilet. Thanks for the violets. Let yourself out."

Chapter 95

"Well, the good news," Tim explained to Cole over the phone the next morning, "is that Theresa had a bowel movement. We've been waiting for this since the surgery and it's a big deal because the drugs she's on tend to clog the drain."

"Okay. Great. What's the bad news?"

"The bad news is that she got furious with your wife in the process."

There was silence on the phone. Tim paced his tiny apartment twice waiting for his friend to absorb the information and respond.

Finally, "I don't know what to say."

"I don't think I'd know what to say if I were you, either. I hope they can work it out, but honestly, and I hesitate to say this, Theresa has always been a little. . . well, . . . uncomfortable with Shara." Tim mentally cringed as he spoke the words.

"Can you explain this to me?" Cole's voice was subdued, atonal.

"I'm going to try. See, you've never met the real Theresa. All that she's been through — all that I've put her through — has changed her. She was happy, positive, and strong. And it wasn't that long ago. But when everything goes wrong, when every single thing that happens is bad . . . and it's stayed bad for a long while . . . Theresa's lost her faith."

"Okay, and what has that to do with Shara?"

"Theresa finds it . . . ludicrous . . . that Shara . . . "

"Is a Christian?"

"Exactly," Tim said with some relief.

"I guess I understand. I'm sure she feels a little picked-on after all that's gone on in your lives lately. I don't know everything that's happened to you; I wasn't there. But I am absolutely confident that God loves you both, and there's a reason for all of it."

"Okay, see, now I find that ludicrous, too."

"Do you, Tim? I'm not sure why. In the few weeks I've known you, and stuff has gone wrong big time, every little disaster has been answered by some unexpected provision to keep you going. You lost your home, but you met Quincy and his sister. Theresa had this horrible accident, but the driver was found and her insurance was made available. Theresa had a life-destroying illness, and it would not have been treated in time, or paid for, if she hadn't been in that wreck. You needed a car, and the insurance settlement got you a car and a little leftover cash. You got the food stamps, you and I earned you a little folding money, and Theresa is going to be all right. Every step of the way, someone has been looking around the corners for you."

"But why the drama, Cole? What was the point of letting all of this happen to us to begin with?"

"Oh, I can't answer that. I'm just guessing, but it looks to me like someone is trying to get your attention and is banging around pretty loudly."

This time the phone went silent on Cole's end. Tim was thinking of the metaphor he had always shared with Treese about being a trapeze artist. It hadn't really occurred to him that it wasn't an accident all the times the swinging trapeze had shown up.

"You there, man?" Cole asked after several seconds.

"Yeah. Here. Hey I didn't tell you my news. I got a job offer."

"You did, man? Really? What's the job?"

"Working for Simon Seloff at the convention center. They need a replacement for the guy who died."

"Hey, that's great."

"You made me think of it because it starts right after Christmas."

"How'd I make you think of it?"

"Cause you told me the music jobs with you would end on December twenty-sixth."

"Oh. So, I did."

Chapter 96

Shara cried for an hour in bed when she learned that her friend, Theresa, was upset at her because of her religion. Cole had broken it to her as gently as he knew how, all the while anticipating the storm that would follow.

"I think the problem is her, not you. She's the one who's mad at God, and you caught the flak,"

"Or else I did wrong. I know she's angry and I know why. But if I wasn't kind enough or if I was too pushy or if I set her off in some kind of way, then it's not the message I wanted to send. It's not the God of love that I mean to represent." Shara sobbed. "I'm going to the hospital." She got up, washed her face and grabbed her car keys.

When she reached the hospital, she stood at the elevators for several minutes watching them open and close three times while picking up and depositing passengers. Shara mentally rehearsed what she would say to Theresa, and nothing sounded right in her head. While she considered turning around and heading home, the elevator door opened again and there stood Tim preparing to push Theresa's wheelchair into the lobby. All three, startled and ill at ease, nodded greetings as the wheelchair moved forward.

Shara took hold of her nerves. "Where are you two headed?"

Theresa looked away and gazed at the floor as if it was fascinating. Tim answered. "To the cafeteria. It has a gorgeous view of the parking lot. Want to come?"

"Yeah. I do."

Shara followed the couple down the corridor, still grappling within herself for what to say. She sat down in a chair next to Theresa while Tim went off to buy a cup of coffee and a sweet roll for himself and his wife. The two women sat in silence until Shara opened her mouth to speak. At the precise moment, Theresa spoke, cutting her off. "I'm sorry for my behavior. I'd like to blame the pain, but the truth is, it was my fault. I'm just so upset about things and I — "

"Hey, let's talk some more about doing Christmas at your place."

"What?"

"Christmas. It's Friday. We talked about this."

"I'll be here."

"Obviously. We'll bring in some food and some wine if you want."

"Wine sounds good," Theresa smiled weakly. "I'll be off morphine, and all I'll get is Tylenol."

"What? You're getting off narcotics? How is that good?"

"The narcotics are constipating me, and the docs want my bowels to move because a piece of my intestine was taken out."

"So, it was a perfect storm of pain inducement."

"Exactly."

"I'll even bring a tree and we can trim it in your room, Shara resumed. "It'll be great. We'll call it 'non-traditional.' Tim can bring his piano and we'll sing carols and open gifts."

"I obviously won't be giving gifts," Theresa stated.

"You are certainly able to give me a gift, and here is what I want: I want you to talk to me about your anger and your feelings about the God Who is love. You can be honest and not spare my feelings, and let me see if I can help you get past this."

"Get past what? There's nothing to get past. I am healing, slowly, and I'll forgive God in time."

"*You'll* forgive *God*?" Shara was appalled. She stared slack-jawed for a moment before recovering`. "Theresa, what do you have to do to get to heaven?"

A bewildered expression flashed across Theresa's face. "Die, I guess."

Shara chuckled. "I mean, what do you have to do to be worthy of heaven?"

"Be good. Be better than I am right now, but I'll improve."

"You won't improve enough. You can't. To be worthy of heaven, you have to be absolutely as perfectly holy and pure as God is. You have to do that from birth to death, and you can't slip up even once."

"Then nobody gets in. That's ridiculous."

"It's not ridiculous. It's how it is, but there's more to it. Jesus died and resurrected so that you and I can be forgiven. The way to get eternal life is to trust Him. That's what He asks."

Theresa stared out the window at the parking lot. After several seconds of watching a black Nissan park, she admitted, "I guess I don't think he's very trustworthy right now."

Tim appeared with a blue plastic tray bearing two coffees and two cheese Danish rolls. He set the tray down and set one of each in front of his wife. "What're you all talking about?"

"Trust," Shara answered quickly. "And trustworthiness. Tim, have you ever thought that everything that's gone wrong in your life might be Someone trying to communicate?"

"I've been thinking about that a lot," he answered, "since Cole brought it up a couple of days ago. It's occurring to me that in our old lives — when we were stable and happy and in our own home and had futures and careers and money — we may have been too comfortable to listen to God. Shara, I'm so rude. Can I get you coffee or anything?"

"Tim, I'm not hungry, but thanks. You're kind. I'm leaning toward agreeing with you. The God Who made the universe is very creative. He has lots of ways of getting to us, but it's up to us to listen. A lot of the world's ills would go away if we would trust Him.

"I was suggesting to Theresa that I pile the gang into my car and bring Christmas dinner to the hospital. What think?"

Instead of answering, he turned to his wife. "What do you think? Are you up for that? We have a lot of blessings to count this Christmas. Are you strong enough for a Christmas party?"

"Name a blessing, Tim. Name one," Theresa spat.

"Here's a whopper: I still have my wife, the love of my life, my partner and best friend. I could have lost her, but I didn't, and I'm thankful."

"Here's another one, Theresa," Shara interjected. "God loves you enough to put Himself on the hook for your mistakes, forgive you, and give you forever, if you want it."

Theresa stared at the two for a moment, lip curled in a scowl, and then took a small bite out of her Danish.

Chapter 97

"Oh, Cole, I've been meaning to ask you something." Shara opened her eyes in the morning and rolled over. "What ever happened with Allen Parker?"

"Who is Allen Parker?" Cole asked drowsily.

"Isn't that the name of the guy at The Dark and Stormy Nightclub? You were going to meet with him weeks ago and I forgot about it till now. What did he say?"

"He was a pretty hard sell, Shara. Bound and determined to avoid the digital music."

"I remember when we went in there, and I saw a gorgeous piano. Maybe we should try again with you and Tim."

"Hmm. Maybe we should if I didn't leave too awful an impression."

"What was wrong with your impression?"

Cole's eyes opened suddenly as he remembered the odd circumstances behind his failed sales call. The question appeared in his mind. Should he lie to Shara about this? Honesty is the best policy, but Shara's temperament changed whenever Cole's mother was involved.

He took a deep breath. "Well, I never made it over to see him when I had an appointment, so he let me know when I called to cancel that he wasn't interested anyway."

"Why didn't you make it over?"

"I knew you were going to ask me that."

"You also know that I want the answer."

Cole told the tale of what happened when he and Forbes had visited Mom to change her lock and she had concealed his keys by sitting on them.

At the conclusion of the narrative, Shara stretched, rolled over again, and muttered, "You know what I think about that. I'm not even going to say it."

Chapter 98

Quincy wasn't due at work until six in the evening, and was at Marietta's to prepare for painting an apartment. He wore overalls — the most ignominious garment he had. What dignified black man would go out in public? But Etta gave him the pants for painting, so he wore them. She had fixed him a fine beef stew and had warmed some soft, yeasty dinner rolls. After the meal, she took his dishes and helped him in the garage by receiving paint cans he handed down to her from the step stool.

"I'll ride over there with you so I can clean the bathroom and kitchen while you paint," she offered.

"I really wish you wouldn't."

"Why don't you want me to come? You got a girl over there?" The quickness of her temper startled him.

"How would *I* have a girl at one of *your* vacant apartments? I don't want you there because the fumes give you a migraine and I don't want to be hearing you fuss all day about it. Stay home. I got this."

"Thanks, baby brother," she softened. "All I've got is you to help me. I hope you know I'm thankful."

"Yes, ma'am. We got us. Always will. Hand me one or two of those stirring sticks right there. Hold up. My phone's going off."

Forbes was talking before the phone even reached Quincy's ear.

"Hey, man, what's happening?"

"Ah, it's all good," Forbes answered. He sounded elated. The underlying excitement was something Quincy hadn't heard from his friend for a long while. "Hey, this girl, Tori, I told you about, man, she's the real deal. Sounds like an angel."

"Really." Quincy attempted to conceal his skepticism. "How old did you tell me she is?"

"I don't know. Twenty-three, I think. She's in college anyway. Getting some kind of theater degree. She's for real, man. I need you to hear her."

"Ah, sure, okay. Where's she playing?"

"Nowhere, man, I haven't gotten us any gigs yet. I just want you to hear her."

"How'm I gonna do that if she's not playing anywhere. At your crib?"

"Not a bad idea. I'll see what I can set up."

"What are you gonna use for music?"

"I'll get Cole to burn a cd off the system. What are you doing tomorrow?"

"Working."

"Okay. What are you doing right now?"

"Painting for Etta. Want to come help me?"

"Not at all. But thanks for the offer." Forbes' tone continued to surprise Quincy. Even being sarcastic, the humor, the lightness in his voice was a cool drink of water.

"What about tomorrow night?" Forbes continued. "Can I set something up for then at my place."

"Tomorrow night's Christmas Eve, man. You wanna louse up the girl's holiday?"

"I'm asking' her for a half-hour meeting with you and Cole. Ain't no thing."

"Fine. But just know goin' in that I'm not real rushed to get a new singer. The piece of the pie I get now is too small. I don't need a trio to be a quartet. It's really a quartet becoming a quintet, 'cause Shara gets paid, too."

"No sweat, Quince. If this works out the way I want, you and Cole can be a duo and Tori and I will be a different duo."

"You said that before, Forbes, but I can't believe you. You'd leave Cole in the lurch like that?"

"What lurch? He'd still have you."

"You know he counts on your ear. You know he depends on your vocal arrangements. He doesn't want to do music unless you do it with him."

"Things change."

"Forbes, man, if this is all about liking this girl, then —"

"No. It's about the music. It's just about the music, that's all."

Chapter 99

"I realize tomorrow is Christmas Eve. I'm just asking for this one small favor. Three songs, that's all I need." Forbes was on the phone with Cole and the topic had turned to Tori Pappas. "If you can drop them off here around 6:30 or 7:00, you can then take Shara to Christmas Eve dinner and I'll leave you alone. Quincy's coming to hear her, and you can, too, but I don't want to interrupt your Christmas." He said the last with unveiled sarcasm which was not lost on Cole. He ignored Forbes' tone and answered directly.

"All right. Which three songs and in what keys? We'll stop by at 6:30 and drop off a disc. I'm not sure what you're doing this for. We're not looking to get a fourth singer."

"I told you before. I'm developing this soprano. If it works out, we'll start our own thing. I'll still sing with the trio until I have enough work to go on."

"You will?"

"Sure man, no problem." The truth was that Forbes intended to keep his musical life compartmentalized and to keep Quincy and

Cole far from Tori. He wanted the young woman to himself without the competition. But, just as much, he wanted their faces rubbed in his new discovery.

"I'll hold you to that," Cole said. "What three songs?"

"'What a Little Moonlight Can Do' — the Nancy Wilson arrangement, 'My Funny Valentine' — the Julie London, and 'I Will Always Love You' — the Whitney arrangement, not the Dolly Parton one."

"Gotcha. Concert key?"

"Better keep the Whitney one keyed down a half step or so. It takes a range."

"Right. I'll bring a cd with me. It won't have graphics, though."

"Thanks, man. See you then."

"Oh, hey, snow is forecast. We'll leave early in case."

"Really? I didn't see the news."

"Predicting two to four."

"Inches or feet?"

"Ha! Inches, I hope."

Cole disconnected the call feeling relieved, but also gratified. Forbes, his friend of many years, was an outstanding baritone and had some chops in the tenor range. He had a great flair and was a consummate showman, but he had his vulnerabilities.

A few years before, Cole recalled, another soprano whom Forbes had been "developing" was rehearsing in Cole's living room, and she couldn't hear her note. She was attempting Linda Ronstadt's part on "Don't Know Much," but the lyric soprano note defied her. Many attempts were made, but the girl, whose name Cole couldn't call anymore, kept missing it. Cole knew it was a hard note to reach, but the woman wasn't helping herself with her own ear.

Forbes, as Cole remembered, was singing Aaron Neville's part of the duet. He stopped singing and looked at her as if sizing her up. Cole's surprise was complete when Forbes demonstrated for her, "Look at these dreams, so beaten and so battered . . " while nailing that lyric soprano riff dead center, on Ronstadt's note — a stretch for most good sopranos, let alone a tenor-baritone.

Years had passed since that failed soprano, but Cole still marveled at Forbes' display of power and range. Surely those attributes, combined with Forbes' ear for harmony, were second to none.

But Forbes couldn't sell a lifebuoy to a drowning man.

Cole had often remarked to those who cared that the music was a small part of his job as manager. The hard part was getting gigs, and that took salesmanship. Sure, he was confident that his singing group was a great product, and club owners should buy it. But a great product is not all there is to selling. It takes a knack. Forbes, as a salesman, was a great cab driver, and it was foolish for him to think he could run off with a soprano, even a good one, and have the success that Cole brought to The Cole Renshaw Trio.

The truth settled in on Cole. He didn't want to do the music without Forbes. But Forbes *couldn't* do it without Cole. Forbes hadn't learned that yet, but it seemed to Cole that he, himself, had. Shara had been banging this drum for years, that he could succeed without Forbes, or even Quincy. Perhaps she was right.

Even so, a huge part of Cole didn't want her to be right.

Chapter 100

Sal Romano opened his pawn shop at eight in the morning. His belly was full after his breakfast with Tori, and she was on his mind.

Like any retailer, he anticipated a last-minute crowd of shoppers to put his fiscal year squarely in the black. One nagging concern was the snow coming in from the northwest, and how that might slow Christmas Eve sales. One could argue that a white Christmas is always lovely, but for those in retail, a black Christmas is preferred. As black as possible. He enjoyed his job. He made it a point to deal fairly with customers, giving them the best return he could afford on items they needed to pawn to meet expenses. Sal wasn't in the high-rent district. His clientele — folks on the fringe, mostly — approached him, often as not, with urgent desperation. His heart was with his impecunious neighbors, unless they were just stupid, and deserved to be cheated. But mostly he was a good egg, a businessman, he told himself proudly, a citizen of the world.

He'd been at the store for an hour when a young man pushed open the door. "Good morning!" Sal called out. "What can I do for you? Merry Christmas!"

The young man was slight of build and had his head shaved clean. A tuft of barely noticeable blond beard grew from his chin, and his eyes, not meeting Sal's, darted about the store. A patch of decorative ink circled his neck and disappeared beneath his jacket collar. One swastika was noticeable, and what Sal knew to be a sign of a prison gang. This dude had done time.

His beige corduroy jacket zipped up the front and a bulge appeared at the waist. Sal, noticing it, became nervous. He tamped down his fear by reminding himself that bad guys seldom hold up stores early in the morning when there's no cash in the kitty. Yet the young man's demeanor was unsettling.

"What can I do for you?" Sal repeated.

"I got this I need to sell." The man unzipped the jacket, reached in and brought out a towel wrapped around a gun. He set it down in front of Sal.

"I see. Where's your paperwork?"

"That's the thing, man. I lost the paperwork."

"Well, I can't buy a gun unless I have a record of the sale to you or some other proof that you are the owner — "

"Yeah, man, I know, I know," he interrupted. "Look, I bought this for my girlfriend, and she got real mad, see, 'cause she doesn't like guns and I didn't know that, so I got to get rid of it quick so's I can get the money to buy her something else for Christmas."

Sal had easily recognized the fast-talking hum as pure fiction. He got guys like this in the store all the time trying to go around the rules, putting Sal's business at risk. They were like freelance used car salesmen, and Sal's policy was to simply get rid of them.

He had to admit, though, the gun was pretty. He picked it up. It was a Glock 9 millimeter, the smaller one, built for a smaller hand. Could the tale about the girlfriend have any truth to it? And it was pristine. He guessed it had been cleaned to a fare-thee-well by someone who knew how.

When the thought popped into his mind about the girlfriend, Sal thought again of Tori. The thought of her going out with that Forbes came to mind, and a surge of jealousy hit him from out of nowhere. He gripped the piece and checked for a magazine. None. The piece was empty.

The customer, seeing Sal's gesture, quickly brought the clip out of his pants pocket. "Sorry. I forgot this." He picked up the towel and wiped off the magazine, a gesture that Sal found most disturbing. Using the towel as a shield, he dropped the magazine into Sal's hand.

Sal looked at it quickly. Two of the 17 shells were missing. Another red flag.

"I'm sorry, sir, but if you don't have the correct paperwork, I can't help you."

"Look man, I understand you gotta be careful. But I'm on the level. I just want to get my girl a nice gift, and I got my money tied up in this. I'll take a hundred. Cash. I paid three hundred. You don't even need to do paperwork. It's 'tween you and me."

During most conversations with questionable customers, this would be where Sal typically walked the guest to the front door and closed it behind him. But as he opened his mouth to utter the script, another man came in the store. It was Danny Doyle, a regular and highly valued customer. Doyle owned a jewelry store in a more moneyed district than this one, and loved to buy dimes-on-the-dollar jewelry from Sal, clean it to a sparkle, and sell it with a grand mark-up. The last thing Sal needed this close to the rush of expected customers was to be seen by Doyle consorting with shady people.

Sal quickly rewrapped the towel around the Glock.

As Doyle approached the counter, he paused to pick up a camera off a shelf and gave it an inspection which took several seconds.

Sal made a snap decision.

He reached in his pocket, pulled out three twenties and four tens and handed them to the shifty-eyed customer. "Bye," he said before turning his attention to Doyle. The young man nodded with thanks and slipped out the front door. As he did, Sal tucked the gun and the clip in a drawer out of sight.

In the seconds following the exchange, Sal couldn't even explain to himself why he had taken the gun. It was idiocy. He couldn't sell it. It was a stupid way to do business, and could only lead to trouble. Sal was certain the gun had been used in the commission of a crime, based on the scent that kid had on him. The guy would not be claiming ownership, and the impulsive decision to buy it was Sal's alone. He was now the owner of an illegal handgun, untraceable to him and completely unusable. He'd wasted a hundred bucks. Damn. As he silently asked himself what the hell he did that for, Tori flitted momentarily through Sal's mind.

"Danny, how ya doing'? Merry Christmas," he effused with a winning smile. "I've got a gorgeous pink sapphire in a gold setting. Just got it in. Wanna have a look?"

Chapter 101

When Shara got home from the hospital, Cole explained to her that his plan for their romantic Christmas Eve dinner had changed. They would be dropping a disc off for Forbes, staying a few minutes in order to feign interest in this soprano, and then they would pick up his mom and take her to dinner. He then braced for the explosion.

"Why, in God's name, is your mother coming to Christmas Eve dinner?" Shara roared.

"Because it's Christmas," he murmured.

"Cole, as long as we've been married, we've had a tradition of Christmas Eve dinner out someplace nice, just you and me. Why are you doing this to me?"

"She asked to go."

"She knows of this tradition. Let's have breakfast with her Christmas morning instead. I have something to give you, and I want to do it without your mother's help."

"She asked to go."

"I understand that. I also understand that it's supposed to start snowing early and I sure don't want to drive way over there, out of the way, on bad streets, to have dinner with someone I . . "

"Don't like," he finished her sentence. "There's no need to conceal it; you never have concealed it."

"Why can't you ever, *ever* say no to that woman? I mean it, Cole. You let her run you. Say no. You are a grown man. I'm not asking you to disrespect or dishonor her. I'm just asking to have my husband to myself on Christmas Eve."

To Cole's surprise, Shara was working herself into quite a lather, and a sinking feeling hit him. "Shara." His voice was quiet, gentle, nearly inaudible. It made Shara cease motion. She stared at him expectantly.

Finally, "What, Cole? I'm waiting. Explain why we can't have dinner alone. Tell me why your mother can't be made to understand. I'm waiting. . .

"I'm still waiting. . .

"Still — "

"All right. Here it is. I owe her a lot of money. She's started fussing at me about it, so I have to pay her something, and I said I'd do it Christmas Eve."

"What money?"

"For the system."

"The *music* system?" Shara was aghast. Her mouth dropped open. "She bought that? I thought you got a small business loan. How much do we owe her?"

"She was cheaper than a small business loan."

"How much?"

Cole stared at his shoes. He was enveloped in the moment he had dreaded since he started The Cole Renshaw Trio. No use any longer prolonging the agony. "I borrowed about fifteen-large. There's eight grand left to pay."

"What on earth cost fifteen thousand dollars?"

Cole took a deep breath. He listed for her the computers, speakers, video and audio monitors, microphones, digital tracks, and assorted items that had comprised his debt.

"You told me you bought most everything second hand."

"I didn't. Shara, a lot of it couldn't be bought second hand. The speakers and head, sure. People in our business, once they've invested, don't sell off their equipment. There was none to buy cheap."

"You lied to me."

"I know you find my mother difficult. So, I kept it from you. Honestly, if I'd gotten an S.B.A loan, the interest would have put us back a lot farther. And the government paperwork alone . . ."

"You will pay her every penny we earned Thanksgiving weekend."

"I was going to give her a thousand."

"Give her every dollar we earned. I want out from under this. I can't believe you lied to me. I'm going to lie down."

Shara left the light off in the bedroom. She cried, her hands over her eyes, thinking of all that had been said and done. Memories of her anger at the Thanksgiving dinner table taunted her. Why had she said those things to Suzanne? Why had she been so impatient? It was all landing on her.

At once, she leaped out of the bed and, with her hand over her mouth, ran toward the toilet, not quite making it, and threw up on the floor. The sickness was actually a welcome distraction. When she finished, and wiped up the mess she'd made, her thoughts of guilt and grief returned. Added to that were her thoughts of her credit card debt, the mortgage, and the many ways she was drowning in a red ocean of not-enough-money. She began to cry some more on her way back to the bedroom.

Shortly, Cole stepped into the room.

"I don't want to talk to you right now."

He stepped back out and closed the door behind him.

She opened her mouth and roared her rage. He had put her in this position, and she was trapped. If he had to borrow this money, fine. If he had to borrow it from Suzanne to save interest, fine. But he should have told the truth. Now he had humiliated her in front of Suzanne not once, but every time Shara had complained about Suzanne's cloying, meddlesome neediness and demands. Shara had had no idea Suzanne was well within her rights. What's more, she had had no idea her complaints against Suzanne had fallen on deaf ears. Even if Cole had agreed with her, he was helpless.

Shara bellowed Cole's name. He opened the door and stepped into the room again, but didn't speak.

She panted sobs, trying to control her anger. At last, in a voice as calm as she could manage, she stated, "You will get a job."

"I know that." He left the room.

Chapter 102

Theresa stood in her kitchen in Columbus. The vivid sky-blue walls fell halfway to the floor and met the antique white chair rail and white bead board lower wall. She could see the plate rail near the ceiling that circled the room displaying her collections of carnival glass and antique dolls. On the wall, her kitchen clock depicted a small ceramic doll fashioned like a blonde girl in a blue dress on a swing with a bucolic painted background. The swing took the doll back and forth mechanically in time with the tick-tock.

The cabinet under the sink was opened and the trash was turned over onto the floor. She wondered how that happened, and made a mental note to pick it up later.

As she gazed about her, she noticed Jason sitting in a chair at the table. He was wearing another black tee shirt bearing the logo of some unrecognizable rock band. He wore no pants, only boxer shorts and white crew socks. He lived there, and had made himself at home. Somehow, she knew it was Jason who had turned over the trash and that it was his mission to disturb and derail her life. He gazed at her with the same disdainful expression of bored disinterest and intolerance he had worn during the abortive job interview downtown.

The image of him filled her with unease. He represented a threat of some sort, a reason to be afraid. But she didn't know what the threat was.

The senseless, random qualities of a dream world explain themselves and convince the dreamer that while the images are odd, they are not so odd that they wake the dreamer up.

Theresa looked around her dream world again. Where her back door should have been, there was a wide corridor surrounding a nurse's station and within the station, Shara Renshaw sat staring at a computer screen. Theresa called to her and called to her, but Shara never looked up. As Theresa walked toward the station, she found herself in a wheelchair. She pushed the wheels forward to move the chair and circled the station to its entry point. She called to Shara again, pleading with her to remove Jason from her kitchen.

Shara did not appear to see or hear her. But in a moment, she rose from her desk and walked into Theresa's kitchen which had morphed into a hospital room. She returned immediately, said nothing. But Theresa was assured, in the way that dreams work, that Jason was gone and her home was safe.

Theresa felt a tug on her arm. She opened her eyes and saw Tim. It took her a few moments to shake off the dream.

"That morphine makes you sleep well, Treese. It took me a minute to wake you up."

"I was dreaming about Shara."

"Was it a good dream?"

"Not really. Do you think she and Cole and everybody will come here Friday?"

"They said they will."

"But will they?"

"They haven't lied to us yet. What is bothering you?"

"It was this dream. I hope they come. I really need them to come. It's important. Can you call them and say they should come early?"

"Okay, sure. I'm not sure what's wrong. You know, it's going to snow."

"I don't care. I'm just afraid. I have a bad feeling."

"It's probably just the morphine."

Chapter 103

Tiffany Pasternak was livid. A civil rights advocacy group which called itself "Cooler Heads" had offered a free seminar at the station to educate the police force on community relations in the wake of racially-charged unrest in many cities. This was all powered by the actions of cops across the country, such as those in Ferguson, Missouri, Chicago, Charleston, Baltimore, Seattle, Madison, and points across the nation. Pasternak felt gratified to learn that her chief had the chance to step to the plate.

Tiffany wished she could speak in a symposium and present the simple headache that results when cops pull   over people on bogus charges simply because of race or some other meritless excuse. The time wasted, and the paperwork alone, were disincentives to her. At least that was one argument. Obviously, department policy should change because it would be the right thing to do. But, barring that, it should be changed because of the labor it costs.

She thought Cooler Heads might have some great ideas on ways for the police force to, for instance, adjust their vernacular when speaking to the public so as to make better, less offensive, less bullying word choices. That, alone, would be a step in a positive direction.

She was bothered by a domestic call Phil Mueller had answered Halloween morning. A single mother of two in a shabby apartment on Terre Haute's north side had called the police because, she claimed, her boyfriend had punched her in the face. When Phil and his then-partner, Garrett Munson arrived, the boyfriend was arrested and put in their cruiser. But then things turned ugly. It was 7 a.m. and the two young boys were still in bed, but not in bed. Munson noticed that the kids, aged about six and seven, he thought, crying and hysterical over the fight, were laying on a thin stack of blankets on the living room floor.

"Where are these kids' bedrooms?" Munson had asked the young mother.

"Right there," she had answered, pointing to the blankets.

"They don't have beds?" Without waiting for an answer, Munson had walked to the refrigerator and swung it open. It contained mustard, a short stack of American cheese slices, and three beers.

Tiffany, hearing the story later from Phil, pointed out that it was the end of the month, and the mother probably had a SNAP card that would be refilled shortly. But it hadn't occurred to the cops on the scene.

"What do these kids eat?" Munson had asked the mother.

I'll take them to McDonalds on the way to school." Her tone was defensive and fearful. She sensed what was coming with tragic exactitude. She began sobbing in terror and dread.

Before long, Family Services had been called, and the terrified, bewildered children were put into foster care simply because their mother was poor — indicted for poverty. Pasternak had shaken her head in disgust when she heard the tale. It would be a herculean task for that woman to get her kids back, made harder by her poverty.

"Way to engender trust in the police," she had complained to Mueller. Mueller had offered no response.

Cooler Heads was staffed by three retired FBI agents, two members of the NAACP, a long-time police chief out of Indianapolis, and a civil rights lawyer.

Pasternak's police chief wanted no part of such a seminar. He shut it down flat. And she was livid.

"Why, Chief?" she had asked. "What is wrong with better training on race relations? Why not get in front of this before we have a Michael Brown in this city?"

"Because it will cost resources, Pasternak," Chief Mark De Lancie responded. The two were in his office, and Pasternak was mouthing off in what she feared was bordering on insubordination — and what De Lancie saw as a hissy fit.

Tiffany knew she was on the verge of losing all credibility, and she was too emotional, but if she didn't stick up for her beliefs, who would?

De Lancie, meanwhile, was fatigued with her constant whining about changing things that don't need changing, and belly-aching about other officers. His patience with her had worn thin before she came in the room. De Lancie kept to himself his personal feelings about Pasternak's, well, proclivities, finding them emasculating. That wasn't the topic at hand, but it was in the back of his mind.

"Chief, the seminar is free," she was saying.

"No, it isn't. When I take officers off the street and sit their asses in folding chairs for a half a day to listen to bleeding hearts help them get in touch with their inner child, those cops are on the clock. My clock. It's not gonna happen, Pasternak. Live with it."

"Let's review what it cost the Ferguson, Missouri PD to host the FBI and a civil rights commission whose findings — and we haven't even discussed Chicago — how'd you like that mess in your lap?"

"Chicago is a unique situation."

"Is it? Oh, never mind. Sorry I said anything." Tiffany had observed De Lancie's growing unease with the direction her complaint was going. He was getting angrier by the minute, and she could see she wasn't doing herself or her cause any good.

"Pasternak, if and when — and this is a huge if and when — Terre Haute has a repeat of Ferguson, then we'll take measures. But I believe in our force. These are good men and women and they use common sense."

"Chief, Phil Mueller and I were on the street last week and he didn't use good sense."

"He didn't pull his service revolver. He didn't arrest anyone falsely. He didn't violate anyone's civil rights. I read the report. I'm satisfied that Mueller followed protocol."

"Oh, you are? Well, that tells me a lot, Chief."

"Start your tour, Pasternak."

Chapter 104

Shara should certainly be feeling the Christmas spirit, but she wasn't. All she could concentrate on was Cole and his betrayal. Her anger rose within her in waves, and concentrating on her job was impossible. She missed three typographical errors and failed to catch a violation of FTC policy in a document on its way out the door. Her boss caught the mistakes and wanted to know where Shara's head was at.

Shara didn't have an answer.

Suspicious and fearful thoughts gnawed at her all afternoon. What else was Cole concealing from her? Were there other women? Other expenses? Other funds? Whether or not there were other secrets, he had humiliated her. She felt like a fool.

On the way home, after cutting out of the office a little early, she said a prayer for guidance, but when the guidance came as a mental recitation of what she already knew, it didn't make her feel much better. She routinely asked God to forgive her trespasses as she forgave those who trespassed against her. So, there it was. She was not only incensed, but she felt guilty about being incensed. And all this while she hadn't done anything wrong.

Or had she? Truth be told, she had built within herself an anger at Suzanne for years that bordered on hatred.

Jesus called that murder.

As the dialogue with herself continued, Shara realized that she had a big mess to clean up within herself, and another within her family. As she pulled into her driveway, she blinked back tears just as she saw in the rear view mirror Cole's van pulling in behind her.

Both stepped out of their cars at the same time and slammed the doors in perfect sync. Cole reached Shara first. "I'm sorry."

"Really? Are you sorry you deceived me, or are you just sorry you were forced to tell me the truth?"

"Honestly, Shara, your attitude toward my mother is so negative, I didn't tell you about the loan because I couldn't see myself stoking your fire."

"Yes, I know. I'm sinning against her, but I'm not by myself. There is plenty of blame to go around. I wish I had known. I wish you had been honest with me."

"And my mother wishes she knew why you are so angry at her when she's just tried to help us."

"I know. But I still think she's manipulative, passive aggressive, judgmental and self-serving."

"But, she isn't."

"Yes, she is. But it doesn't matter that she's wrong. I can't fix her; I can only fix me."

"What about Christmas Eve? Are you going to be okay going to dinner with her?"

"No, I am definitely not. But I intend to call her right now and try to mend some fences. Don't try to stop me. After what you pulled, you need to hush up. You seriously do."

Shara stormed in the house with Cole on her heels. He lay on his back on the cat-hair-filled sofa and squeezed his eyes shut in dread.

Papa Kitty, resentful of his bed being crowded, took his place on Cole's head and purred loudly as Shara dialed Suzanne.

"Momma, it's Shara. I need to talk to you."

Cole heard a pause before Shara continued. She revealed that she just found out that Cole had borrowed a lot of money, and she wanted Suzanne to know that he had done it without her knowledge or consent.

Cole listened as Shara explained that she would never have said certain things to Suzanne if she had known about the loan. She went on to explain that she would never have *taken* the loan if she had known about it. That's when she fell quiet.

Suzanne, out of Cole's earshot, was annoyed by Shara's honesty and resolve to make things equitable. Suzanne's long-held pattern of coaxing her son gently with manipulations like the offering of money or the expressed need for a favor, or the flagrant reminder of what a horrible son he was had been ingrained carefully since her husband passed when Cole was a much younger man.

The year was 1969. Cole, with a shiny new driver's license had taken the family car for a ride to show his friends. Hours passed while he drove by several domiciles. He stopped by his girlfriend's house. He smooched on Laverne in the back seat for a long while.

He dropped by Forbes' house and told Forbes' father untruthfully that his dad had bought the car for him. He hoped Forbes' dad would do likewise for Forbes, but he didn't.

He cruised by the high school where he knew basketball practice was about to end. His friends all liked the '71 metallic blue Chevy and wanted a ride.

When Cole got home at 10:30, the house was deserted. He called two of his mom's friends and couldn't find her.

Undisturbed, he sat back and turned on the television. "Gunsmoke" was on Channel 2, and Cole pulled a bag of chips out of the kitchen pantry, sat back and chilled.

At a quarter to midnight, the phone rang. Cole stumbled into the kitchen out of bed to answer. "Cole, my God, where have you been?" It was Suzanne's voice, and the panicked, hysterical timbre set him on the defensive. What was he being accused of now?

"Your father died tonight. Heart attack. He collapsed three minutes after you left. Three minutes! I have been at the hospital ever since. Come get me. Do it now."

And that was the start of it. From that day, the Widow Renshaw established a methodology for getting what she whimsically desired, and it always included a mind game that tapped Cole's neglect of his father in time of need as ammunition in an unending cycle of guilt, manipulation, and submission that would continue for decades. If Suzanne had said, "If you'd been with me when your father died . . ." once, she'd said it a hundred times, and it always worked. The guilt was a powerful tool, and it didn't matter that the teenager had no way of knowing his father was in trouble.

Here it was decades later, and the process of guilt-baiting and demanding was as efficacious as ever. On some deep level, Cole recognized that he had had no way, all those years ago, to know that responsibility was at his home, and that he should not have been joy-riding when he was needed. But Suzanne had planted the guilt with finesse. Knowing what he knew, he still couldn't shake off the sense of shirked responsibility. It was deeply ingrained, soldered to his heart.

Until Shara walked into it.

A frank acknowledgment of the dynamic between Suzanne and the couple threw in a good monkey wrench. Suzanne's process had just been derailed. Shara was onto her.

Suzanne couldn't bring herself to be as frank. She deflected the sincerity as best she could. "It's fine, dear. I'm glad I can help. I am certainly looking forward to dinner tomorrow night. Where are we going? I think I'll wear my brown pants suit."

Shara exhaled. She had no ground to stand on now, and would have to put up with the dinner even though she had railed at Cole against including the woman. She made one last ditch effort: "Suzanne, I hope that you can understand that returning to you the money we owe depends on how much work Cole can do getting us jobs. If he is busy all the time helping you, well, then, he can't do that. We want to pay you back as soon as we can, but it has to start with you."

"Sure, dear, I don't want to be any trouble."

"But it is trouble, Suzanne, when Cole can't work because he's at a doctor's office instead."

"Well, I don't mean to be any trouble, dear," she repeated, "Maybe after Christmas he can take me to an after-Christmas sale. It will be hard for me to get out for dinner with you both if it snows. I really need new boots. Do you think he'll do that for me?"

Like talking to a brick wall, Shara was thinking. "Sure, Suzanne," Her statement was unapologetically wooden and insincere. Calling her mother in law "Suzanne" was her only pinch of dignity left. She seldom used the woman's name, but called her "Mom," as Cole did. This was a subtle protest. "We'll pick you up. Cole has an appointment at 6:30, but it shouldn't take more than a half hour. Expect us around 7:30, though the streets might be bad by then." Shara had reached her limit at that moment, and she decided she was in for a penny and in for a pound.

"Suzanne, while you were talking, it occurred to me that I haven't known you and Cole as long as you and Cole have known each other. Is there something I don't know about the two of you? I ask this because of this very honest fact that I need his help, and I can't get it because he is helping you. Now, given that he loves both of us, yet the scales are always tipped in your favor, I am honestly asking why you don't want to understand that I need you to stop calling him for small little petty chores that eat up his whole day. I need him to work, and I told him to get a job — to pay you off as much as anything. He won't hear me, and I think you know why."

"Oh, my goodness, Dear," Suzanne replied with a sort of condescension that enraged Shara further, "Don't worry about the money now. He can pay me back ten dollars a week if he wants. He doesn't need a job."

"What happened, Suzanne? Tell me *now*."

"Nothing, dear. Nothing at all happened. I just get lonely sometimes, and want my boy, that's all."

"So, what I'm hearing from you right now is that your loneliness, and wanting your boy trumps the deep financial hole we're in, the danger we're in if his music doesn't succeed before I lose my job. My troubles, which drive my migraines and my blood pressure don't compare, *at all*, to you wanting company."

"You seem upset."

Shara bit her lip. Her exasperation was complete. "Yes, Suzanne, I seem upset for a good reason. You and Cole have a good time at dinner. I won't be joining you. Good-bye."

Shara hung up the phone and stood still, eyes closed, arms at her side. She wished her anger would wash over her, cleanse her cathartically, and be gone, but she knew it wouldn't happen that way.

Cole had sat up quietly, and folded his hands, elbows on knees, looking at the floor. He feared meeting his wife's gaze.

"Cole?"

"Yes, baby, I wish you hadn't done that."

I know what you wish. When you take your mother to dinner tomorrow, use your own money. My credit card will not be available. I suggest you take her to Taco Bell. That's what you can afford."

Shara went into the kitchen and began preparations for easy side dishes to take to the hospital Christmas Day.

Chapter 105

Barb woke up Wednesday with the urgency for which the occasion called. When her dad had told her she would be off with pay between Christmas and New Year's, the guilt was strangling. She would quit today. She had gotten the green light from the church to assume the music directorship, and her satisfaction was rich. There was this singular loose end and she was anxious to be done with it.

She dressed and went to work. Marching straight to the office of Dr. Glenn, she knocked after a moment of hesitation.

"Yes," came a distracted reply. He was at his desk, face to monitor, reading the thesis of a master's candidate. He was deep in concentration, but broke it when Barb entered.

"Dr. Glenn?"

"Oh, yes, hello, Barbara. How can I help you?" He rose to his feet and gestured to a chair for her. "Is all going well with your lesson planning? Is there anything you need?"

"Sir, I have to tell you something and I'm, well, here it is. I've received a job offer for a job that I want very much, and I am here to tender my resignation. I am sorry for the inconvenience I am causing." She set a typed piece of paper on his desk, and waited for his reply.

He looked at it briefly. "All right. Very well, then. I'll have Gabriella help you pack up your things. Is an hour enough time?"

An hour? What is the rush? Vitriolic of him, but she realized she had that coming.

"Yes, sir, thank you."

Glenn took his seat and resumed his work. Barb left. She went directly to her father's office and stepped in without knocking.

"Hi," she offered.

Lloyd stood from his desk, smiling broadly. "How are you, Ms. Baxter? I hope you find the campus and amenities to your liking." The twinkle in his eye and the light note of sarcasm could have been charming if Barb had not had the burden of her news to bear.

"Dad, I quit the job. I just gave Glenn a letter of resignation, and I am taking the job at church. I'll go now and pack my office. I've got an hour."

He was wordless. His face articulated the emotions he didn't utter. "I guess I'll see you at home, then."

"I'll have a nice dinner ready for you."

Chapter 106

Frank Glenn had looked forward to the break between Christmas and the New Year when the college was out of session. His wife's planned trip to south Florida had been canceled, of course, and replaced with a plan to fly out to Denver. Either way, Glenn's bags were packed. All that corralled his concentration was Frankie and his injuries

Glenn had packed books, not knowing how conscious Frankie would be most of the time. A new biography on the life of Mozart beckoned, though Glenn wondered what more could possibly be written. A biography of Jule Styne also beckoned, though Glenn knew far less about the American Songbook composer. . .

Now the trip out west had a new wrinkle.

With the unexpected departure of the new hire, Glenn would be burdened with the task of teaching her assigned classes until he could find her replacement.

The thought of Tim Shelton hit often and hard. But weeks had passed since his interview with Shelton, and he had grown confident that the man had, by now, returned to Ohio and was probably gainfully employed. Truthfully, Glenn wanted to believe Shelton had landed on his feet without any direct evidence to that effect. He wanted that exculpatory assurance.

Glenn could start over. He could post the job on the school's internet site, perhaps rework the job description a little, and in so doing, buy time. He'd still have to teach Baxter's courses, but starting from scratch had a certain comfort when he considered never having to eat crow with Shelton.

Glenn effectively talked himself into a certainty that Shelton didn't matter. Surely, he was employed somewhere by now and Glenn need never think of him again. Surely there were more candidates out there as qualified as Shelton, and who, if hired, would not be a continuing reminder to Glenn of his own bad judgment. Surely. the next try would be more effective. Surely, he could put a new candidate search off until the new semester.

While considering his options, Glenn also thought of Barbara Baxter. He admitted to himself that if he scored a job opportunity a few days after starting a new position and wanted it with the same ardor she expressed, he might do the same thing, even if it was inconsiderate **and unprofessional.**

Glenn's thoughts turned also to Lloyd Fuller. Looking back on the hiring process, it occurred with the clarity of hindsight that Fuller had pushed Glenn to hire the attractive blonde. Surely, Fuller had not been smitten by the woman. She was half his age. Still, Glenn recalled, the pressure to look very hard at Baxter had been coming from Fuller. Glenn wondered why.

Glenn loosened his necktie. On a whim, he opened up the file on Baxter and gave it another look. He read through what he already knew about the young lady, and a second glance provided no insight. What the hell, he told himself, he'd see if she was on Facebook.

It took mere moments for him to find her page. Apparently, she was a big Facebook user, and her page was truly an eyeful. When it opened, photos of her with a dark-haired man decorated many posts. Her husband, obviously. He clicked on photos of her playing a concert at her church in Rolla; of her picnicking with the husband; of her directing a large choir; of her dressed as Mary Magdalene in a Maundy Thursday play; of her and the husband poised to blow candles over a birthday cake. All innocuous and unindictable until Glenn saw the last picture. He clicked to enlarge it.

There stood Baxter, smiling and happy, with her arms around the corpulent waist of his own assistant department head, Lloyd Fuller. The caption said he was her dad.

"Well, I'll be damned," Glenn said out loud. He picked up the phone.

Chapter 107

Christmas Eve morning, Tim woke up only partially alone. He had spent the night in Theresa's room. The hospital, assured by the insurance company that coverage was in place, had moved another bed into Theresa's room and was bringing a food tray for every meal for Tim as well as Theresa.

The humming and buzzing and chirping of equipment surrounding his wife had soothed him to sleep, and the industrial-strength mattress on the hospital bed was decidedly more comfortable than the lumpy mattress at the apartment. Tim woke up feeling better than he had felt for a while.

He changed clothes in the bathroom and went to Theresa's bedside.

Theresa wasn't asleep. She looked at him with recognition and fear. She was sopping wet and tense. Her hair clung to her face with sweat. A little cry came out of her mouth, plaintive and miserable.

"What's wrong, baby?"

"It hurts a lot, Tim," she whispered. "A lot."

Tim slipped on his loafers and marched to the nurse station. "My wife is in trouble. Something's wrong with her," he barked at no one in particular.

It was a maddening five seconds before a nurse looked up from her computer screen. "I just checked on her not ten minutes ago," she remarked with a scarcely satisfying look of concern.

"She's sweaty and I think she's delirious."

"Please go to the waiting room. I'll come get you when we know something." Then, to another nurse, she instructed, "Call Dr. Baumgardner's cell. She's in Chicago for the holiday, but see if you can get her." She then walked swiftly into Theresa's room as Tim watched. The color was draining from his face.

He heard the nurse on the phone leave a message for Dr. Baumgardner. Surely, doctors liked to have a holiday sometimes, too, Tim told himself. He mentally demanded the doctor return the call. He insisted. It was almost a prayer.

The wait was 45 minutes, but it seemed like days to Tim. Not a nail-chewer, he had picked up the habit after Theresa's accident and sat tearing at his cuticles with his teeth. He gazed out the window at the parking lot, now white with falling snow. The thought flitted past that this snowstorm might be worse than predicted. No matter. He was staying here.

When the nurse approached Tim and casually sat down next to him, he held his breath. "I've got good news and bad news. The bad news is that she's picked up a little staph infection, but it's little, and we're giving her antibiotics. She's lucky we found it at an early stage so we can treat it before it's out of hand. This happens a lot in hospitals, Mr. Shelton." The nurse smiled reassuringly. "The other bad news is that she's in a lot of pain. This is in part due to the staph, but mostly due to, well, everything else. The good news is that we have been giving her only the pain meds she says she wants, and it turns out she has been trying to wean herself off of them. Said they were giving her nightmares. She has had nothing but Tylenol for two days, but she may not have understood that she's not ready to be off of opioids. As you know, we stopped them until she was able to go to the bathroom. Now that we know that the colon surgery was successful, she can return to morphine, but she fibbed when she said she didn't need it. That's all. We've got a morphine drip back in place. She's comfortable.

"She's a strong woman, Mr. Shelton, and just a little stubborn."

"Tell me about it. We've got friends coming over Christmas Day. Will she be able to see folks?"

"Given the amount of morphine, she's subject to have a really good time," the nurse smiled.

Chapter 108

"So, what time are you coming over tonight?" Forbes asked Tori on the phone.

"Oh, I forgot to tell you. I can't." Tori, wearing only pajama bottoms and her bra, was fidgeting on the phone. She wished to hang up and finish dressing.

"You can't! I've got the whole trio coming and our sound engineer to hear you. What's the hold-up?"

"Oh, I see. I didn't realize. Well, it's not much of a hold-up," Tori hedged. "It's just that my car needs some brake work and if I don't get back there to pick it up, well, they're closed Christmas Day, of course . . . "

"Here's what. I'll come pick you up, bring you over, and then take you to get your car after. This won't take long. I just want Cole and Quincy's take on your possible contribution. I'm thinking maybe you could appear with us as a guest vocalist sometime."

"Really?" Tori squealed. "That would be fantastic. You tell me when you're coming, and I'll be ready."

"How about if I buy you dinner afterward?"

Tori fell quiet. Having dinner with Forbes on Christmas Eve would no doubt annoy Sal, but Sal would be at his shop, so there really was no harm. It seemed odd that, when she had spoken to him, he was inexact about when he'd leave the store, but it was Christmas Eve, so everything was extraordinary. It was her first holiday with him as her boyfriend, and she didn't want to second guess.

On the other hand, a voice in the back of her mind whispered that a Christmas Eve dinner with a man who wasn't Sal may be just a little inappropriate. And Sal, when he heard about it, would blow a gasket. But Forbes stood to do so much for her music career, she dare not disappoint him. The possibility of being a guest vocalist for the Cole Renshaw Trio was the carrot on the stick.

"Tori?"

"Hmm, yes, okay, I'm here. Sure, I can have dinner with you. What time are you coming?"

Chapter 109

Barb got up early on Christmas Eve. Her father, having stayed up late, had slept late, and it had pleased her to knock on his door and wake him up. Just a little care-taking had made her feel purposeful again, and connected to family, diminutive as family was.

Something had been bothering her, and it had taken her a while to put a name to it. But now that she identified the trouble, she wanted Dad up and at the breakfast table to talk about it.

Chapter 110

Cole had just gotten off the phone with Christine Berthold. It had been an effort to get through the conversation with her while remaining civil. This kind of thing happens all the time in Terre Haute — and most other cities, too, Cole imagined. But when it happened to him at such an inconvenient moment, well, he was grinding his teeth.

He went in the bedroom-turned-office where Shara sat at the computer. She was writing a song list for the job the Sunday after Christmas. There would still be holiday music at the show, but less of it and more of the smooth, crooning fare that was Cole's specialty.

Cole looked over her shoulder. "Shara, you don't have to do that."

"I won't have time the rest of the weekend."

"No, I mean, you don't have to do that at all. Christine's on the Green just let us go."

"Why on earth? They loved us. What did you do?"

Shara's anger at him was stubbornly still in place, and Cole felt sure he would be taking heat for everything that went wrong for a long time. This time it wasn't his fault, but he doubted that it would matter whose fault it was. "We were undercut."

"By whom?"

"Chaz Sinclair found out we were playing the room, and he called Christine. He offered to do it for half the price, and is throwing in Monday nights. She bit down."

Sinclair was a piano-playing vocalist who ran the circuit across most of the piano bars in town that catered to a baby-boomer clientele. He usually lasted a couple of months before his repetitive, monotone repertoire and escalating bar tab lost him the job. But in the wake of his scorched-earth tactic, venue holders would get skittish about hiring more musicians. Christine's would not be the first venue Cole had lost to Sinclair, nor would it be the last water Chaz poisoned.

"I don't know why I asked you that. I knew you were going to say his name before you half-finished the thought. What are you going to do? Offer her $50 less than he offered and do Monday nights also?"

"Hell, no, Shara, this has got to stop all over the city. Leeches like Chaz, if they get their way, will be having every musician in the county paying the venues to let them play."

"I agree. It's the first thing you've had right in a while, but I agree."

"What are you talking about? I've had one thing wrong. One. I should have told you about the loan, and I didn't. I've apologized to death. How long are you going to hold this over me?" Cole's voice was raising uncharacteristically. Anger welled up as his lip curled into a scowl. His long fuse was burning down to its end, and Shara was aghast.

"Don't even think about yelling at me. You put up with Forbes and Quincy coming to shows stoned, and you don't say a word. You don't even dock their pay when they're late. You endure the manipulative crap from your mother and *refuse* to even talk to her about taking a cab to the damned doctor. You won't raise your voice to the people who are actually hurting you, but you've got nerve enough to get mad at me for being mad at you and you turn hateful." She stood from the computer, turned toward her husband and leaned against the side of her desk before continuing. "Let's review who in your world is really on your side."

Chapter 111

Frank Glenn was not one to be humiliated lightly. He had been doing a slow, quiet burn since he discovered that Barbara Baxter was the daughter of his colleague. Glenn had holed up in his office, door closed, to avoid Lloyd Fuller.

He'd have to get over it. At some point, interviews must resume to fill the position, and he would need Lloyd for that. He'd have to steamroll over his irritation at some point. But for now, he was happy to get through the holidays without being reminded of how he had been played.

It was Glenn, after all, who had set the rule for not hiring family members within the department. Felicity Cramer, the president of the university, had signed on after a spirited debate, and Glenn's department policy had become policy for the whole university. Therefore, to have it violated so flagrantly behind his back, and in his own house was an acute embarrassment, and, well, he didn't want to talk to Lloyd for a while.

Add to that, there was the matter of his son. The report had reached him that the accident in Denver had been Franky's own fault. Seems the 22-year-old Environmental Science major had gotten stinking drunk at a frat party and thought it would be fine to go for a drive in the mountains with his girlfriend.

Dr. Glenn had just learned of a girlfriend when his wife called him in the morning. Apparently, her name is Jen, and she was a chemistry student just out of high school. She had been even drunker and had walked away from the accident in the ravine unharmed, called for the paramedics, and may be responsible for Franky still being alive.

Frank kept a photo of his family sitting on his desk. He stared at it while conflicting thoughts spun in his head. The photo was taken when Franky was 14. A mall photographer had used the bromidic blue backdrop and the boy had insisted on wearing his favorite orange sweater. On one hand, Glenn mused, the color was awful on the photo, and after only eight years, he wished the 8 x 10 would fade. On the other hand, it was a priceless memory of a happier, healthier time.

Franky, if he lives, may be paralyzed from the neck down.

Glenn considered the lengths he would go to if his boy would be healthy. He fantasized about physically climbing to the stars, grabbing God by the collar, and demanding his boy be okay.

Glenn's eyes began to tear and his nose burn. The panic, the fear, the hope, the love for his son — it all welled up in him.

He picked up the phone. "Gabriela, hold calls and visitors until I call you."

"Certainly, sir —" and he hung up on her.

Glenn laid his head down on his desk for ten full minutes, and let himself cry.

As he sobbed quietly, the thought returned to him. *I would do anything on earth for that boy. I would lie, steal, cheat, murder, commit mayhem and genocide for —*

I would lie.

Glenn sat up in his chair and watched the door. He saw in his mind his colleague and friend, Lloyd Fuller, who had stood on that spot inside the door just a few days ago and lied to him to put his daughter in the best possible light.

Glenn picked up the phone and called Fuller's office. His friend picked up the phone.

"Hey, Lloyd, it's Frank. How's Barb doing with her new job?"

Silence.

"Lloyd, you there?"

"Uh, yeah."

"Merry Christmas, my friend. How about we head on out of here early this afternoon and stop on the way home. I'm buying. We have a lot more in common than I realized about us until a minute ago."

"I think you've had a belt or two already."

"Nah, just the holiday blues and a small epiphany. I'll tell you about it. What think? Three? You'll be done by then?"

Chapter 112

Barb drove down to the grocery at the end of her street. The little family-owned store had been there since she was a child. Her mom had shopped there weekly when Barb was in kindergarten and her dad worked for the Terre Haute symphony. It was a family Mecca when she was in high school and college when Dad directed the symphony chorus. Now, Barb walked through the doors once again. Much had changed since she'd moved to Rolla. The white walls were now pale gray, and all the walls were lined with grocery-themed wallpaper border. The meat department and dairy had switched places, and patrons could now pay their bills with their iPhones. Barb grabbed a shopping cart and began the sojourn through the aisles. Her intent was to fix her dad an amazing Christmas Eve feast, healthy, but not too healthy, and finish off the meal with a supplication for him to move Dr. Glenn into hiring that man she had overheard at the seafood place.

Frank Glenn listened to her dad; she knew he did. That's why she was called for the interview, for Pete's sake. Now, she wanted him to use that same influence to get that man hired. She didn't know the man's name, and could barely even describe him. His wife had reddish-blonde curly hair. That's all she could remember. But surely Dad knew who she meant.

She had gotten as far as the canned soup aisle when she became aware of a person following her. She gave it a few seconds and was about to spin around and confront the stranger when he spoke.

"Barb? Barb Fuller?"

A man near to her age stood alongside her. "Yes?"

"Barb, it's me, Don Witte, from Sherwin Banks Elementary. I believe you once poured blue and green tempera paint down the front of my shirt, oh, say, 30 years ago."

Barb laughed. "I most certainly did not do that." She lifted her arms to hug the tall figure, and breaking away, looked him over. His blonde locks were long and curly. His blue eyes were engaging. He was a handsome man and bore no resemblance to the child she remembered from first grade. "I had already stirred the paints together. It was entirely aqua, and I want the credit for my creativity," Barb laughed.

"Tell me why you did that all those years ago."

"'Cause I liked you, of course! Isn't that the protocol when you like somebody, and you're five? Aren't you required to pour paint on their shirt?"

Don laughed. "I guess it is. Thirty years have been kind to you. What are you doing in town? I thought you moved to southern Missouri. Is there no place like home for the holidays?"

"Actually, I've moved back. After my husband died, I realized there was really nothing for me in Rolla, so I came back to Dad's and I've taken a job at a church over on Fremont Street."

"A job? What job?"

"Music director."

"Really?" Don's tone was one of exaggerated, nearly ridiculous interest, and Barb took note.

"Yeah, good church. Look, I've got to go or I'll never have dinner on the table. It was nice to see you." She started to move away.

"Barb, wait. We should get together and catch up." Barb then noticed the twinkle in his eye. She'd seen it before in many men's eyes.

"Sure, okay. How's Robin? You're married to Robin Blaine, aren't you?"

"I'm not. Robin left me after I, well, I sort of got religion. She couldn't handle it. Long story." He paused, looked at her as if deciding something, and finally said, "Why don't I call you? You're at your dad's?"

"Sure. I'll look for your call." Then, dismissing him, she walked away.

As she hurried through the store picking up supplies, she thought of Don. Interesting what he said. Should she take his call if he actually made one? A brief glance into her heart revealed the answer. The main reason she had come home to Terre Haute was obvious. She was lonely.

Barb got back to the house and began marinating the beef tenderloin in Italian dressing. She cut potatoes into spears and prepared them for garlic roasting. A green salad with grape tomatoes, fresh mushrooms, and dried cherries would complete the festive dinner for Dad. There was a cheesecake. She dug out the Christmas dishes. She found candles and placed them in holders on the dining room table. She set the Pinot Noir in a prominent place for Dad to open on his arrival. There. All set. If this doesn't persuade him to hire that guy, nothing will.

The phone rang. When she greeted the caller, her father's voice sounded weird. "I'm not going to be home on time, baby girl. I went out with Frank for a holiday drink. I should be home by 7 or 8."

"Frank Glenn?"

"Yes, Barbie, he's right here. He knows who you are and he's fine with it. Here, say hi to him —" Lloyd handed off the phone. This was bizarre and out of character, all of it, Barb thought.

"Dad? DAD! Where are you?"

"It's me, Barbie, Frank Glenn. How you doin'?"

They're both drunk, she concluded.

"I'm fine, Dr. Glenn. Thank you for asking. Where are you guys? I'd like to come join the party!"

Within 45 minutes, Barb was helping her father into the house. She planned to leave the tenderloin marinating in the fridge. She'd make her dinner for Christmas Eve and would order a small pizza for herself tonight. Her dad, who seldom finished his first glass of wine, was heading off to bed early. She'd spend the evening alone again. At least he was off work Christmas Eve. She'd spend the day with him and make her case for his forgiveness, and for the stranger whose future she ruined. She would make a strong case that someone else would make a better candidate anyway. She'd smooth it all over.

By happenstance, she noticed the phone on the kitchen wall. It had once been a beige instrument with an old-fashions rotary dial. Today, it had a modern face, but it was still beige, in its first location, and the springboard for a million memories. The one memory hit her suddenly and most acutely.

She had answered the phone several years ago when she had visited home for a long weekend. She'd left Bill in Rolla and was staying four days to see old friends, so she assumed the phone call was from one of them.

Today, the memory was clear and artfully painful. It had been Smitty Rollens from the factory calling to tell her Bill was dead. "He severed his hand on the equipment, Barb. I'm so sorry to tell you this. He was alone, the factory was closed, and the coroner said he had gone into shook and bled out."

Darkness enveloped Barb in that moment, and years later, it had not completely lifted.

The dichotomous reality had confused her, as she recalled that horrible day. How on earth could Bill, a sustained, eternal presence, an immutable constant of her life, be gone? How could the universe have changed so fundamentally, but still look the same? Cars were still driving up the street. A pigeon was sitting on a fence post in the yard. The soft drink she had just set in the refrigerator was still there — just as if nothing was amiss. Didn't the universe know that absolutely *everything* had shifted?

A few minutes later, after she'd talked to Dad, she'd jumped in her car and headed back to Rolla. She'd left her suitcase behind.

Returning to the present, Barb shook off the memory. *Block it out, stop thinking about it. Stop it. Stop it!* she scolded herself.

Still gazing at the phone, she wondered if Don Witte had a telephone listing, and if he was spending Christmas Eve alone.

Chapter 113

Cole helped Shara prepare for Christmas Day. He wrapped up the yellow flowered bed jacket she had bought Theresa for Christmas, and decorated it with a green bow. Cole enjoyed wrapping gifts. He would pinch the wrapping paper along the corners of the box being wrapped and make a fine, sharp line. He rendered the ribbon himself into elaborate bows rather than use the dollar-a-bag ones.

Shara had told him she thought Theresa might like something to wear that hadn't been owned by someone else, and he had agreed, making the wrapping of the gift a particular extravagance.

He wrapped a book of charts he'd purchased at the music store. A collection of Cole Porter standards Tim may not know very well that the implied directive to learn the pieces for live shows should serve as an assurance that Cole intended to continue his musical partnership with Tim.

He made a salad while Shara combined canned green beans, mushroom soup and milk in a casserole dish and set it in the fridge for baking tomorrow.

Shara made cherry pie, but she cheated with cherry pie filling in a ready-to-fill pie crust. She unpacked the Pinot Grigio and chilled it for tomorrow.

"How are we going to fit all these dishes, plates, napkins and flatware in the car tomorrow as well as Quincy and Forbes?" Cole wanted to know.

"I don't know. How do we routinely fit a thousand tons of music equipment in that van? We just do," she replied. "Quincy and Forbes could drive themselves if the roads were all right."

Cole was listening. The quip about fitting everything in the van was light and airy. He guessed the Christmas spirit had gotten to her, because he knew she was still angry at him. But the lightness in her tone was a relief.

"Shara, put that down."

Shara set aside the can of yams she was holding and looked at him curiously. He came to her and put his hands at her waist, drawing her near to him. "Look at this, woman. I know my mother is a pain in your keister, and I know she has her flaws. You think I don't see it, but I do. It's just that I owe her, and I have owed her years before I knew you. It's a long debt, and I have to respect her because of it. But I love you, and I want your understanding. I favor her because I *owe* her. I favor you because I love you. And that's the difference. Do you understand?"

I do, Cole. I understand the difference between your mother and me. I am far less passive aggressive and ugly to you. What I don't get is the *why* of it. What does she have on you? What happened in your life that caused so much guilt? That, I don't understand."

"Why do you think I have guilt?"

"Because I know you. You are a good man and I can't believe you have so much to be sorrowful for. The guilt has been put on you. I want to know how. I want to know what, besides money, do you think you owe Suzanne."

"It's a long story."

"Bore me. But while you do, make that onion dip you like to make."

"What did my mother tell you when you talked to her?"

"Nothing. She skirted around the issue. You said she likes to come in sideways, and she did. Look, if this is a case of boys being boys when you were young, you should have forgiven yourself ages ago. God forgives you, whatever it is."

"Shara, she blames me for my father's death."

Shara paused several seconds, watching him, expecting more. Finally, she asked, "Why?"

"When he had the heart attack, I wasn't there. He collapsed minutes after I left the house — with the car — and didn't get home for hours. No one had cell phones then, of course, and I came home and went to sleep while she was at the hospital with him. She blames me that I wasn't there to help."

Shara continued to stare. Surely, she thought, there is more to this story.

"I can think of eight or ten different ways none of that is your fault, especially at a time when there were no cell phones. How on earth were you supposed to know?"

"I just was. I don't know. I was off hanging with my friends, and I shouldn't have been. It was funny; I'd just gotten my license and it was my first chance to take the car out. That hacked her off, too. I wasn't taking her along. Plus, she was mad that I even had a license because it meant I was going to leave her alone. Plus, we knew my father was prone to heart attacks. He had nitroglycerin pills on him . . ."

"She didn't put one under his tongue?"

"She told me she couldn't get the lid off the bottle. And I was blamed for that, too. I wasn't there to open the bottle."

"Honey, surely, you can see you weren't to blame for his heart attack."

"Shara, on the surface, I can see it. At a glance, sure. But I had it pounded into me every day since I was 16. If anything is said often enough, you start to believe it, and that wasn't the end of it."

"What was the end of it?"

"Because I wasn't there that night, she had to leave her home and go back to teaching. There wasn't enough money for me to go to college, so I had to work, and study, and pay my own way. I was blamed for all of this, and I was pressured to go to school in town so I could look after her.

"My dad had hoped I'd go to law school, or at least get my bachelor's degree at Morehouse College in Atlanta. That's what he told me he hoped for me. Morehouse is the largest all-male black university in the country. He used to talk all the time about wanting me to go to school where he went. But that all ended after he died. She needed me to stay home. A lot has happened in forty years, Shara. You are coming in late."

"Okay. A death of a parent always has fall out. I can't help think, though, that even if she hadn't started out being passive aggressive and manipulative, doing so served her pretty well. She got used to it."

Chapter 114

"Are you bringing Isaiah for dinner?" Marietta, on the phone with Quincy, wanted a table count for her holiday dinner. Isaiah, her nephew, part-time apartment cleaning help and full-time radio broadcaster could be off or on the air on Christmas Eve, so she needed to know.

"Here's what, Etta girl. Isaiah will be there before I will. He gets off the air at 6:00 and will go right to your place, unless the weather gets in the way. It isn't but eight miles to your house from his studio. But I've got to stop at Forbes' and hear a soprano."

"A soprano? What for?"

"It's a Forbes thing; that's all I can tell you. I'll be around about seven-thirty or eight unless the roads are too bad. I hope the salt truck drivers hit the streets early."

"Glad you told me. I planned an early dinner.

"Hey, get you a bottle of Rumchatta and pour it on rocks. That'll make the wait shorter."

"You know I don't drink liquor."

"Yes, I do, big sis, and I think a stiff belt would do you a lot of good. I'll be there by eight.

"Oh, come before you go to Forbes' and I'll have a slice of pumpkin pie for you to take him."

"Shit, girl. I'll come beforehand, and you'll have pumpkin pie for *me*."

"That's right," she sang. "You come on. There'll be pie and coffee and a bowl of chocolate hazelnuts. I know you love those."

"Etta, why don't you come with me to Forbes'? I'm gonna listen to this soprano for a minute, and you and I can leave. I just want to settle Forbes down. He's all hot and bothered for me to hear her."

"How many girls does this make?"

"I lost count. Then we can come back to the house and have Christmas Eve with Isaiah. Three of us. Family. Coming? I'm gonna pick you up around six."

"Oh, no, I'll have things on the stove. You go on without me and I'll be here when Isaiah shows. He might just eat all the pie, though," she teased.

"Better not!"

Chapter 115

Quincy Garland had gone to church as a youngster at St. James African Methodist Episcopal in Lafayette from the time he was old enough to walk on his own. His sister, Marietta and mom, Bea, encouraged the youngster to take part in all the programs offered to youth, and by the time he was eight years old, he knew all his books of the Bible in order, by heart.

It was early that year, however, that Bea Garland had her first epiphany regarding her son. On a Sunday in March, when the weather was inclement, Pastor Stewart asked all the kids to stand at the altar and sing, "Jesus' Little Lamb" for the congregation in an effort to delay the start of services. He hoped the crowd would fill in as an ice storm had, no-doubt, delayed the arrival of many. Thirteen children, aged four to eleven, answered the call to the altar and began the song with the pianist accompanying. With the first note, Quincy's voice came forth, strong and sweet, rich and tuneful, until most of the other children stopped singing and simply watched him.

Bea was thunderstruck.

To Quincy's recollection, that was the last moment of peace he ever knew. From that day forward, his life was a whirlwind of choirs and choir rehearsals every Wednesday and Thursday night. He was invited to join the boys choir, the children's choir, and as he aged, the men's and main choir.

He did many solos, and at Christmastime, his treatment of "O Holy Night" became an experience that parishioners were still talking about the following Christmas.

Quincy reveled in the recognition, and it was fun. He grew to realize his own in-borne ear for harmony, and when he entered high school, he stepped up when the faculty advisor of the music department sought to do a production of *The Little Shop of Horrors*.

Quincy learned years later, that when he got the part of Audrey II, that the faculty advisor chose that musical simply *because* of Quincy's voice.

Quincy made friends in high school, but none who left a more lasting impression than Thurman Walsh. "T," as he preferred to be called, introduced Quincy to the darker side of Lafayette when he started a small in-home business selling mescaline. Seems T had a cousin in Arizona who took to mailing T large packages of mushrooms, and T took the initiative to render them as mesc and start a cottage industry.

It was one night Quincy's sophomore year when he accompanied T to the west side of town to meet a friend, Arturo, for a quick sale and for a sales pitch that there was more where this came from.

The neighborhood was the territory of an up-and-coming drug gang. As the two walked away from Arturo, T realized he may have been hasty in dismissing Arturo's warnings about the meeting place. When a car stopped in the middle of the street, and when another stopped right in front of it, and when three guys exited the cars and walked straight toward Quincy and T. T knew to panic.

He kicked Quincy in the back of his knee, which buckled, knocking him down behind a car. As two shots rang out, Quincy hid his head. That kick to his knee was the last beneficent act Thurman Walsh would ever do, saving Quincy's life, and it stuck with Quincy forever.

Chapter 116

Cole's phone rang in the middle of the afternoon. As always, when a call came in, a part of Cole's mind hoped it would be a venue holder calling about a job. Unlikely on Christmas Eve, but hope springs eternal.

"Hello?" he chirped with his friendly business voice.

"Hey, Cole, it's me. I've got a little problem."

"Tim, hi, what's wrong?"

"Well, the car won't start."

"The brand-new car you just bought won't start?"

"Now, you and I both know this thing is a long way from brand new. I think it's the battery."

"Not that much of a surprise. It's in single digits out there, and it it's already started snowing. You want me to jump start you?"

"I'm at the hospital, and, honestly, I was going to go home and get clothes. I've worn the same two changes of clothes for four days, and I need something, uh, fresher."

"Okay?"

"So, here's my fear. Not only do I need a jump, I really don't want to drive in snow on these tires. They're next to bald, and I'm a little concerned on these roads . . ."

"I got you. You want me to run you home for clothes?"

"If it's a big imposition, I'll do without, but with you all coming over tomorrow, I don't really want to stink up the place."

Cole laughed. "No, no, we don't want you to funk up the place real righteous. Here's the thing, though. I'm helping Shara with the food for tomorrow, but we're going over to Forbes' early in the evening. Since it's not too far away, I could swing by the hospital on the way and get you, run by your house for a minute before we head to Forbes' place. I'll ask Quincy to run you home so Shara and I can go to dinner."

"You think Quincy would mind?"

"No, man, where you stay is not far from his crib, and he goes by there every day anyway to check on the building for Marietta."

Chapter 117

Forbes started out early cleaning his apartment to a fare-thee-well. He even changed the bed sheets, reasoning that you *just never know* who might want to spend the night. It was a pipe dream, but it was his own pipe dream. Mid-morning, he looked out and realized the snow was really coming down.

Good! He told himself smugly, he would prefer that Tori not drive in this. He was glad he'd offered to go get her. His taxi cab tires were worn bald, and he had paid a mechanic $50 under the table to pass his last safety inspection. Yet, his superior male skills as a driver would certainly prevail better than hers would in that new-model car she drove, he convinced himself.

Self-delusion and over-confidence continued as he made a run to the store to purchase 7-Up and bourbon for the cocktails Tori enjoyed. A five-dollar bottle of wine in case Shara wanted to celebrate was an afterthought.

Dusting and vacuuming began when he got home. The snow was piling up, and Forbes sliced open a bag of rock salt he'd gotten while he was out. He threw half a bag on the sidewalk leading to the street.

He lit a pumpkin spice-scented candle to freshen the apartment air. His fingers were crossed that the scent would overcome any residual bud aroma and lend a sense of festivity.

At four o'clock, Forbes showered and shaved. He chose a white button-down shirt under a deep burgundy sweater that could be regarded as Christmas-y. He enacted the customary baptism in cologne, and hoped it blended well with the pumpkin spice.

He left early to pick up Tori. No way to predict these roads.

Chapter 118

"Let's leave a little early because of the roads," suggested Cole.

"I can't agree more," Shara told her husband, "Especially if we are picking up Tim at the hospital. But on the other hand, I'm not in that much of a hurry to get this dinner underway."

"Shara — "

"Look, Cole, I had envisioned giving you this over a romantic candlelight dinner with a glass of wine and a filet, but that idea went the way of the do-do bird. Since I am no-doubt eating at a family-style buffet that doesn't have a liquor license, but does have crowds of noisy children and no serenity, I'm giving you this now."

She presented a small box wrapped in purple foil.

Cole offered a curious look and took it from her.

Shara, still unsettled and resentful about the way her Christmas Eve was ruined, missed Cole's reaction when he opened the box. It was a gold ring with a diamond centered inside a square. Thick, but not massive, tasteful, not gaudy. "It's beautiful," he told her.

"I wanted to give you something you'd never buy for yourself. I hope you'll wear it."

He slipped it on his right ring finger, a mirror to his wedding band. "I'll never take it off. It fits perfectly."

He continued, "I have something for you, too, but I have to wait until later."

"Understood. I'd be happy if Mom stayed out of the presentation."

"Well, that's not it; It's just —"

"Cole, whatever you bought me, it would be a better gift to me if you would return it, with my thanks, and give that money to your mother. There isn't anything I want for Christmas more than being out of debt to her."

"I can't take it back."

"Why?"

"Because of what it is."

"Explain."

"I bought you a new study Bible, and I'm having your name imprinted in gold on the leather cover. The store didn't get it done in time."

"Oh. I love it. Thank you. What kind is it?"

"An English Standard. I love you, Shara, and I'm going to try to shake off my mother. I heard what you said. It's not my fault Dad died. But, when something is pounded into you for so long — "

"You said that before, and I understand. We're going to work on this together, okay? We're going to get you past this guilt. If you had murdered your own father, God still forgives, and if you did nothing wrong at all, you are still in need of His forgiveness, and so am I. We're going to trust Him, and we're not going to be manipulated."

Cole wrapped his arms around Shara and hugged her for a long time. Then he kissed her. When he broke the kiss, he looked in her eyes. "Shara, I do trust Him. But, exonerating myself, well, I wish it was that easy."

Chapter 119

Late in the morning, after Lloyd had slept in later than any morning in his memory, he rose with just a touch of a headache. Lucky, it was only a touch, he told himself. He had really overdone the night before.

In the throes of getting well-polluted, Frank Glenn had confessed his investigation into Barb's Facebook page. He further confessed his realization that he would do anything for Franky, and he could hardly blame Lloyd for his peccadillo about Barb.

Lloyd was pleased to let go of the subterfuge and move on. But he had a question to ask his boss.

After two cups of coffee, he had left Barb in the kitchen and took the third cup to his office. He phoned Glenn at home.

"Ho. Ho. Ho," he said to Glenn when he picked up the phone. His delivery was an overly-serious, bordering on atonal deadpan that cracked Frank up.

"How do you feel, Dr. Fuller?" Frank laughed. "Ready for the hair of the dog?"

"No dog hair," Fuller smiled. "Not even a Mexican hairless."

"I didn't know you had it in you to drink that much."

"I don't. That's the problem."

They laughed together.

"What's on your mind this Christmas Eve morning?"

"Well, I'm calling to be duly penitent, and to ask you what you plan to do about the position."

"The teaching position? Well, my plan is tentative. What are you penitent about?"

"I pushed you into hiring Barbara, and I nudged you away from Shelton."

"All known. All agreed to. Don't you think Shelton has gone back to Columbus long ago and is now gainfully off of our radar?"

"How do you know that?"

"Because of how qualified he is."

"Frank, my sister dates a guy with a doctorate in poli-sci in Cincinnati, and he's managed a coffee shop for two years. Let's call Shelton."

Chapter 120

Quincy arrived first at Forbes' apartment. The sprinkle of rock salt on the path to his building door was losing the battle, and snow was piling up. Quincy noted to himself that the forecast of four to five inches was wrong, as it often is, and there must be eight inches on the ground already, with no sign of stopping. On his way over, he had hit a slick spot and narrowly missed careening into a parked car. The wind was fierce, exacerbating the drifts. Quincy pulled his wool scarf up high around his ears and he set his shoulders toward the frigid air. At once, his foot hit ice, and he skidded, flailing his arms for balance. Pain shot through his ankle as he twisted it. A moment later, Quincy was on his back in a pile of snow.

He cursed long and hard. Seeking to assign blame, he found the scapegoat in Forbes whose home he did not wish to visit on a night like this. He wanted to leave, arrive safely at Etta's, and eat his holiday meal.

Quincy could see himself crashing on her couch tonight rather than drive home after hours' more accumulation was on the roads. That was a given, but now he'd be crashing with an ACE bandage around his swollen ankle. He rolled over on his knees and regained his feet, careful to walk on the grass for traction. His ankle hurt, but not too badly. Maybe it would be okay.

Once at the door, he knocked snow off his feet, and removed his wool hat when he stepped in the outer door. He hobbled up the two steps to the apartment door, grasping the railing as he did. The stairs were wet from snowy feet before him. He knocked.

The door immediately burst open, and a triumphant Forbes stood with a drink in his hand. "Come in, man, come on," he effused. "This is Tori Pappas, she's a friend of mine, a soprano, and I want to see what we can do for her. Why are you limping?"

"I fell on your walkway."

"I salted it."

"Not enough, man. Do you see how it's coming down out there? A county road truck couldn't put down enough salt out there. Your landlord should have done something."

Then, noticing the young woman, Quincy nodded at her. Forbes had just said her name, he knew, but he couldn't call it; it was a total blank. He couldn't help, though, acknowledging her allure. He stifled the many sarcastic responses he could have rendered. "What do you mean, 'we'?" or, "A soprano would be as useful as tits on a boar hog," or, "Drop the pretense, Wilson. Have you gotten laid yet?" all came to mind. Instead he said, "Pleased to meet you." He neither shook her hand or looked in her eyes.

"You want a bourbon and seven?"

"Uh, no, man, I'm due at Marietta's in a minute for Christmas Eve dinner."

With that, a knock sounded on the door. Quincy grabbed the knob and let Cole and Shara enter. Forbes was surprised to see Tim trailing in right behind them. The new arrivals' shoulders and hair were all snowy, and Forbes reached for their coats as they disrobed. He made introductions to Tori, and the Renshaws each shook her hand. Tim stepped forward and said, "Hi."

"Shara," Forbes said. "Do you want a glass of wine."

"Absolutely. I'm not driving, but I am lubricating. It's Christmas Eve and I'm in a mood to drink myself stupid."

Forbes and Quincy wondered what that crack was about, but didn't say anything. Tim looked at her with a quizzical expression.

"Cole, help me get her wine in the kitchen, huh? Bring the coats; I'll hang 'em up."

Cole wondered what on earth Forbes needed help for, getting a glass of wine.

Upon getting out of earshot, Forbes asked conspiratorially, "Well, whaddya think? Is she hot?"

"Yeah, she's hot, but that doesn't matter, does it, if she can't sing?"

"But, she can, man. You'll see."

"Then let me see so I can get out of here." He picked up the wine glass and gestured for Forbes to return with him.

Entering the front room, Forbes said to Tori, "Well, I had hoped we could all sit down and get to know one another, but Cole and his wife have somewhere to be — "

"And, so do I, Forbes," Tori said.

"Tori, I'm taking you to dinner and then to your place. I'm not letting you drive in this. We'll get your car next week."

Shara noted his tone, both paternal and pedantic. She knew Forbes, knew what he wanted and needed in his life. His words and intents were manipulative and false, and she doubted the young woman could see it yet. Forbes was virtually Suzanne. But she kept silent. It wasn't good for anyone to drive in this. At least Forbes had that much sense.

Tim had been told in the car that this audition was for a soprano that the Cole Renshaw Trio had no need for, but Shara was not stingy with her articulations of this waste of time. Tim thought he would help out by saying nothing, or nearly nothing. He snuck a peek out the window, and worried.

"Tori, I brought you here to sing for my partners, so let's let you do that," Forbes continued. "Let me put in a cd."

When the music came up, Tori felt a little helpless and naked. She had no mic, just the music. She would need to power these songs as there was no electronic help. And she was singing for a trio she admired. The onus was on her to do her best, and she felt she was at a disadvantage.

Nancy Wilson's arrangement of "What a Little Moonlight Can Do," was the first to come up. She could have it keyed a little lower, but it was such a simple, repetitive, fun song that she got through it easily. Sensing the jovial timbre of the song, she sang with personality and rhythm, snapping her fingers and swinging her hips.

She noticed that the woman, Shara, gazed at her as she sang with a critical eye. The men were being kind and accepting, and it didn't hurt that they were men. The woman, though, was honest. The white guy she didn't know stared at the floor, trying to be inconspicuous.

The second song, "My Funny Valentine," was simple and unchallenging. It was a good choice for a singer with little experience. There were no huge jumps, and it didn't take much range. It also didn't prove much. During her rendition, she concentrated on tone depth and phrasing.

Her last song, the Whitney Houston piece, was the most difficult. It took power, range, precision, and passion to do well. Tori attempted to render it well by thinking of someone she had once loved desperately and passionately in hopes of improving her performance. But she came up empty. There had been no one she had ever loved like that.

Sal? No. Not yet.

At the conclusion of her performance, the spectators offered encouraging applause. Forbes, of course, clapped with great enthusiasm. The others were just polite.

"Thank you," Tori said, reading the room. "I would appreciate your honest thoughts and criticisms." She would expect, with an invitation like that, for the four to look at each other uncertainly to ascertain who should speak first, but no one did. They eyed the window and the outdoors.

After an awkward moment, Shara stepped in mostly to hasten the end of the meeting. "Well, Tori," she ventured, "You have a strong, lovely voice. But you are making some rookie mistakes which are easy to fix. If you were working with us, I would insist on corrections, and I couldn't let you out on a stage of mine if I was uncertain of you.

"For instance, do not breathe in the middle of a phrase. And never breathe in the middle of a word. That makes me a little crazy. For instance, on the Rodgers and Hart song, you breathed in the middle of 'unphotographable," and I cringed.

"And look at your feet. Stand as if you are firing a gun. Feet planted, breathing enabled. Make yourself wide. Let your diaphragm have all the room it wants." Shara looked at the floor, thinking, and measuring her words.

"Here's a biggie. This drives me over the edge. Do not clip off the end of a phrase in order to breathe and rush into the next phrase. That's about as amateurish a mistake as I can think of.

"I think you have great potential, and you can be going places, but you need to stretch your range. That Whitney song may not be the best choice at this stage, but you can grow into it. Self-knowledge is important. If you get to a stage in a song where you hear yourself lose tone depth, then work on that song until you don't lose tone depth before you sing it in public. You can get there.

"That's all I have. Guys?"

Cole and Quincy knew better than to criticize a female Forbes was stuck on. They both demurred. Quincy said he needed to go. The couple agreed.

Forbes was furious at Shara. He hid it as best he could, but there would be words later for how she jumped down the throat of that poor, beautiful girl and crushed her dream. He abandoned all attempts at objectivity, even though Shara's criticisms were much the same as his own. He hadn't criticized Tori at all to her face, and in the depth of his soul, he recognized he had done her a disservice by humming on her instead of actually guiding her. Could it be possible that Cole and Quincy were onto him? Could he really be deprioritizing his work to mentor in favor, well, . . . getting her to like him? Could it be that his best friends knew him better than he knew himself?

He fetched the coats of his guests, and thrust Shara's into her arms with a pinch of vitriol.

Meanwhile, Tori had hoped for much more. Sure, the words of the woman stung, but she had asked for them, and the woman was actually constructive in her criticism, and helpful. Tori didn't resent honest criticism, never had, but she wished the men had said something. She wished it weren't snowing; she wished no one was in such a hurry to leave.

When everyone was bundled up and ready, Forbes turned off lights and brought up the rear out the door.

Tim, who remained nearest the door, went out first, with Quincy behind him. Quincy turned to say something to Shara and Cole as he noticed a slightly built man coming toward him up the walkway through the snow. "Uh, hi," he started to say as he attempted to step out of the man's way. The man was white, but swarthy, and had a flattened-out, crooked nose.

As Tori and Forbes stepped out of the building and onto the stoop, Forbes offered the young woman his arm to hold. She smiled briefly as she stepped into the snow, careful to watch her footing. When she looked up and saw the newcomer, Tori's mouth fell open in surprise. "Sal! What the devil are you —"

Without warning, Sal pulled a hand gun from his coat pocket, aimed, and fired three times at Forbes.

The loud cracks rang out, echoing among the apartment buildings through the silent air.

Quincy dove at Shara, knocking her down and landing on her. He bellowed, "Get down!"

Tim, adrenalin suddenly rushing, dove into the snow and lay quietly. The sense of panic, now familiar after months of unease, settled in like an old comrade.

Quincy, then, reached up with one leg and slammed his foot into the back of Cole's knee, knocking him down just as Thurman Walsh had knocked him down decades before.

Cole felt a sharp stab in his thigh as his legs were knocked out from under him. A stray bullet had ricocheted off the brick building, and caught him. He screamed out as he fell in the snow. Blood shot from his upper thigh, and he grabbed the wound. He screamed again. His cries sliced through Shara. She tried to push Quincy off her, but he grunted quietly, "Stay still."

The gunman took off, running imprudently on the snowy grass. He slid and slipped, falling once and regaining his feet. The thought would occur to him later that Tori had seen his face; there was no point in trying to flee from the crime. But the deed was done; he had accomplished his goal. Forbes Wilson would never bother Tori again.

Tori and Shara were screaming in horror. Tim, with a renewed sense of being under siege, froze in terror.

When the gunman was out of sight, Shara pushed Quincy off of her, and grappled for her purse and her phone. In moments, she was screaming at the 911 dispatcher to send help as she stumbled across the slick walkway to Cole's side. He was still screaming. Shara yelled above him into her phone.

Quincy, confident that the gunman would not return, regained his feet and limped to Forbes who lay very still.

Tori merely stood in place, shrieking and crying. Forbes' blood had splattered on her coat. It shocked her. She had never seen so much blood. She had watched her baby sister be born ten years ago. It wasn't as awful as this.

Tim Shelton, prostrate in the snow, squeezed his eyes shut, and imagined how Theresa's life would be if he weren't there to care for her.

Chapter 121

It was fine with Pasternak that she drew a solo tour on Christmas Eve. Folks usually stayed home on the holiday and crime was low. Mueller had asked off and she was happy to start the tour without him. Plus, she reasoned, there was no one to go home to.

Tiffany heard three shots ring from a distance from her cruiser. The sound was ubiquitous, bouncing off the many tall apartment buildings in the surrounding blocks. She pulled out, but didn't turn on her sirens, anxious for another sound clue. As she turned the corner, she saw people laying face-down in the snow and two women screaming.

She called for back-up and then paramedics once she saw the blood-stained snow. She barked her location at the dispatcher as she skidded in to the curb behind a minivan.

She rushed to the scene, looking about her carefully for signs of a perp. Seeing none, she triaged. Two men were hit. As she rolled one of them over to check his wound, he looked familiar to her, but she couldn't place the face. A woman was kneeling next to him. Yes, Tiffany noted, she'd seen these people before. He was hit in the thigh and was losing blood fast. Her first instinct was to worry for his femoral artery.

She hollered at the woman to find her something to wrap this wound. The woman stood and marched to the younger woman and snatched the wool scarf from around her neck. Both women were sobbing, but the older one was at least trying to function.

Pasternak used the scarf to secure a makeshift tourniquet and pulled it as tight as she could.

It was wholly inadequate and the blood soaked it and continued oozing into the snow. "Ma'am, do you have a belt, or is your friend wearing a belt?"

Tori stepped forward as she unbuckled her braided leather belt, pulled it out of the loops, and handed it to the officer. Her hands were shaking so hard she could barely hand the thing off.

Pasternak used the belt to tighten the hand-made tourniquet. Then, she got on her shoulder radio, requested an estimated arrival time for the paramedics. "I've got a shooting. Two victims have gunshot wounds."

"Roads are bad, Pasternak," came the reply.

"Thanks, Ellison, I hadn't noticed. How soon?"

Out of the corner of her eye, she saw a beige sedan driving slowly away. The car moved slowly either because of the road conditions or because the driver didn't wish to be noticed. She couldn't be sure. Visibility was low, but she could make out the plate number, which she memorized before returning to her task.

The man closest to the door was hit twice. The wound in his neck looked bad. She knelt near him.

People were coming out of the building, she noticed, and out of buildings next door and across the street. She bellowed, "Stay back. You're standing in a crime scene. Go back inside. Now! We'll want statements from everyone, but now you are compromising the scene!"

Turning her attention to Tori, she asked, "Did you see who fired at you?"

"It was my boyfriend," the younger woman admitted between sobs. "I had no idea he was so . . . "

"What's his name?"

"Sal Romano."

"What does he drive?"

"A beige Buick."

"That Buick there?" Pasternak pointed at the slow-moving car.

"Yeah, maybe," she admitted. "I think so."

A small group of spectators had formed on the sidewalk near the street. Tiffany rolled her eyes in exasperation. Well, maybe, she thought, with this witness identifying the boyfriend, tracks in the snow won't matter.

Tiffany pressed her hand hard against the gushing blood at Forbes' neck. She used her other hand on the shoulder radio. "I need cruisers to search for Sal Romano, a male. Copy this Indiana plate number PAWN66, in the neighborhood surrounding the corner of Impala and Justine. Attempted murder suspect. I've got two down at 1236 Impala. Where is my ambulance?"

"Ambulance is two minutes out," came dispatcher Ellison's crackling voice. "They're having trouble negotiating these roads."

"I heard you the first time. I'm going to lose two men here from GSWs if I don't get help now! Ellison, send cruisers to Sal Romano's address and place of work."

At the suggestion of losing two men, Shara collapsed into renewed hysterics. Tiffany could only tell her that an ambulance has the equipment and crew to stabilize the victims. Shara was inconsolable, though, until she saw the blessed ambulance turn the corner and drive up onto the lawn.

Tiffany questioned the wisdom immediately. If the ambulance lost traction on the grass, they might never get it back on the street. She swore under her breath. At that point, she noticed another man standing near the one with the femoral artery. His face was blanched white, and his panic was etched on his face.

Shara knelt in the snow next to Cole. She touched his face, stroked his forehead, and whispered, "I'm sorry," over and over. She kissed his face.

"What are you sorry for?" Tiffany asked. "Is this your husband?"

"Yes. I'm sorry that I have been so mad at him lately. I never dreamed I might lose him . . . I never thought . . . ."

"The ambulance is here, ma'am. You'll want to ride to the hospital with it." She rose and went to the other victim.

Quincy was at Forbes' chest next to Pasternak as she was pressing her hand against his neck. The blood was everywhere, and Quincy was hearkening back to his high school friend, shot to death in a place he shouldn't have been.

He grasped handfuls of clean snow to wash off the blood that was forming a red, gory paste in the frozen air. As he did, snippets of memory flitted through his mind.

Twenty years ago, at a street show outside of a Lafayette hospital, a woman — Theodoro, Quincy thought was her name — asked Quincy and Forbes to sing "Knock on Wood." An unnecessary amount of discussion followed. While both men knew the song, Theodoro seemed puzzled for some reason. Quincy couldn't remember why.

"You guys can sing, 'Knock on Wood' for me?" she wanted to know.

They nodded in unison. The hospital held the show yearly on its parking lot to generate interest in its services. Forbes and Quincy didn't care about that. They just wanted to sing.

"Will you guys sing it for me?" Theodoro pleaded.

"Sure."

"Okay, after this country singer finishes, I'll call you on stage, k? 'Knock on Wood,' right?"

"Sure." Quincy had repeated, "Knock on Wood."

The two sat down on a retaining wall nearby and waited for Theodora to signal them.

At one point, she sent a young woman who had just sung a Barbara Mandrell song earlier, to approach the two. "Theodora wants to know if you're going to sing, 'Knock on Wood.'"

"Wow, man," Quincy told Forbes. "I told that woman three times we'd do it. What's her damned problem?"

"Her problem is that she doesn't know Eddie Floyd from Jackie Wilson, or from Doris Day for that matter. Ten bucks says she doesn't know the song."

"Solid."

"So," the young woman repeated, "You're going to do the song she said."

The two ignored her.

After the call came, the digital accompaniment began. The two men, now on stage, heard the familiar music and laughed so hard they nearly missed the start of the vocals. Quincy did a pantomime of laying dollars in Forbes' hand as the two jumped into the Isley Brothers' "It's Your Thing." The two destroyed the song with their amazing singing chops, and Quincy was bound to hold that satisfying memory in his heart for all time.

Now, in Quincy's mind, the sweet memory rushed to his defense, blocking out the images before his eyes. Let this not end the memories, Quincy prayed. Let this not be the end. He squeezed his eyes shut, blocking tears.

As paramedics Dickson and Bruce leaped from their vehicle, Pasternak barked facts. "I've got a gunshot in the thigh here; possible femoral artery, and over there a neck wound, and I don't know if he's hit anywhere else. Neck looks bad. The two knelt in the snow and applied a proper tourniquet to Cole's leg. Tiffany stood to help Bruce lift the gurney, but the uninjured white man nudged her aside. "Let me," he told her. She returned to Dickman who was traching Forbes.

The wife, Tiffany noticed, was completely in the way and would not stand aside. Tiffany vaguely hoped that, if she were ever shot, someone would be in the way to worry about her. Her heart went out to the mortified woman who could do nothing but panic.

Quincy helped Shara climb into the back of the ambulance before he hoisted himself into it. Tim climbed in last.

Dickman was now kneeling at Forbes' chest. Pasternak, reaching his side, communicated to him with a glance. They non-verbally exchanged a message that was too clear.

Dickman bellowed at Bruce, "I'm traching this victim!" In a moment, Bruce was rushing over with supplies. Pasternak looked away as Bruce sliced through the front of Forbes' neck and applied the bag and device to force air into his trachea. Having taped the trach in place, Dickman found another gunshot wound in his chest and an exit wound leaking blood into the snow. Bruce applied a dressing. That should get him to the hospital.

"Let's get this man on board. I'll hold the trach in place," he said to Pasternak and Bruce.

Tim imagined that hours were going by as he watched the paramedics tend to Forbes. Shara, at his side in the ambulance, cried, and her tears were small stab wounds to Tim as well. He looked at Cole, and Cole, cringing with pain, met Tim's eyes. He mouthed something inaudible. Tim leaned his ear against Cole's mouth, but couldn't make anything out.

Tim was afraid to touch his friend, afraid he would cause more pain. The drenched tourniquet, red and greasy, turned Tim's stomach over. It struck him hard that he could easily lose the only friend he had left in the world, and that his view of his circumstances had gone from not good to horrific in a matter of seconds.

Bruce, at the wheel, tried to move the ambulance.

Pasternak, knowing time was crucial, could not call herself surprised when tires spun in the snow. Everyone on board heard the tires spinning, but felt the vehicle moving not at all. As Pasternak watched, the rear door opened and the uninjured white man jumped down at her side, slamming the door behind him. He and Pasternak positioned themselves against the rear of the ambulance, planted her feet and pushed with their shoulders.

Maybe, just maybe, Pasternak hoped, the help of the man would be enough to get this buggy back on the street. She cursed silently the decision to drive up on this slick lawn.

Tiffany looked at the man next to her. His face was red with effort as the two bore down. There was more to him, though. A stress she didn't expect to see. This man was committed. He became her best hope for success.

The truck began to move. The tires spun and spun, spraying snow and mud out behind itself, but the vehicle slowly made progress. Abruptly, it got its traction somehow, and moved off the lawn.

Tiffany fell into the snow. As her shoulder impacted the ground, waves of pain hit her, but she mentally walked it off. This shoulder might be dislocated, was the thought that occurred to her. She held her bad arm with the good one as she struggled to her feet.

Tim, meanwhile, as the ambulance advanced, landed on his knees, not softly. As he stood, he held out a hand to the woman and helped her to her feet.

As the ambulance got back onto the pavement, it paused. Tim realized it was waiting for him, and he trotted carefully to the street, opened the back door, and got back in.

The only victim left behind was the young woman who was sobbing on the sidewalk. This was the one who said her boyfriend was responsible for this murder attempt.

"Your car is here?"

"No, I'm stranded. Forbes was my ride." The young woman descended into another crying fit.

"I'll get you a ride home after you make a statement at the police station. What's your name?"

"Victoria Pappas."

Pasternak looked over Tori's shoulder and noticed two police cruisers and an evidence truck pull into snow-covered parking spaces on the street. She walked toward the first driver and greeted him.

"Ambulance just left with two victims and three witnesses. I've got one uninjured victim here. She knows the perp."

"Romano, right?" asked Dave Palance.

"Right. Is his name and license on air?"

"All cruisers searching for him. Baker and Trefenbach are on their way to his place."

"The witness, Victoria Pappas, needs to be medically checked out and then should go to the house and make a statement while the rest of you process the scene." She watched as two technicians she didn't know stepped from the evidence truck holding equipment cases.

"Why don't you take her, Pasternak?"

"Because I'm going to the hospital. I think I dislocated my shoulder."

"Ouch," Palance sympathized. "I wondered why you were holding your arm that way. Get in. I'll take you and the other victim both."

"Look, thanks, but can I go to St. Mary's?"

"Regional not good enough?"

"St. Mary's is closer to my crib."

"Square."

While Pasternak and Tori got in the cruiser, Palance stepped out. He spoke very briefly to Relaford and Anders in the other cruiser. On his way back to the car, Palance slipped and fell on the sidewalk, landing on his buttocks, and spewing a stream of cuss words.

Yeah, it's real slick, Pasternak said to herself. Any other time, when her shoulder wasn't screaming at her, she'd laugh behind his physical comedy. Nothing at all funny had happened today, though.

Chapter 122

When Marietta opened the door at seven o'clock, she was nearly bouncing up and down in panic. She glanced at Isaiah and shrieked, "Let's go. Hospital. Your father's been in a shooting!"

"What?"

"Drive the car."

On the way out, Isaiah drove imprudently on the slick roads, as Marietta described to him the phone call she had gotten from his father. She explained that there had been an incident at Forbes Wilson's house and shots had been fired.

As she explained, Isaiah pressed the accelerator recklessly, scarcely caring if he hit anything. He slid through stop signs and a few red lights, grateful that most other drivers who would have been on the road, were home with their families on Christmas Eve.

His dad, it seemed, had called Aunt Etta from the hospital. He had given little by way of explanation, but mentioned that blood would be needed. It was then, Marietta told Isaiah, she had begun bouncing up and down, waiting for him.

She intended to give blood. Would Isaiah do so also?

"Of course, I will."

As they pulled into the emergency room drive, Isaiah skidded to a stop at the door. "Go," he commanded. "I'll be in when I park the car." Marietta grabbed her purse and head scarf and exited the car.

She immediately slipped and fell in the snow.

"Etta!" he bellowed.

"I'm all right. Turned my ankle." She pulled herself to her feet and hobbled into the ER. "They ought to salt this parking lot better," she muttered under her breath.

Once inside, Marietta limped to the desk and blurted, "I'm Marietta Washington. My brother, Quincy Garland is here. I want to see him."

The clerk had no chance to respond. Quincy appeared behind her and took her hand.

"Oh, my God! You're all right!" She flung herself into his arms and he held her close.

"I'm cool, Etta. It's Cole and Forbes. They were hit. Cole has lost a lot of blood, and they won't tell me anything about Forbes because I'm not a relative."

"You aren't Cole's relative either. How do you know about him?"

"Shara's here and they told her."

"I see."

"Isaiah with you?"

"Parking the car. Roads are bad. I fell outside."

"Yeah, I know I fell too, earlier. The ambulance was driving slow. It was maddening. You okay?"

"Hurt my ankle. It's gonna swell, but I'll be fine. Where is everybody?"

"This way."

It was a good twenty minutes before Isaiah found a way to park and make his way to those gathered in the waiting room. Shara was white with fear and worry. Her hands were shaking and Quincy, seated next to her, was holding one of them. Marietta sat on the other side of him.

When Quincy saw Isaiah, he let go of Shara's hand and stood. Isaiah, with his coat thrown over his arm, dumped the coat on a nearby chair and hugged his father. "Are you okay? You look okay."

"I didn't get hit, son. It's okay for me. Forbes and Cole were hit. Cole's in surgery and we're waiting for word on Forbes. His mother is on the way."

"Okay," Isaiah said. "What happened?"

Quincy sat down and quickly explained the events outside Forbes' apartment. As he did, Shara began to cry again, and he reached for her hand.

Isaiah said to Marietta, "Where do I give blood?" He noticed that her coat was off and her sleeve was rolled up. She was pressing on a cotton ball and bandage in the crook of her elbow. She pointed him to the clerk behind the desk. Isaiah strode to the clerk, tearing off his thick wool sweater as he did so. After he spoke, she opened the gate and permitted him into the back.

In Shara's mind, time had slowed to a crawl. She had been in this waiting room for ten years, it seemed like, and the people around her moved in slow motion. She prayed like she had never prayed before that her husband would be okay. She had been at the site of the shooting. She had seen the blood-soaked snow and Cole's blood soaked coat and pants. She couldn't banish the images. They repeated in an endless loop through her mind's eye, and she searched her memory for what she could have done differently. What should she have known? Why did this happen? What is the meaning? What can she do now but trust and pray that Cole and Forbes would make it?

Shara's own history was unhelpful. This was not her first emergency room visit. There had been other family members in crisis, and those memories flitted through her mind. But none like this. None of this magnitude. None of this terror. None of this unexpected, incalculable, senseless evil. Her sobbing resumed.

Quincy, watching his son enter the gate into the emergency treatment area, noticed a familiar sight. There was Genevieve Wilson, Forbes's mother, entering the emergency room. She was dressed, as was her practice, in blue jeans and a leather jacket. Her matted, wet hair was covered in a leather helmet reminiscent of a World War II fighter pilot, and Genevieve, as always, bore the air of a lady truck driver, but not as feminine.

Quincy rose to greet her, but before he could get to the counter where she stood, she rushed through the gate to the back. He returned to his seat and said to Shara, "That was Forbes' mother. We'll know something pretty soon."

Chapter 123

Shara checked with the front desk four times before she got definitive news about her husband. The surgery was long, and a vascular specialist had been called in at the last minute to assist. The surgeon's drive, usually a fifteen-minute trek, took an hour, and Shara was sure she had aged ten years during the drive.

In the waiting room, Shara was numb and aghast at the turn of events. How? Why? The questions had no answers. Shara and Quincy, holding hands in the waiting room, were less than encouraged when Genevieve, from inside the examination room, cried out so loud that the sound was jarring. All motion stopped as nurses, technicians, visitors and patients were chilled.

Both Shara and Quincy knew what the plaintive, miserable wail meant. Forbes was gone, and there would be no recovering from this. Everything changed with Forbes' demise, and there was a darkness in front of both of them.

Shara became physically cold and sick. She excused herself to a bathroom and filled the toilet with vomit as she grappled to understand her loss. She grieved for Genevieve, whom she had met only once, ten years ago, and she grieved for herself, a potential widow, and prayed, and prayed, and prayed.

She never thought of calling Suzanne.

Chapter 124

Pasternak didn't go to the same hospital as Cole and the others. St. Mary's was much closer to her house, and if they drugged her, she wanted a short distance to get home.

True, no one was on the roads to speak of, but the conditions were so bad, she dreaded the four-block sojourn to her apartment.

Within a few minutes of her arrival, she was in an examination room, gritting her teeth. A triage nurse came into the room. "Are you Officer Tiffany Pasternak?" the nurse asked.

"Yes."

"What is your birthdate?"

Tiffany told her. She stared at the woman who was perhaps 40, and quite beautiful. She was large, even horsey, a lot like Tiffany, herself, but with flawless dark chocolate skin and large, expressive, scintillating eyes with long lashes. The lashes had to be fake, Tiffany noted, but they made her eyes gorgeous.

"What's your name?"

"You can call me Nurse Beth," she replied. "How did you dislocate your shoulder, Officer Pasternak?"

"Pushing an ambulance off a slick lawn in falling snow while two men bled out on board. What's going to happen?"

"Sounds heroic."

"Yeah, well, don't let the cop uniform fool you. I'm actually an Amazon warrior."

"You're just disguised as a cop."

"It's my secret identity."

Tiffany was sweating and miserable, as evidenced by the tension in her voice even as she tried to be flippant. But Nurse Beth took her mind off of things just for a minute.

"Seriously, Nurse Beth, what's going to happen?"

"Well, when I get a doctor in here, she's going to manipulate your arm and try to get the bone to pop back into the socket. The pain should ease after that. How's the morphine doing?"

"Not that great."

Beth reached for a control on the IV stand and punched the button for another dose. "What about now?"

"That's a little better."

"You said you were saving people who were bleeding out?"

"Yeah, I happened on a crime scene. Two men shot, both life-threatening wounds."

"They in here?"

"No. They're over at Regional. I sure hope they're okay."

"Why? They nice guys?"

"I have no idea. You like nice guys?"

"Not that much," Beth confessed. "I'm not really a guy kind of girl."

Tiffany's eyes widened briefly. "May turn out we have a lot in common. How long have you been nursing?"

"Twelve years. How long have you been doing a job that gets you needing nursing?"

"This is my first dislocated shoulder, Nurse Beth."

"It won't be your last."

"What in hell does that mean?"

"Slow down, Amazon princess. I mean that once a shoulder has been dislocated, it tends to get dislocated again and again."

"How long am I going to be out of work?"

Beth stared at Tiffany for several seconds, measuring her words. "I don't know, but I think, long enough to take me out for a drink."

"You like Evie's?" Tiffany asked, mentioning the lesbian bar in midtown.

"I've shut it down several times. But you'll have to wait until you're off narcotics before you can tie one on."

"Then, I'll need your phone number."

Chapter 125

Within an hour, Tori Pappas had been transported to district headquarters to answer questions by police. She spoke to three officers and Chief De Lancie, who scarcely concealed his resentment for being called back to work on Christmas Eve.

She told the cops four or five times that her guy, Sal Romano, was a wonderful guy, wouldn't hurt a flea, gentle and kind, but had a bit of a possessive streak. She resisted the use of the word "jealous," as that left a harsher impression. But she feared the temptation of wholesale lying.

After an hour of questioning, Tori realized she would not be able to save Sal. And she shouldn't. There was no doubt; Sal had pulled the trigger. There was no whitewashing it. She'd seen it with her own eyes.

It was then that the realization hit her. The blame was squarely in her lap. It was she who had repeatedly gone out with Forbes, who had led her boyfriend to believe that Forbes was a threat, who had preferred Forbes' company believing he could enhance her musical standing, all the while knowing, but not caring, that Sal was clearly enraged.

Had she not flaunted her relationship with Forbes, had she not let her pride and Forbes' flattery influence her, perhaps this could have not happened.

Sitting in an interrogation room that reminded her far too much of some crime drama, Tori put her blood-soaked coat back on for warmth. The realization of her culpability chilled her blood. She wept and wept.

Chapter 126

As it was the holiday, and De Lancie wanted to get back home, he gave a lick and a promise to his interrogation of the witness, Victoria Pappas, before asking a uniform to drive her home.

De Lancie sympathized. The woman, young, inexperienced, and pretty dumb-ass, did not grasp that boyfriends tend to object when their women go out with other guys. De Lancie did all the correct things: he put a notification out on the wire with the car description and license tag with a physical description of Romano that the Pappas woman had provided. He imagined Romano would be arrested soon, and he hoped his holiday could be redeemed.

De Lancie had to hand it to Pasternak. She was not his favorite officer, but he admitted she had stepped up to save two lives this evening, and had put herself in danger to do so. He'd write himself a note to remind him the next time she got on his last stinking nerve. But he'd do that after the holiday.

Meanwhile, the young woman had a ride home on the horrible roads, so he congratulated himself for well-managing the situation. Pasternak was always going to be a work in progress, but this evening told him she could be a good officer.

Chapter 127

Romano had just started to turn down his street, thinking he'd stop and throw some clothes in a bag, when he saw Greenback and Baker's cruiser pull into the street from the far end of the block. He had caught his turn in time to straighten his wheel and keep going.

His thoughts were a jumble of self-defense and fear. His last run-in with the police had been twelve years ago. There had been a disagreement at a local watering hole in Indianapolis and he had spent the night in jail.

This was far different, he knew.

Tori had seen his face as he pulled the trigger, and, while it was worth a lot to get rid of Forbes Wilson, all hope of getting away with murder was extinguished.

Traveling on these roads was next to impossible, but it would be impossible for the police as well. He'd head out of town, and if lucky, would eventually drive out from under the snow. He'd go east as the radio had said the storm was going east. He'd get on I-70 and take Route 41. It should be plowed and salted.

Sal shook all over. His face was drawn with tension, and his need to piss was acute.

He could stop at the pawn shop, grab a few things, and use the bathroom.

No, and damnation, he told himself. If they knew where he lived, then they'd be at the shop just as well.

Sal resigned himself to owning only the clothes on his back. He'd stop at an ATM and get as much cash as he could.

As the machinations flowed through his head, his fears increased, and his sense of loneliness set in. He surely did not think this through, he lamented. The tension of merely driving on these roads would exhaust a titan, but combined with, well, the situation, he doubted he'd get far before he'd have to pull over.

The cops would be contacting his mom in Indianapolis; he can't go there. They'd be after his dad in Fort Wayne. Hell and damnation, he repeated to himself. He sure didn't think this through. He had only gotten as far as getting rid of that ape. He hadn't thought one inch past that.

What about Bucky?

His childhood friend, still in Indianapolis, was always glad to see him, but as far as Sal knew, he wasn't in contact with anyone Sal knew. He'd head there. This, at least, this was a plan.

Chapter 128

Suzanne waited until 8:30 before she microwaved a breaded chicken patty with steamed broccoli and rice for dinner. It was a shabby meal, and not what she had anticipated at all. Or, what she had been promised. She had begun calling her son's mobile phone at 7:15, but there had been no answer all night. She had left about seventeen messages in ascending levels of anger. No one ever called her back, and she had a sneaking feeling that it was that Shara who was behind Cole's standing his mother up.

It occurred to her briefly that there may have been trouble on the roads. But, they both had cell phones and there was no excuse. She turned to her default position of blaming Cole for everything that went wrong, ever, and she'd speak her mind at some point, just watch her.

Her appetite was all ready for a big steak and a baked potato, but as the minutes passed, her craving became a resentment that her Christmas Eve meal, accompanied by the check Cole had promised her, was not going to materialize, and she'd be darned if she didn't find out why.

She called to the cat. She opened a can of cat food and poured it out in the cat dish, talking sweetly to her companion and friend. She considered the things that could have gone wrong, but she centered the blame on Cole and Shara, not imagining what they would say when she reached them.

Chapter 129

Sal continued east on Highway 70 towards Indianapolis. A part of him was grateful that the visibility was so low. He could probably be well on his way to losing himself in the large city before any of the authorities were able to see his license plate in the snow and darkness. He only needed to be careful and safe. If there were a traffic incident, and the police were summoned, his goose would be cooked. He'd be very careful.

He reminded himself that he was a good boyfriend, and even though he would doubtlessly pay dearly for his actions tonight, he did it for Tori, and she would certainly stand by him once she recognized his loving sacrifice. Obviously, he had done it all for her. There was no doubt that she would see that and honor him for his effort to save her.

The gun was in his jacket pocket. Its position called to mind the young man he had gotten it from and his suspicious demeanor. Now it was Sal who was suspicious, but his heart was in the right place, and he hoped everyone would understand that. Obviously, Forbes Wilson was the wrongdoer, and everyone would eventually come to realize that, exonerate Sal, and reward him for his intentions.

These circuitous self-examinations and excuses ran through Sal's head as a repeating loop for the hour it took to get to his friend's house.

He hadn't been to Indy for years. Thirty miles outside of the metro area, the snow stopped, and he had only to find the house and start a new life. He had left a lot behind. But it was for Tori. Just think about Tori.

He dared not use his cell phone. Pulling into a Quik Trip just off the interstate, he asked the clerk for a phone directory and called his buddy on a cell phone he borrowed from a pretty young customer.

Bucky picked up the phone, and, recognizing Sal's voice, was elated. "Hey, man, merry Christmas. Glad you called. What are you doin' this Christmas?"

"Hey, Buck. I just got to town. I'm wondering if I could crash at your place for a little while?"

"Uh, geez, I wasn't expecting . . ."

"It's a last-minute thing, that's all. I would've called earlier if I'd been thinking right. Whaddya say? You got a couch for me to crash on for a night or two.

"Yeah, Sal, hold on for a minute. I just want to run this by Angie." Bucky covered the phone with his hand so that his voice was reduced to muffled pleas. It was a full two minutes before he spoke to Sal.

"She says okay. But all we got is the couch. You comin'?"

"Sure. I'll be there. But give me directions. I'm on the highway east bound at Emmett Grove. Where do I go from here?"

Bucky explained the simple route to his house, and Sal promised to be there before it got too late. He said to tell Angie thanks, whoever Angie was supposed to be, and breathed a sigh of relief as he gave the phone back to the pretty young girl.

Chapter 130

Quincy could not process the grief. He sat in Cole's hospital room and waited for Cole to awaken. He knew that the telling of the bad news about Forbes was on him. He wouldn't put that on Shara. Shara was passed out in a chair, exhausted from the ordeal, and Quincy sat in the chair next to her, her head resting on his shoulder.

Etta and Isaiah had gone. There might still be some Christmas dinner left after all these hours, and they should have some. But Quincy had no appetite. He only had a dreaded fear of the black abyss before him.

Cole was going to be all right. He had lost a lot of blood, but the hospital had transfused a lot. He was out of danger, and he had that to be thankful for. But his thoughts were on Forbes, and his memories and fears and joys related to his friend ran in sequence through his mind.

At some point, Quincy wondered who the gunman had been. He recalled vaguely that the girl — what was her name — Tori? She seemed to know the guy. He dismissed his curiosity. He didn't know or care who the man was. Quincy only knew that his dear friend was gone, and nothing was bringing him back.

It wasn't his first death. He'd lost his parents at early ages, his friend, Thurman, from high school, three cousins, and an uncle. Why did this one hurt so much?

He looked at the pictures in his mind's eye of Forbes laughing, eyes crinkled up in mirth.

He thought of the time Forbes and Shara had hilariously argued about what would be the best way to turn around Forbes' car in Shara's driveway. Forbes had said he wanted to turn around the front end and face the taxi out so Cole could get up close with the jumper cable. Shara had argued the practicality of turning the whole car around rather than just the front end, and the senseless argument had eaten up minutes until Cole had screamed, "Stop!"

Quincy called to mind the time many years ago at Shara's parents' house.

The Cole Renshaw Trio had been there celebrating some birthday or other, and had performed Sammy Davis Jr.'s "I Gotta Be Me." Cole was on the tonic note while Quincy was on the third interval and Forbes was on the fifth. One half second before the final, climactic harmony note, Forbes had looked at Quincy, and Quincy just knew, he just knew that Forbes wanted to switch parts. So, when that note came, Quincy hit the fifth, fully expecting Forbes to take the third. And he did. The note sounded better than ever. Later, Cole had said, "What made you change?"

Forbes had said, "We just decided."

Quincy, in a hospital chair with a frightened and exhausted Shara on his shoulder, and a comatose Cole, in the bed, sporting a large bandage and dressing on his left thigh, squinted his eyes shut to block out his sobs. Grown men don't sob when someone dies. Except that they do.

Chapter 131

It was ten o'clock Christmas morning when Shara Renshaw peeked in the door of Theresa's hospital room. Theresa was dozing. There was a finished, but uncleared breakfast tray on her rolling cart. Tim was flipping channels on the television. As she approached, she noticed that Tim smelled like sweat. She touched his shoulder from behind.

Tim jumped to his feet when he saw Shara. Theresa, smiled dutifully as each of the Sheltons welcomed the visitor.

She bore the angst of a million worries, and Tim braced for the worst.

"How are they?" His question was half of a deep concern and half of a demand.

Theresa merely stared. Having grown used to pitfalls and calamities, she looked at Shara with apprehension and fear. Her hands stayed still.

"Well, quite a lot, I'm afraid," Shara replied. Her eyes were red from crying, and the timbre of her voice almost cracked. "

"Cole lost a lot of blood. His femoral artery was hit and he nearly bled out, but the hospital got to him in time, just barely. The ER is still asking for blood donors. I gave blood and so did some of our friends, but, anyway, Forbes didn't make it."

The couple sat silent. After half a minute of watching Shara bury her face in her hands, Theresa whimpered, "That nice man died?"

Shara inhaled and exhaled loud and hard before answering. "Yes, Forbes was a nice man. And, yes, he died. The shooter got away, but the police are on his trail. Forbes' mother is still in the ER, I think, crying like the damned, and, Theresa, I don't know, I'm so thankful that Cole isn't dead, too, I can hardly think of Forbes. It's wrong of me."

"What did your mother-in-law say? Is she down in the ER?"

Theresa's innocent question stung Shara.

"Oh, my God!" Shara cried, shock all over her face. She followed the cry with a long string of curse words the Sheltons never dreamed would come out of her. She fumbled in her pocket for her phone.

"Not in here, Shara," Tim said, guiding her outside. "They don't like cell phones next to these monitors."

"Oh, hell's bells," she replied, frustrated, "I'll just go over there to her house."

"You won't do that either. There's twelve inches on the ground. Let's go to the cafeteria and you can call." Tim grasped Shara's elbow and led her into the hallway. "While you do that, I'll go down to the ER and offer blood."

"Kind of you, Tim."

"No, it isn't. He's my best friend in the world, Cole is. Tapping a vein is the very least I could do. Call me if he needs a kidney."

"You're kidding, but I don't know that he won't."

Chapter 132

Officer Terry Blackwell sat in his cruiser next to a liquor store in suburban Indianapolis. A twenty-five-year veteran of the Indy P.D., he smelled retirement on every breeze. It was the end of his tour, and he had minutes to kill before heading to the station. Most of his Christmas could be spent with Ric, Julie and his five grandkids who would all be over at the house by noon. His wife, Sophie, had gotten up early to cook, and she'd have a bite for him before he laid down for a few hours.

Terry was parked in his usual place. He didn't even know that two houses up the block was the domicile of one Bucky Bianchi, childhood friend of Salvador Romano.

Blackwell noticed the beige sedan parked in front. He hadn't noticed it before on any of the mornings he'd parked here waiting for his shift to be over. He thought nothing of it. Those people had guests for Christmas morning, it appears. Out of town guests at that, he mused, based on the county indicated by the license plate.

As he observed the house, its front door opened and a slightly built man stepped onto the stoop. He thanked the people inside for the place to crash, laughed at something one of them said, and turned to go down the stairs. He saw Terry at the same moment Terry saw him.

Sal's crooked, flattened nose gave him away. Terry recognized him from the description that had come over the wire of a man wanted for murder in Terre Haute. He immediately ran the plate, and it came up fast, as the network wasn't busy on a Christmas morning.

As Sal stepped to his car with haste, the police car at the corner sounded its siren. Sal froze, and fingered the trigger inside his coat pocket.

The report out of Terre Haute had called this man armed and extremely dangerous, Blackwell realized. He called for back-up, gave his location, and, he hoped, his sense of urgency. With lights flashing, and siren wailing, Blackwell put his car in gear and pulled forward.

Sal stepped into his car.

He's going to make a break for it, Terry thought. Quickly, before Romano could get his engine started, Blackwell pulled in front and angled his front fender just ahead of Sal's, blocking him in. He opened his driver's door, and stepped out, crouching down. He duck-walked to the front of his vehicle. His intention was to put the cruiser's engine between himself and Romano.

"Halt! Police!" Terry bellowed unnecessarily.

Sal knew what was coming. As he raised his gun and pointed it at Officer Blackwell, the veteran cop fired several times directly at Romano's windshield. As Blackwell knew they would, the first three shells ricocheted off the glass, creating a tight spider web of cracks. The fourth shot penetrated.

Salvador Romano's last thoughts before he greeted death were of Tori. She would be happy to know that he loves her so, and he did this for her.

Chapter 133

A groggy Suzanne answered the phone early Christmas morning. She had planned to be up early for Christmas breakfast, but after her horrible son and his wife stood her up Christmas Eve, there would be no counting on them. She turned off the alarm and slept in.

"What happened?" were her opening words to the caller, whom she assumed would be Cole.

Instead it was Shara. "Cole's been shot."

Silence.

"Did you hear me, Mom?"

"I don't think I did. What?"

"Cole was shot last night at Forbes' house, and so was Forbes. I've been at the hospital all night. You can get out of bed and come over here. We're at Regional."

"Are you going to come get me?"

"No, Ma'am, I am not leaving here for the foreseeable. You can call a taxi."

"What happened?" Suzanne repeated.

"We were leaving Forbes' house, on the way over to get you, and we were ambushed outside his door. A short little white guy with a crooked nose had a gun. He killed Forbes. I don't know, yet, if he killed my husband. So, I'm going back to him now, and I can't be on the phone. Come over if you want to."

She hung up.

The moment she disconnected, Shara realized she had been unnecessarily harsh, even mean to her mother in law. She hadn't intended that, but she knew where she went wrong. When Suzanne suggested Shara drive in a foot of snow, that marked the end of Shara's patience.

Her phone rang. She looked at the caller ID, and wasn't surprised it was Suzanne calling back.

"Yes," she answered.

"Shara, I don't need the tone," Suzanne scolded. "I want to know exactly how my son is. What did they tell you? Is he going to be all right?"

"I'm sorry, Suzanne, you're right. The doctor said that, had he lost even a small amount more blood, he would have gone into hypovolemic shock."

"What the hell is that?"

Shara's mouth dropped open. She had never heard Suzanne say "hell," or any other unfriendly word. The severity of the situation wasn't lost on the old woman, she realized. "It means that the tissues of his body would not have had enough oxygen, and there would be organ damage. But they transfused him in time," she added. "I can't tell you it wasn't close. A vascular surgeon managed to repair a major artery that was hit. Are you coming over here?"

"Shara, I honestly don't think I will. Trying to get out in this weather, well, isn't safe for me, and if I managed to get all the way there, I'd just be more work and worry for you. But I want you to call me every time something happens. Promise me."

"I'm walking back to his room now, Suzanne. I promise I'll keep you up-to-the-minute. And thank you for understanding."

"Oh, dear, I understand quite a lot more than you think I do."

"What does that mean?"

"I hope you'll never find out. You almost did, but I hope you don't."

"Seriously, Suzanne, I'm not following right now, but I'm here at the ICU, so I have to turn off the phone."

"What I mean is that I hope you won't ever find out what it is to have your husband die, and be left all alone with no one to help you, and with all the burdens he left behind for you."

"Oh."

"I hope you never learn what a lonely time that is, or how you are forced to do things, take steps you never thought you would ever take. I hope you don't find out exactly how hard it is, or how desperate it makes you, and how many actions you feel forced to take that might appear selfish to those who don't understand. Good-bye." Suzanne hung up.

Chapter 134

"It's the most joyous day of the year," Barbara effused Christmas morning as she wrapped her arms around her father's neck and hugged him, "except for Easter Sunday."

"So, it is, my beautiful girl. How about if I go to church with you?"

The two stood in the kitchen of their home. Lloyd wore a bathrobe and slippers while Barbara wore sweatpants and a tee shirt. The Christmas service would start at ten o'clock, and the two were finishing up breakfast.

"I would love that, Daddy. I hope you know, though, that while I will be conducting the choir, it won't be my choir yet. I've only rehearsed with it once."

"I'm sure it will be beautiful."

The two talked a few minutes about Edith Evringham, the eighty-year-old soprano who could still nail a high C, and how Barb had no doubt the woman could master a first soprano part of a DesPrez motet. Three more singers of that caliber, she bragged to her dad, and she'd take the quartet on the road.

"I'll miss you. Don't be gone long."

"Dad, hire that guy."

"I'll call him tomorrow. Let's let him have his holiday to himself before I bother him."

"What did you tell me his name is, again? I'm going to pray for him."

"Shelton."

"Call him now, Daddy. For all you know, it could be the best Christmas present he could receive."

Chapter 135

Tiffany's shoulder put her out of work, and she took the opportunity to do some things she'd let slide. Mopping the kitchen floor was a trick with only one good arm, and doing the bathroom wasn't much easier. Way to spend a Christmas Day, she told herself.

She'd like to celebrate the holiday, of course, but she wasn't invited anywhere, and there were these narcotics that stood in the way of alcohol, so this may turn out to be the dimmest Christmas yet.

She could wash uniforms. There were three that needed a going over, including a bloody shirt she had worn the day she picked a dog up from the middle of the street. It had been hit by a car and she couldn't stand to see it suffer any more. She'd taken it to a vet and paid to have it put down.

That was it. She could catch up on laundry. Folding and stacking would be a challenge, but she'd do the best she could.

It looked like a tedious holiday in front of a lot of tedious unwanted days off work until the phone rang.

"Pasternak," she answered, just in case it was police business.

"Sterling."

"I'm sorry. Who is this?"

"It's Beth Sterling. Nurse Beth from St. Mary's Hospital. I figured you might be in the mood for some holiday cheer. I'm off work in an hour, and I thought I'd get you and bring you to my place to eat, drink, and be merry. Or maybe just eat and be merry, in your case, given the narcotics."

"You gonna have the game on?"

"What? Football? Really? You want to watch football on Christmas Day?" Beth's voice was both facetious and ebullient.

"Damned straight."

"Hey, there's nothing about me that's damned straight. You comin'?"

"Damned queer, then."

Chapter 136

Marietta's mostly-cooked Christmas Eve meal was cold on the stove, fit only to be thrown out when she and her family got back to the house. Her brother was completely bereft. When he had processed the meaning of Genevieve Wilson's cries in the ER, Quincy withdrew. It was ten o'clock Christmas morning, and Quincy hadn't said a word in hours. Upon getting to Etta's, he had plopped on the sofa, and put his sore ankle up on the coffee table. He was staring at a television that was broadcasting light-hearted Christmas news about therapy dogs at a hospital in Maine.

"I guess none of this is fit to eat," Marietta told Isaiah as she looked around her kitchen. I guess I'll fill up trash cans.

"You might could save the green bean casserole."

"No, it has milk in it, left out all night."

"What about the Jell-O salad?"

"Yeah, that's okay; it's in the fridge. But it's not much breakfast."

"Ooh, pumpkin pie for breakfast!" Isaiah suggested.

"I'll make a pot of coffee."

A few minutes later Isaiah offered a hot coffee mug to his father who shook him off.

"Dad, come in the kitchen and have some pie with us, man. It's going to be okay."

"No, it isn't. My best friend is gone, and my other best friend may not live, and if he does, he may not sing again."

"What do you mean?"

"Shara said they intubated Cole."

"So?"

"Sometimes when that happens, if the doctors aren't careful, the procedure scars the vocal chords."

"I never heard of that."

"It's true. I might be the only Cole Renshaw Trio singer who can still sing."

Chapter 137

Tim stepped into Cole's hospital room at lunch time. Cole was awake, but covered with blankets that were pulled up around his face. Shara was busy tucking the bed covers under his limbs and torso, securing them.

"Hi," Tim said. "How's my friend doing?"

Shara looked up at him for a moment as if she didn't recognize him before she came to herself. "He's going to live, Tim, and the doctor doesn't think there is organ damage to speak of."

"That's great news. Why aren't you doing the happy dance to John Phillip Sousa music?"

"Because we don't know if he'll ever be able to sing again."

"What?"

"When they intubated him, they were in a big hurry. They may have damaged his vocal chords. I am told that is a big fear in singers who undergo surgeries. As it is, he can't talk. But, you can talk to him."

Shara sat in a chair and put her face in her hands. She was processing her grief, worry, and exhaustion. Cole watched her movements; he looked distressed.

Tim moved to Cole's side. Cole's eyes were crinkled up with pain and angst as Tim gazed at him. He mouthed a word to Tim, and Tim nodded at his friend. "I know. It's Forbes."

Shara wailed.

"I'm sorry, too," Tim mumbled. "Did they ever catch the guy?"

"It was on the news," Shara told him between sobs. "He was found in Indianapolis. He pulled a gun on a cop."

"So, he's dead?"

She nodded, and resumed crying. She reached for a tissue, and Tim picked up a box and put it in her hands.

"So, Shara, here's an age-old question I'd like to ask you, since you are religious, and I'm not. Why do bad things happen to good people? Doesn't God ever protect good people?"

"You're right, that's a big question. I don't know if I have an answer, but here lately, it seems like bad things happen when people do them to each other. We all do bad things because we choose to."

"And God does nothing?"

"I hardly think He does nothing. But what He chooses to do, He does because it's right. I can't see around corners like He can, so I can't judge. I guess He could snap His fingers and all evil would vanish. But that would mean we all give up our free will. Do you want to do that?"

"Of course not. But isn't there any middle ground?"

"You tell me. Where is it? God should allow you to be angry at Him, but He should have gotten you that job? He should tolerate the anger I've had toward my mother in law, but He shouldn't have let Theresa be in an accident? The only thing I'm sure of is this: trusting Him is better than not trusting Him. Everything else is a crap shoot."

Cole was watching Shara as she wiped her nose. He closed his eyes and shifted his weight under the covers as if he wanted to speak, but couldn't.

She stood and went to him.

"Do you need anything, baby?"

Cole shook his head, dismissing her.

She looked in his eyes and knew what he wanted to say. She just knew.

"Cole, I did talk to your mother, and I got an earful. For the last two years, I have blamed her for taking so much of your time, and if you get through this, and we still have the Cole Renshaw — well, Duo, I guess, now, we still need to work some things out.

"Where I was wrong, I just never looked at her or what she had been through with your father dying the way he did. I never saw her, or her pain, from her vantage point, and I was wrong. She brought it right to me on the phone. She told me that I almost lost you in this mess with Forbes. So, I imagined how that would be, and I saw it for the first time."

Cole spoke, and when he did, Tim Shelton felt a release in the tension he hadn't known was there. Cole's voice was stronger than Tim expected. "You weren't there, Shara. For my mother, it was a punch to the gut that she hasn't gotten over yet, and when she looks at me, she sees my dad." He reached toward the drinking water. "Give me that," he coughed.

Chapter 138

When his phone rang an hour later, Tim Shelton stepped into the hallway outside Theresa's hospital room and strolled down to a waiting lounge. He answered with a hearty, "Merry Christmas," hoping it was Shara with good news.

It wasn't.

"Merry Christmas, yourself, Tim, how are things going for you these days?"

"Uh, fine, I guess. Who is calling, please?"

"This is your old friend Lloyd Fuller from the university in Terre Haute."

The information made no sense to Tim for several seconds. He remained quiet, processing what this might mean.

So, Fuller continued. "I know it's Christmas Day, and you must have obligations, but my daughter has been on me non-stop until I call you about the position."

Tim, gathering himself, asked, "What does your daughter have to do with the position?"

"It's kind of a long story, Tim, but here's the crux: If you still want the job, I am authorized by Dr. Glenn to offer it to you." Fuller waited through the seconds of silence on the phone, as he became increasingly bewildered. "Did you already take another position, then?" he finally asked.

"That's another long story, Dr. Fuller."

"Lloyd," he corrected.

"Okay, Lloyd, the short answer is this: yes, I'd like to take the position, and I've already moved to Terre Haute permanently as I am working in music here." Tim hedged. Not too many needless details, he told himself. "However, my wife has been injured in an accident, and I am seeing to her."

"I'm very sorry to hear that. I think, though, that you would have some sympathy here for your situation. Frank Glenn flew out to Denver this morning."

"Oh, right. I forgot about his son. How is he doing?"

"We're waiting to hear. You and I will sit down some time and talk about the changes that have happened around here, partially because of you. There has been something of a renaissance in the department, and I hope you'll embrace it."

"I don't think I know what you're talking about."

"You will, my friend. It's a new day. I feel better than I have for a long time, and you will, too. Hey, how about lunch tomorrow, you and me. We've got a friendship to build."

"That sounds good to me, Lloyd, more than you know."

Chapter 139

Shara asked the hospital to move another bed into Cole's room so she could stay the night, just as Tim had been doing two floors upstairs. She had showered and brought some sweat pants from home to sleep in. Quincy had been by earlier, and had reminded her of how precious he was to her, now that Forbes was gone.

"Hey, man," Quincy effused to Cole when he came in the room. He clenched Cole's hand and shook it. "Whaddya got for me?"

Cole offered a weak smile. "My voice is coming back, for one thing. I think I'll be able to make the show at Tin Pan Sally's in two weeks."

"That's great, man. But, what about . . ."

"We're a duo for now, Quince. And I'm going to lean on you hard for a few shows until I'm back to a hundred percent."

"Square."

Quincy then told Shara and Cole that Genevieve had talked to him about a memorial service, and had asked him to sing.

"What are you singing?" Shara perked up.

"My Heart Will Go On."

"From 'Titanic'?"

"That's it."

"But that's sung by a woman to her dead lover!"

"Yeah, and I'm gonna kick its ass. It's like Cole always told Forbes, you change some pronouns if you need to. And my heart will be in this, Shara."

Chapter 140

Tim, having spoken to Shara and Cole, went back to Theresa's room, tense and depressed. It seemed to him that everyone in his world — everyone — was in a bad way. He was affected more than he had ever dreamed by the death of Forbes Wilson, even though he had hardly known the singer. But his friend, Cole Renshaw, one of the few who had been kind to him in months, had suffered a setback he couldn't imagine. It occurred to him that he was feeling the way many innocent people must feel when a terrorist attack happens in their world. The wind was knocked out of him; and he was afraid.

As he went into the familiar hospital room, Theresa was dozing. He stood at her bedside and watched her for many moments, thinking and considering until Theresa stirred.

"Hi," he said, leaning over and kissing her.

"Hi," she replied, "Your breath is bad. Brush your teeth."

"Oh, okay, sorry."

"And, while you're at it, quit going to the Renshaw's room. Just leave those people alone. We don't need them now."

"What? What are you talking about?"

"Cole and Shara. I'm talking about Cole and Shara. What's hard to understand? If you're starting this new job, there's no reason in the world you have to play music with him or do anything else that puts me in their company."

"I see." He looked at her, trying to look through her. Finally, "How is your pain right now?"

"Not any worse than usual. Why?"

"Treese, you're kind of, I don't know, off today. It's Christmas. Try to find some joy."

"Ha!" she blurted way too loudly. "That's real funny, Tim. Look at my Christmas. I'm totally stuck here like every day. I don't even get the Christmas party that your friend, Shara, promised me!"

"Well, her husband was shot, almost died. I don't think you can blame her for not staging a party in this room."

"I'm not assigning blame to anyone. What happened, happened. Can't you just leave them alone?"

"You are absolutely assigning blame. You've blamed Shara and Cole for weeks because you're mad at God. I'm ready to stop being mad. This shooting has made me realize that people do bad to each other, but it hurts the most when we're poor. Last night, I saw horror. I came within inches of dying, and I've realized that I am afraid of death. I saw my only friend's leg splashing blood into snow. I saw innocent people have their lives turned to sewage before my eyes. You weren't there, but take my word. That event changed me.

"Treese, I think I'm going to try going to church with Shara and Cole. See if God's got anything for me. He may not, but I'm going to find out."

Theresa stared, her mouth agape.

"I'm not asking you to go, and you can't right now anyway, but I'm going to try. I've come to see that some of our problems are our own fault."

"If you do that, Tim, you will certainly do it without me. I don't see how you can possibly let this Jesus Christ off the hook and blame yourself. Go, then, and don't come back."

"Treese, you've got it backwards. The way Shara tells it, I'm the one who's off the hook, and Jesus Christ, whom you revile, is on the hook for my mistakes. I get that now. I wish you were on board."

"I'm not."

"I am. And I'm coming back to you. And when I do, I might be a better man."

He strolled out of the room and rode the elevator to the lobby. Busy for a holiday, the lobby was crowded with visitors carrying poinsettias and gifts to patient rooms. He walked outside, his mind a jumble of images and memories, and sat in his car. The parking lot was well cleared, but the adjacent streets were still a mess as evidenced by the slowness of the traffic and the daunting drifts.

Tim wanted to drive to clear his head, but the car was still unusable, and unlikely to be used any time soon.

At the end of the parking lot, he could see a drop off of terrain into a wooded area. Beyond it, a good quarter mile away, a series of identical blonde brick residential buildings, covered in snow, defined the horizon. Tim got out and walked to the parking lot's limits. Ordinarily, when feeling this way, Tim would take a long drive, leaving Theresa at home, and think his thoughts. But he had nowhere to go and shoes that were unsuitable for this weather. So, he'd not tromp through the snow as he wished. The sun was high in the sky and bouncing glittery rays of light off snow-covered branches in the woods. There was utter silence. He stood there a long time. Okay, he told himself at last, here goes.

"God, I'm glad Theresa is going to be all right. I wish she would be all right in her heart, and I wish she wouldn't be so [his mind wandered briefly and he thought of her] . . . oh, and I'm glad we met Cole and Shara, and I really wish he could be okay and could keep singing, and I guess I'm glad I finally got this job, though I don't know why it took so long and so much heartache and worry. [The thought occurred to him that he really *did* know, and that the worry was part of drawing him closer to the Person he was talking to now.] And I hope Lloyd and I can really be friends [His thoughts wandered again as he considered the cryptic remark Lloyd had made about his daughter] and, well, I hope you'll speed up Theresa's healing, and, I don't know, I guess that's all. Uh, amen."

Pretty lame, Shelton, he told himself. The author of a master's thesis, several articles on music history, and hundreds of cover letters, he couldn't remember when he had ever expressed himself so badly. He smiled with the irony.

He then saw movement out of the periphery of his vision and looked toward it. There, at the bottom of the hill maybe a hundred feet away, a small female deer with white spots speckling her back, stepped gingerly through the snow. She looked up at him and their eyes met. They watched each other for many seconds, and neither moved. Then, not able to help himself, Tim raised a hand and waved at her. She stared back at him, her forepaw raised tentatively for several seconds. Then, she blinked, turned and darted away through the trees.